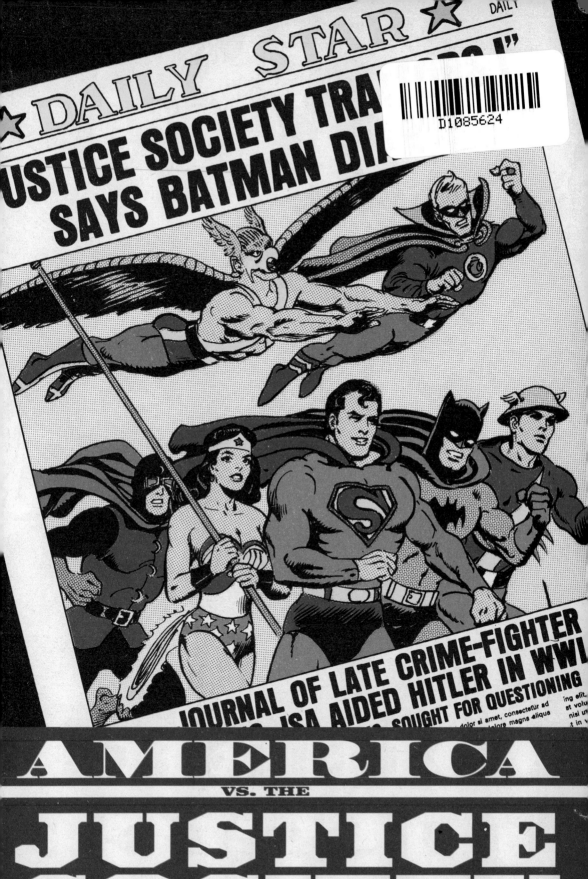

DAILY STAR ☆

DAILY

D1085624

JUSTICE SOCIETY TRA...
SAYS BATMAN DI...

JOURNAL OF LATE CRIME-FIGHTER
...JSA AIDED HITLER IN WWI
...SOUGHT FOR QUESTIONING

# AMERICA
## VS. THE
# JUSTICE
# SOCIETY

# AMERICA
## VS. THE
# JUSTICE SOCIETY

**ROY THOMAS** WRITER

**RAFAEL KAYANAN**
**RICH BUCKLER**
**JERRY ORDWAY**
**MIKE HERNANDEZ**
**HOWARD BENDER**
PENCILLERS

**ALFREDO ALCALA   BILL COLLINS**
INKERS
**DANN THOMAS**
CO-PLOTTER
**DAVID CODY WEISS**
LETTERER
**ADRIENNE ROY   CARL GAFFORD**
COLORISTS

**AMERICA VS. THE JUSTICE SOCIETY**

Published by DC Comics. Compilation Copyright © 2015 DC Co
All Rights Reserved. Originally published in single magazine fo
in AMERICA VS. THE JUSTICE SOCIETY 1-4 © 1964, 1965 DC Com
All Rights Reserved. All characters, their distinctive likenesses
related elements featured in this publication are trademarks
DC Comics. The stories, characters and incidents featured in t
publication are entirely fictional. DC Comics does not read or
accept unsolicited ideas, stories or artwork.

DC Comics, 4000 Warner Blvd., Burbank, CA 91522
A Warner Bros. Entertainment Company.
Printed by RR Donnelley, Owensville, MO, USA. 6/19/15. First
ISBN: 978-1-4012-5509-1

SUSTAINABLE FORESTRY INITIATIVE
Certified Sourcing
www.sfiprogram.org
SFI-01042
APPLIES TO TEXT STOCK ONLY

Library of Congress Cataloging-in-Publication Data

Thomas, Roy, 1940- author.
  America vs. the Justice Society / Roy Thomas, Jerry Ordway,
Howard Bender.
    pages cm
  ISBN 978-1-4012-5509-1 (paperback)
  1. Graphic novels. I. Ordway, Jerry, illustrator. II. Bender, H
illustrator. III. Title.
  PN6728.J89T48 2015
  741.5'973—dc23
                                            2015007661

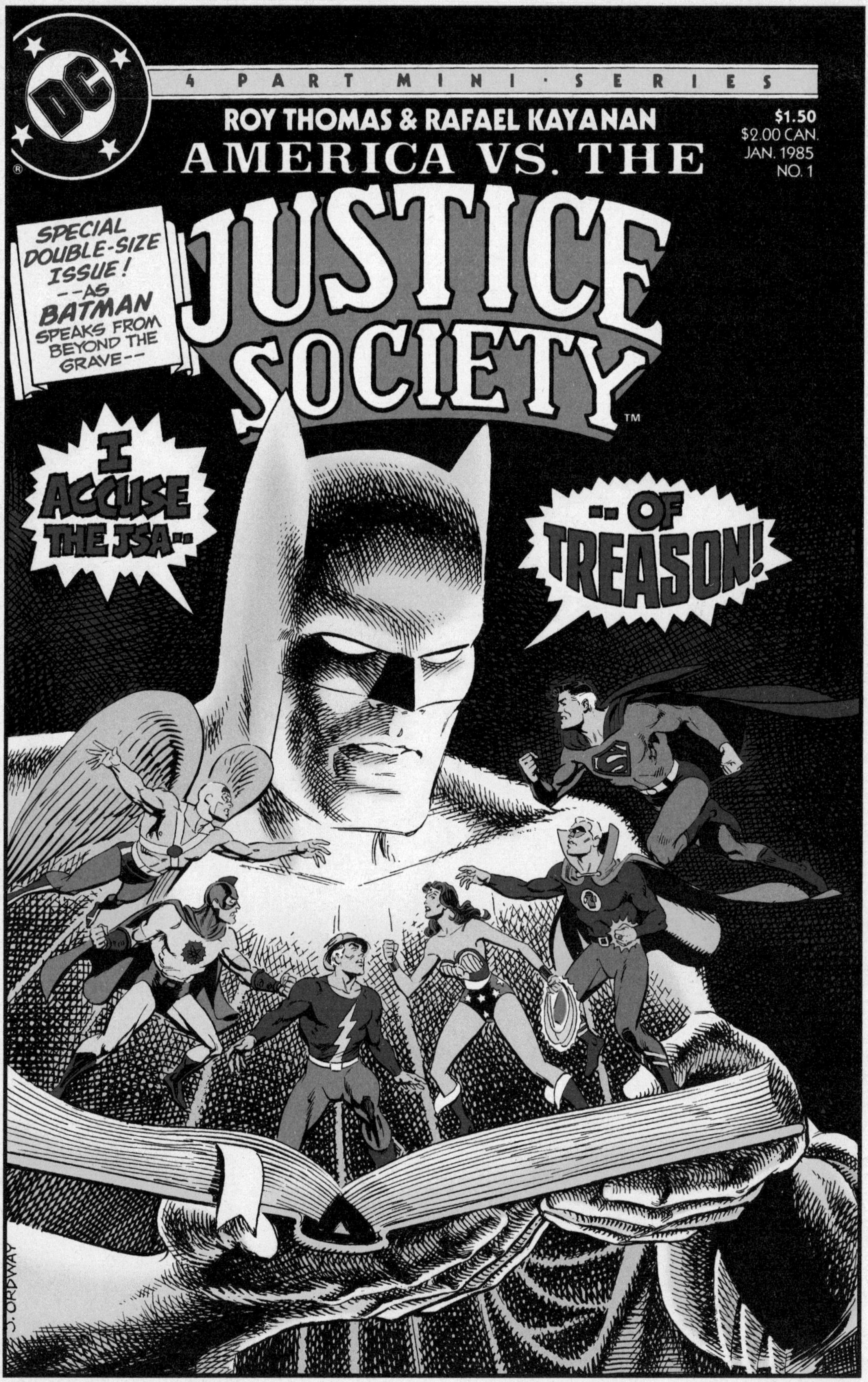

4 PART MINI·SERIES
ROY THOMAS & RAFAEL KAYANAN
$1.50
$2.00 CAN.
JAN. 1985
NO. 1
AMERICA VS. THE
JUSTICE SOCIETY
SPECIAL DOUBLE-SIZE ISSUE! --AS BATMAN SPEAKS FROM BEYOND THE GRAVE--
I ACCUSE THE JSA--
--OF TREASON!
J. ORDWAY

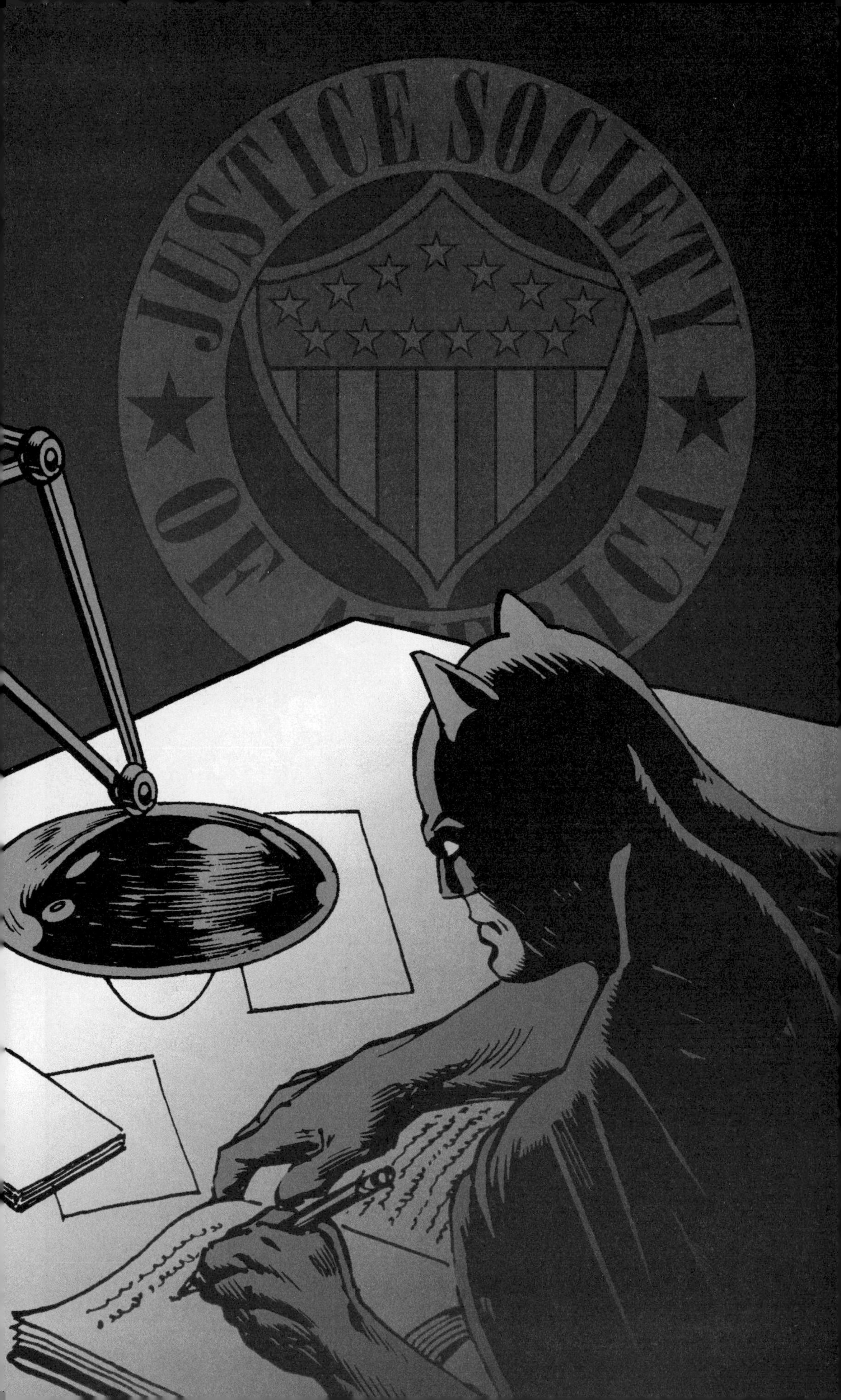
JUSTICE SOCIETY
OF

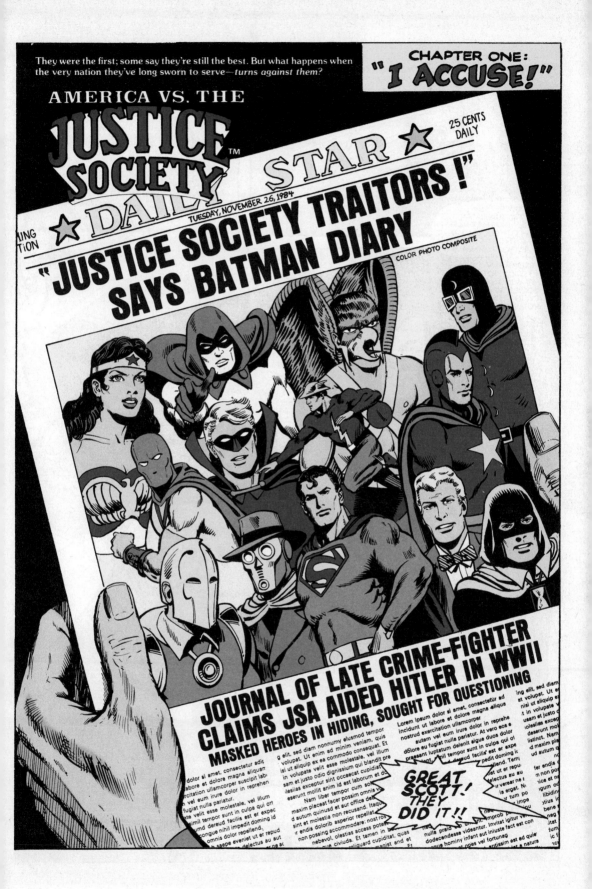

They were the first; some say they're still the best. But what happens when the very nation they've long sworn to serve—*turns against them?*

**CHAPTER ONE: "I ACCUSE!"**

AMERICA VS. THE

# JUSTICE SOCIETY™

★ DAILY STAR ★

25 CENTS DAILY

TUESDAY, NOVEMBER 26, 1984

## "JUSTICE SOCIETY TRAITORS!" SAYS BATMAN DIARY

COLOR PHOTO COMPOSITE

## JOURNAL OF LATE CRIME-FIGHTER CLAIMS JSA AIDED HITLER IN WWII

### MASKED HEROES IN HIDING, SOUGHT FOR QUESTIONING

GREAT SCOTT! THEY DID IT!!

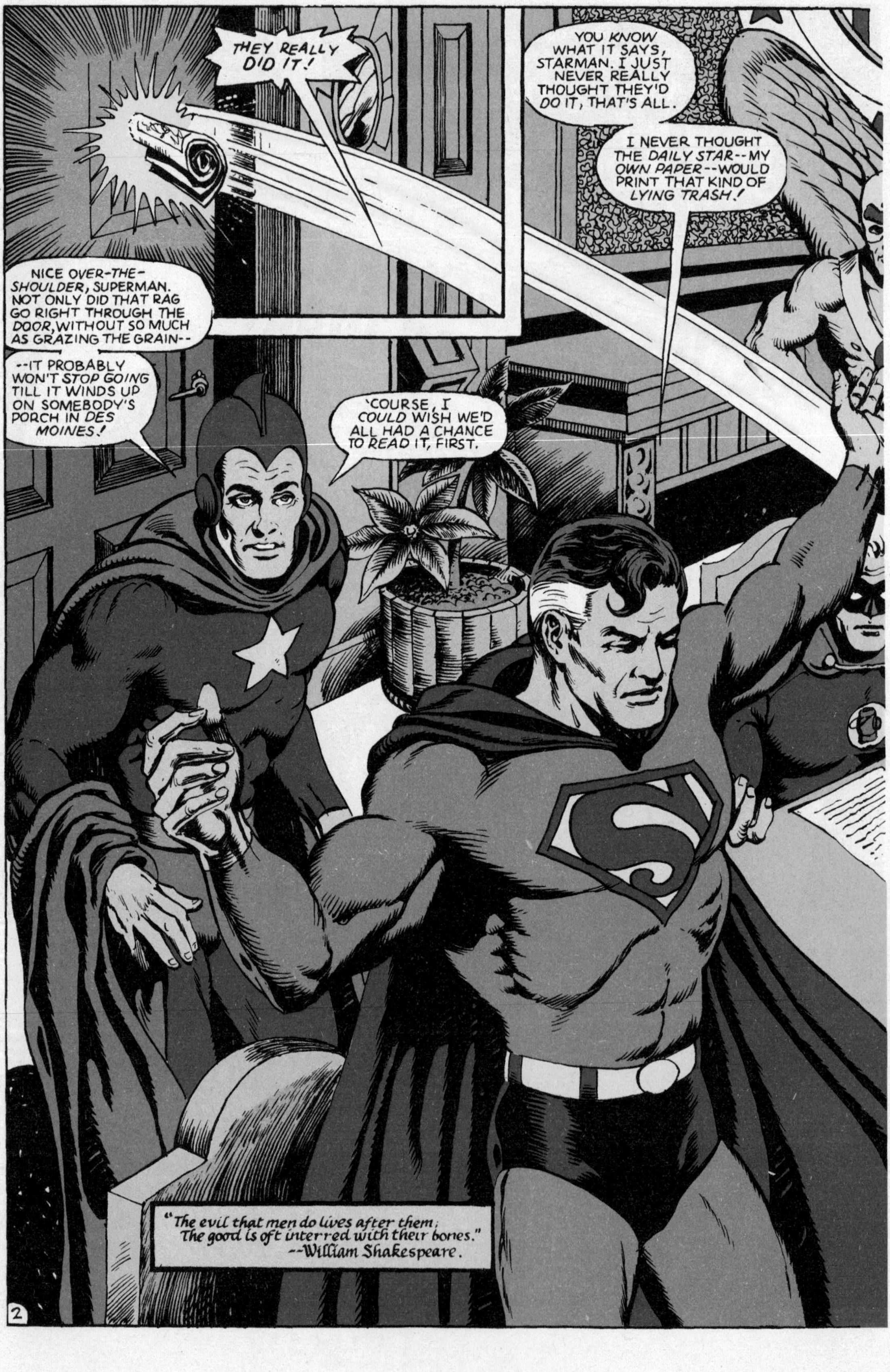
THEY REALLY DID IT!
YOU KNOW WHAT IT SAYS, STARMAN. I JUST NEVER REALLY THOUGHT THEY'D DO IT, THAT'S ALL.
I NEVER THOUGHT THE DAILY STAR--MY OWN PAPER--WOULD PRINT THAT KIND OF LYING TRASH!
NICE OVER-THE-SHOULDER, SUPERMAN. NOT ONLY DID THAT RAG GO RIGHT THROUGH THE DOOR, WITHOUT SO MUCH AS GRAZING THE GRAIN--
--IT PROBABLY WON'T STOP GOING TILL IT WINDS UP ON SOMEBODY'S PORCH IN DES MOINES!
'COURSE, I COULD WISH WE'D ALL HAD A CHANCE TO READ IT, FIRST.
"The evil that men do lives after them; The good is oft interred with their bones." --William Shakespeare.
2

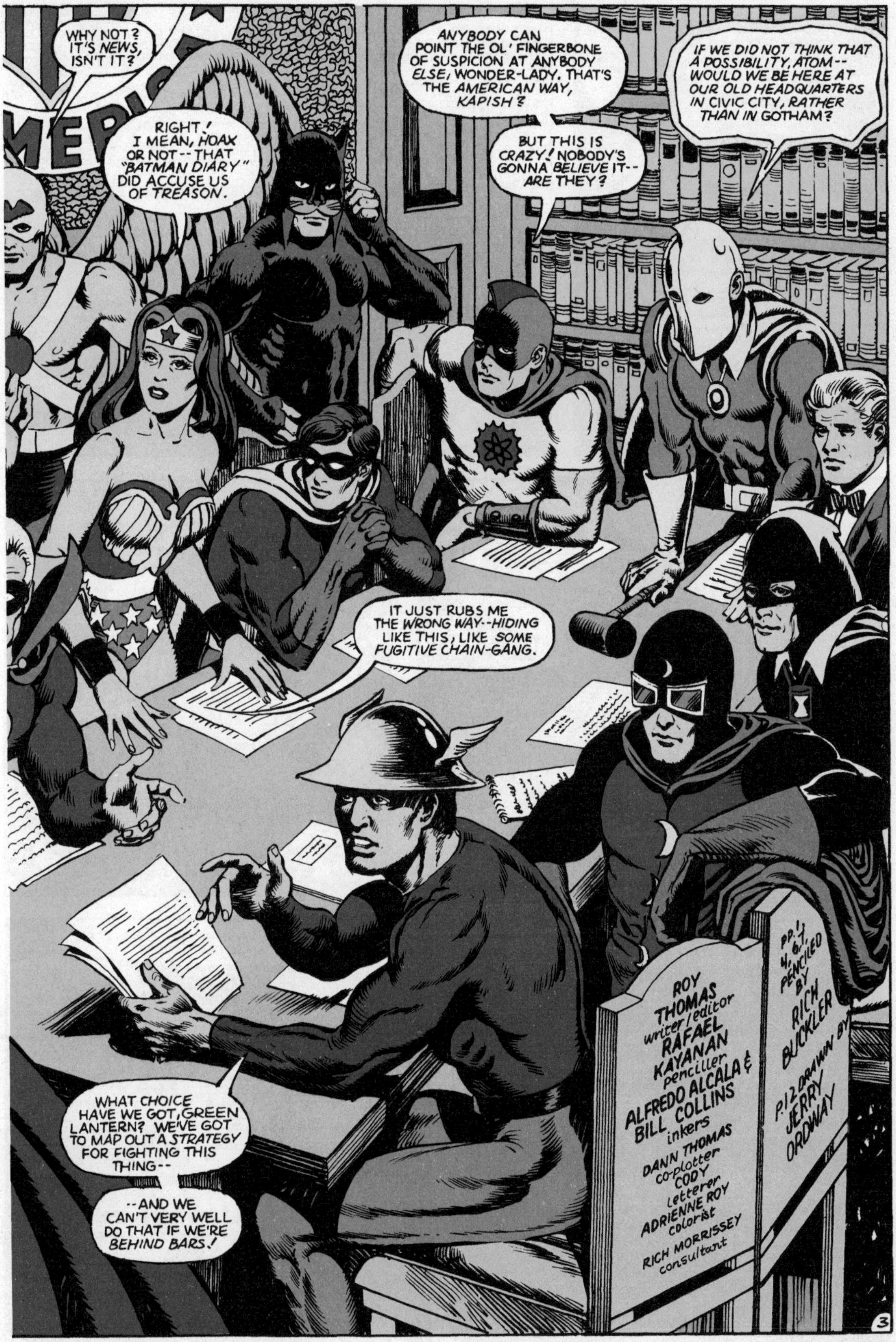
WHY NOT? IT'S NEWS, ISN'T IT?
RIGHT! I MEAN, HOAX OR NOT--THAT "BATMAN DIARY" DID ACCUSE US OF TREASON.
ANYBODY CAN POINT THE OL' FINGERBONE OF SUSPICION AT ANYBODY ELSE, WONDER-LADY. THAT'S THE AMERICAN WAY, KAPISH?
BUT THIS IS CRAZY! NOBODY'S GONNA BELIEVE IT--ARE THEY?
IF WE DID NOT THINK THAT A POSSIBILITY, ATOM--WOULD WE BE HERE AT OUR OLD HEADQUARTERS IN CIVIC CITY, RATHER THAN IN GOTHAM?
IT JUST RUBS ME THE WRONG WAY--HIDING LIKE THIS, LIKE SOME FUGITIVE CHAIN-GANG.
WHAT CHOICE HAVE WE GOT, GREEN LANTERN? WE'VE GOT TO MAP OUT A STRATEGY FOR FIGHTING THIS THING--
--AND WE CAN'T VERY WELL DO THAT IF WE'RE BEHIND BARS!
ROY THOMAS writer/editor
RAFAEL KAYANAN penciller
ALFREDO ALCALA & BILL COLLINS inkers
DANN THOMAS co-plotter
CODY letterer
ADRIENNE ROY colorist
RICH MORRISSEY consultant
PP. 1, 4, 6, 7 PENCILED BY RICH BUCKLER
P. 12 DRAWN BY JERRY ORDWAY
3

EVERYBODY *KNOWS* WHERE OUR GOTHAM CITY *DIGS* ARE; THEY POINT 'EM OUT ON *BUS TOURS,* FOR CRYIN' OUT LOUD.

HERE, AT LEAST, WE CAN BUY A *LITTLE TIME.*

TIME? TO DO *WHAT,* FLASH? TWIDDLE OUR THUMBS WHILE THEY GET A *FIRING SQUAD* READY FOR US?

IN YOUR *CASE,* THEY'LL NEED *KRYPTONITE* BULLETS, RIGHT, SUPES?

*WHOMP!*

NOW, *LOOK--!*

SORRY, OLD FRIEND. GUESS I'M NOT IN THE PROPER MOOD FOR *GALLOWS HUMOR.*

MY *FAULT.*

WHAT COUNTS IS, WE WERE *SET UP,* SOMEHOW-- FRAMED BY SOMEONE WHO'S TRYING TO PASS HIMSELF OFF AS *BATMAN,* ACCUSING US FROM THE *GRAVE.*

WHOEVER IT IS, HE SURE PICKED HIS *SHOTS*--SINCE IT'S BEEN ONLY A FEW MONTHS SINCE SOME OF US NEARLY *WRECKED THE WORLD.*

THAT *WASN'T* OUR FAULT, WONDER WOMAN.

YOU WANT TO TRY EXPLAIN-ING THE *STREAM OF RUTH-LESSNESS* TO A MASS AUDIENCE, ROBIN?

LOOK, THIS IS GETTING US *NOWHERE.*

PERHAPS IF WE EXAMINE THE *FACTS* ONCE MORE--SUCH AS THEY *ARE?*

MIGHT AS WELL, DR. FATE--THOUGH I KEEP WISHING WE WEREN'T *SHY* A FEW JSAers.

NO SENSE DRAGGING *POWER GIRL* AND THE OTHER YOUNGER MEMBERS INTO THIS; THEY WEREN'T EVEN AROUND BACK IN *WORLD WAR TWO.*

AT LEAST *SANDMAN'S* STILL TOO WASTED FROM HIS *STROKE* TO BE HASSLED--THANK HEAVEN FOR SMALL FAVORS.

THOUGH I DOUBT *WES DODD* WOULD SEE IT THAT WAY.

THERE'S GOT TO BE AN *ANSWER*--SOME CLUE, JUST WAITING FOR US TO *FIND* IT!

FUNNY. THAT'S WHAT *BATMAN* MIGHT'VE SAID WHEN HE WAS *ALIVE*-- AND NOW HE'S THE ONE SUPPOSED TO BE CALLING US *TRAITORS.*

I KEEP GOING OVER THE WAY IT ALL *BEGAN*--

4

"--ONLY *YESTERDAY*, IN MY-- *CLARK KENT'S* OFFICE AT THE *DAILY STAR*:

CLARK KENT MANAGING EDITOR

"I SEEM TO RECALL I WAS PRAYING SILENTLY FOR A *NEWS BREAK*...

"AND, LORD KNOWS, WE GOT ONE...

WHAT THE--?

*PLOP!*

MY...APOLOGIES, MR. KENT.

TAKE IT EASY, DOC.

DR. NICHOLS!

THANK YOU, JAMES. YOU SEE, MR. KENT, I'M *NOT WELL*. PERHAPS I SHOULD HAVE HAD MY *CHAUFFEUR* COME ALONE.

WHAT BRINGS YOU HERE, SIR?

THIS *JOURNAL*, MR. KENT! I BELIEVE YOU'LL RECALL THAT, YEARS AGO, I HAD DEALINGS WITH SOCIALITE *BRUCE WAYNE* AND HIS YOUNG WARD, *DICK GRAYSON*...

...THAT, BY *HYPNOSIS*, I SENT THEM INTO THE *PAST* ON NUMEROUS OCCASIONS.

I RECALL, SIR... BECAUSE YOU SENT *ME* ALONG WITH THEM, A TIME OR TWO.

YES, THOSE WERE WONDROUS DAYS. WELL, THROUGH MR. WAYNE, I MET THE *BATMAN*. I PRESUME HE MUST HAVE COME TO *TRUST* ME, AS POOR MR. WAYNE DID.

"...FOR, ONE NIGHT ONLY MONTHS BEFORE HIS *DEATH*, THE CAPED CRUSADER CAME TO ME ONE *FINAL* TIME...

GOOD EVENING, DR. NICHOLS. DIDN'T MEAN TO STARTLE YOU.

EVEN *PLEASANT* SURPRISES ARE NOT GOOD FOR ONE WITH A VERY OLD, VERY WEAK HEART, SIR.

WHAT MAY I DO FOR YOU... AFTER SO MANY LONG YEARS?

5

I NEED YOU TO DO ME A FAVOR, DOCTOR--IN THE EVENT OF MY DEATH.

DEATH? NONSENSE, MAN! YOU'RE FAR YOUNGER THAN I AM!

THEN LET'S JUST CALL IT... A PREVENTIVE MEASURE.

BATMAN THEN GAVE ME THE JOURNAL HE WAS CARRYING-- AS WELL AS SOME SPOOLS FROM A WIRE RECORDER. *

HE ASKED ME NOT TO READ THEM, BUT IF HE WERE DEAD BEFORE THIS DATE, I SHOULD--ON THIS VERY DAY--THEN TURN THEM OVER TO THE DAILY STAR--TO YOU, MR. KENT, IF YOU WERE STILL ITS EDITOR.

ASTONISHINGLY, HE WAS KILLED ONLY A FEW MONTHS AFTERWARD. HE AND MR. WAYNE ARE BOTH GONE NOW, POOR SOULS.

*PREDECESSOR OF TAPE RECORDERS. --Roy.

AND NOW... I'M QUITE TIRED. GOOD-BYE. JAMES WILL HELP ME TO MY CAR.

GOOD-BYE, DR. NICHOLS... AND STAY WELL.

"USING MY X-RAY VISION, I SCANNED THE BOOK AT SUPER-SPEED...

IT'S BRUCE'S HANDWRITING, ALL RIGHT.

HE'S EVEN PASTED IN A FEW PHOTOS.

BUT THE STORY HE TELLS--IT'S INCREDIBLE!

"It is with profound regret that I must pen these dark revelations about my former friends, the Justice Society of America...

"As most people know, they began their long careers as individual crime-fighters, before the JSA existed as such.

"Even in those early days, there was a strong element of vigilantism in their--in our work.

"Superman was the first of us to appear--and in his premier exploit he took the law into his own hands...

"...using fear of falling to force a confession from a corrupt lobbyist in Washington in 1938.

"I am ashamed to confess that on occasion, I myself used illegal methods-- including a handgun--in '39 and '40--

"--before my relationship with Commissioner Gordon gave me semi-official status in Gotham City.

"No such reassessment seems to have bothered The Spectre, however--a grim ghost who claimed he had been instructed by higher powers to deal out justice--

"--even if that often included taking human life.

"He wasn't really much different from the rest, though--whether it was the 5'1" Atom--

"--Dr. Fate, who seems at times almost to have been possessed by the awesome Helmet of Nabu he wore--

"--The Sandman, who was hunted by the police for his methods, as well as for wielding a dangerous gas-gun--

"--or The Hawkman, who claimed to be the reincarnation of an ancient Egyptian warrior--

"--and had about as much respect for due process of law.

"Not that the other charter JSAers--The Flash, The Green Lantern, and The Hourman--had any more!

7

"Still, only when such self-appointed avengers decided to unite did they truly become a menace to America."

"That occurred in November 1940, under conditions still little-known, even decades after the end of World War Two -- in an America still officially neutral --"

"-- when, in Commissioner Gordon's Gotham City office, I first met the Flash and the Green Lantern -- as well as a 'Mr. Smythe,' who represented the now-famous British agent code-named 'Intrepid'."*

GENTLEMEN, YOUR PRESIDENT HAS AUTHORIZED ME TO ASK THE THREE OF YOU --

-- TO UNDERTAKE A SECRET MISSION WHICH MAY WELL DECIDE THE SURVIVAL OF THE BRITISH NATION -- AND YOUR OWN.

GO ON.

*SEE USA ORIGIN, 1977 (REPRINTED 1982), AS WELL AS SIR WILLIAM STEPHENSON'S OWN ACCOUNT.

"'Smythe' sent us to attack Adolf Hitler himself, in Berlin -- where we were joined by the other six mystery-men I named before --"

"-- all but Superman, that is."

"Yet, whether it was because such authoritarian types were already predisposed toward a fascist/Nazi world view, or because of the Führer's well-documented persuasiveness..."

"...things didn't work out exactly as 'Smythe,' 'Intrepid,' and President Roosevelt had hoped."

"The nine of us came... we saw..."

"...and were conquered!

<I HAVE BEEN EXPECTING YOU, AMERIKANER HEROES! YOU HAVE BEEN SENT BY MY ENEMIES, THE BRITISH--AND BY THAT JEWISH WARMONGER ROOSEVELT--TO PREVENT MY RIDDING THE EARTH OF INFERIOR RACES--DYING EMPIRES!>

IF THAT'S THE TWISTED WAY YOU WANT TO *LOOK* AT IT!*

< NO! GIVE UP YOUR FUTILE ATTEMPT! INSTEAD OF OPPOSING MY NEW ORDER, USE YOUR MIGHTY POWERS--YOUR STRONG RIGHT ARMS--

*TRANSLATED, OF COURSE. HITLER SPOKE NO ENGLISH.    --R T

<--TO FIGHT FOR THE GLORY OF THE GREATER GERMAN REICH!>

"Much has been written else-where of the magnetic, almost hypnotic effect of HITLER'S GAZE.

"I can swear--it's all true.

"Perhaps his gaze was reinforced, this time, by the SPEAR OF DESTINY he held--that spear which, legend says, pierced the side of Christ on Calvary.

"Perhaps not.

"I only know that, looking into those clear blue eyes--listening to that strident Nordic voice--

"--I suddenly felt that ADOLF HITLER, Austrian-born creator of Nazism, was the predestined SAVIOR OF THE TWENTIETH CENTURY WORLD!"

9

"Nor was I alone!

"I can no Conger remember the words he used. I don't think they were important.

"Yet I could sense the others, standing near me, being swept along, just as I was, by Hitler's harangue against modernism--the Jews--the Treaty of Versailles that had ended World War One--and God knows what else.

"Maybe, as authoritarian types, we were already predisposed to the world view he expounded; again, I just don't know.

"All that matters is that, in the end, the mystic prowess of Dr. Fate and Green Lantern was no more proof against Hitler's spell-binding oratory than were the rest of us.

"I don't claim that makes us blameless for what followed. I only document that it happened.

10

"I only wish I'd had the presence of mind to get a photograph of what happened next:

HEIL HITLER!

"and so, an unholy alliance was forged--American-born mystery-men and the dictator of the Third Reich.

"Then, Der Führer used his Spear to summon up actual Valkyries from some other-dimensional Valhalla--and sent both groups to destroy the U.S. government.

"Only one thing prevented that day from being the darkest in American history...

"His name was Superman.

"He intercepted Valkyries and a long-range German bomber over Washington.

"Later, secret F.B.I reports would say that the Atom was wounded saving FDR from a Valkyrie.

"The truth is--the Mighty Mite merely stumbled into her path.

"When Superman collared her a moment later-- still unaware the other nine so-called 'heroes' had been the Valkyries' allies--the masked men pretended they had been trying to stop the warrior-women.

"None of them was particularly eager to take on Superman to get to Roosevelt.

"And so the President put his seal of approval on this Nazi fifth column which named itself--in his presence--the Justice Society of America.'"

MY GOD IN HEAVEN!

THAT'S OUR ORIGIN, ALL RIGHT-- BUT SO WILDLY DISTORTED--!

11

"On the 22nd of that month, with superman and myself only honorary members by then, the JSA had their first meeting--and reveled in the media attention, even though all they did was sit around in a hotel and swap tall tales of their individual exploits, with the Flash as chairman.

"It was neither the first nor the last time that a supposedly hard-hitting law-enforcement group in this country substituted press releases for action.

"Still, FBI chief Hoover was taken in, to the extent that he sent the JSA on their first real mission--to round up the alleged head of all Nazi sabotage in the U.S.

"They brought back one Fritz Klaver--a distinctly second-string spymaster, for whom Hitler had no more use--and it was hailed as a major triumph.

JUSTICE SOCIETY of AMERICA

FOR AMERICA AND DEMOCRACY

JERRY ORDWAY '83

12

"In mid-1941, when Der Führer found other Axis work for the Flash to do, Johnny Thunder took his place--a strange choice, until you realize that Thunder, too, was loyal to the Reich.

"As new chairman, the Green Lantern came up with a noble-sounding plan to raise $1,000,000 to benefit European war orphans.

"Seven of the JSAers had little trouble procuring $100,000 each from patriotic Americans...

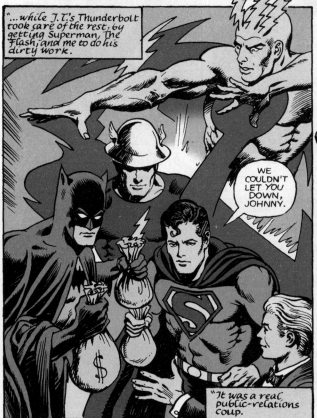

"...while J.T.'s Thunderbolt took care of the rest, by getting Superman, The Flash, and me to do his dirty work.

WE COULDN'T LET YOU DOWN, JOHNNY.

"It was a real public-relations coup.

"But check it out--the money never helped any war orphans.

"The Lantern took it to fill Hitler's coffers.

"Soon afterward, he and the Hourman were replaced by Dr. Mid-Nite and Starman--but no matter.

"They were Nazis, too.

13

"Need proof? By using the Freedom of Information Act, any private citizen can look up what happened in late 1941 when Hawkman, Sandman, and Dr. Mid-Nite saved a gathering of theoretical scientists from presumably Axis agents.

WOK!

"I cannot prove one truth I later discovered--that the men were, in fact, agents of the Soviet Union...

SLAMM

"...still, it afforded the JSA the chance to befriend these brilliant, loyal scientists, for their own purposes.

"The men of science revealed a plan for sending people 1000 years into the future...

"...where a formula could be obtained that would make the United States bomb-proof.

"The group included Prof. Damon Everson... Prof. Malachi Zee...

"...and an assistant named Per Degaton.

"We shall hear more of him later.

"Leaving Flash and G.L. to guard the scientists, the others let themselves be sent into the future.

HAVEN'T YOU FELLOWS GONE YET?

THEY'VE BEEN, AND RETURNED, FLASH--TO THE VERY SECOND THAT THEY LEFT.

"The device utilizing the future-formula worked the first time it was tested, even large bombs having no impact on the protective force-beam...

BLOOM!

"But when they tried it a second time, later--it failed.

"What other conclusion is there but that the JSAers rigged it to fail--not a difficult task for beings like the Spectre or Green Lantern?

WHAT WENT WRONG, DAMON? IT SHOULD HAVE WORKED!

I--I JUST DON'T KNOW, MALACHI. I--

"None of them suspected the truth--JSA sabotage!

14

"Gaining entrance to the brain trust's lab that night, I found that both the formula and the prototype had obviously been tampered with -- just as I'd suspected.

"I'd never told Robin about it -- and I didn't tell my JSA 'friends' about this.

"That was the turning point for me. Now that America and the Axis powers were on a collision course, I mentally renounced my oath of allegiance to Hitler.

"That would have been a fatal mistake."

HMMM... AT THIS POINT, THE JOURNAL REFERS ME TO THE WIRE RECORDINGS.

NO SENSE BORROWING A RECORDER...

...WHEN I CAN UNSPOOL THE WIRE AT SUPER-SPEED, AND MY SENSITIVE FINGERS CAN "READ" IT.

GOOD LORD! IT'S A RECORDING OF PRESIDENT ROOSEVELT HIMSELF --

-- AND HIS FRIEND AND CONFIDANT, HARRY HOPKINS!

STILL NO ANSWER FROM THE JUSTICE SOCIETY, MR. PRESIDENT?

I'M AFRAID NOT... AND TIME IS RUNNING OUT-- FAST!

FROM BATMAN'S JOURNAL: "Correction: time had already run out...

"...at a place called Pearl Harbor.

"And the whereabouts of the JSA on that day of days has never yet been established -- nearly four decades later!

15

"FDR didn't mention the JSA in his speech the next day...

YESTERDAY-- DECEMBER 7, 1941-- A DATE THAT WILL LIVE IN INFAMY--

"...but they were very much on his mind when I visited him secretly that very night.

MR. PRESIDENT...?

WH--? THE BATMAN!? I WAS JUST WORKING ON MY STAMP COLLECTION; CALMS THE NERVES, YOU KNOW.

WOOF

QUIET, FALA. I DON'T THINK THE BATMAN AND I WANT ANY SECRET SERVICE VISITORS.

"I laid my soul bare that night. Roosevelt understood...and forgave!

YES, I AGREE WE MUST PLOT OUR COURSE CAREFULLY.

...SWEAR TO YOU, SIR, THAT FROM THIS MOMENT, I'LL KEEP YOU ADVISED OF THE JSA'S TREACHERY, WHENEVER I LEARN OF IT.

EVEN IF SUPERMAN SEEMS INNOCENT OF WRONGDOING THUS FAR --

--WE MUST BE CAREFUL NOT TO AROUSE THE SUSPICIONS OF THE SPECTRE AND THE OTHERS, TOO SOON.

"To this day, I've no way of knowing if the eight unregenerate JSAers suspected I was no longer on the same side as they -- yet only a few nights later--

I HEREBY DECLARE THE JUSTICE SOCIETY OF AMERICA DISBANDED -- FOR THE DURATION!

MEETING ADJOURNED!

THWAM!

"The official story they gave out to the press, of course, was that each of them--except the deceased Spectre--wished to join the Armed Forces to fight the Axis...

16

"Yet, for reasons never explained, they--and new recruit Wonder Woman--did fight abroad in costume before long--"

"--but only against the Japanese, despite America's official 'Germany First' policy."

"Admittedly, I'm at a loss to say why a hero such as Superman--"

"--remained on the home front fighting easily dispatched hoodlums."

"When the JSA finally 'allowed' itself to re-group as the Justice Battalion--"

"--again their foes were only Japanese such as the Black Dragon Society, not Nazi spies."

"Apparently, like their master, Hitler, they were loyal to no cause but their own."

THIS IS MAD-- INSANE--!

AND NOW-- THIS NEW BIT ABOUT ME--!

"Secret archives even tell of an epic battle between Superman and Wonder Woman--"

"--over the possession of a new and terrible weapon."

"Superman wished to save it for the United States, and the Amazon-- well, one can only conjecture about what she wanted."

17

"Yet, so similar are Amazon Heritage and Nazi doctrine--each being an elitist, racist group--that one can easily imagine the hellish result--

THE FACTS ARE TRUE, UP TO A POINT-- YET THE WHOLE THING JUST MAKES UP A FABRIC OF FANTASTIC LIES!

"--if she had succeeded in giving Hitler the atomic bomb that exploded off the coast of Mexico on June 12, 1942--five years earlier than official accounts!"

"And so this bloodiest of wars went on--and on--

"--while the super-beings who could have stopped it contented themselves with fighting against lesser apolitical foes:

"The King Bee and his human insects...

"The so-called 'Monster'...

"The Brain Wave...

"The original Psycho-Pirate...

"Yes, it may be charged that I did the same... but I had no super-powers to unleash against the Axis hordes!

18

"Many of those who did were tricked by the All-Star Squadron--that JSA-dominated wartime group--into fighting the Axis powers of other, parallel earths, instead of this one.

"This took care of the so-called Freedom Fighters, who have been seen back on this earth in recent years.

"Some of those JSAers lured away, of course--didn't live long enough to return.

"Just as Hitler's realm was toppling, Green Lantern and Flash returned to wallow in the JSA's headline-grabbing glory...

"Perhaps the last time they were all together before the 1960's was at FDR's funeral.

"...replacing various heroes who had left the Society.

"But did they gather to mourn--or to gloat over how they had deceived the nation's leader?

"In any event, though most of the others retired, the seven regular JSAers of the period stayed in business-- the business of covering up their wartime tracks, mostly.

"One man who was onto them was THE WIZARD, in 1947.

"He knew they were, in truth, villains like himself, not heroes at all--

"So naturally they closed ranks to put him out of business, to avoid the competition."

(19)

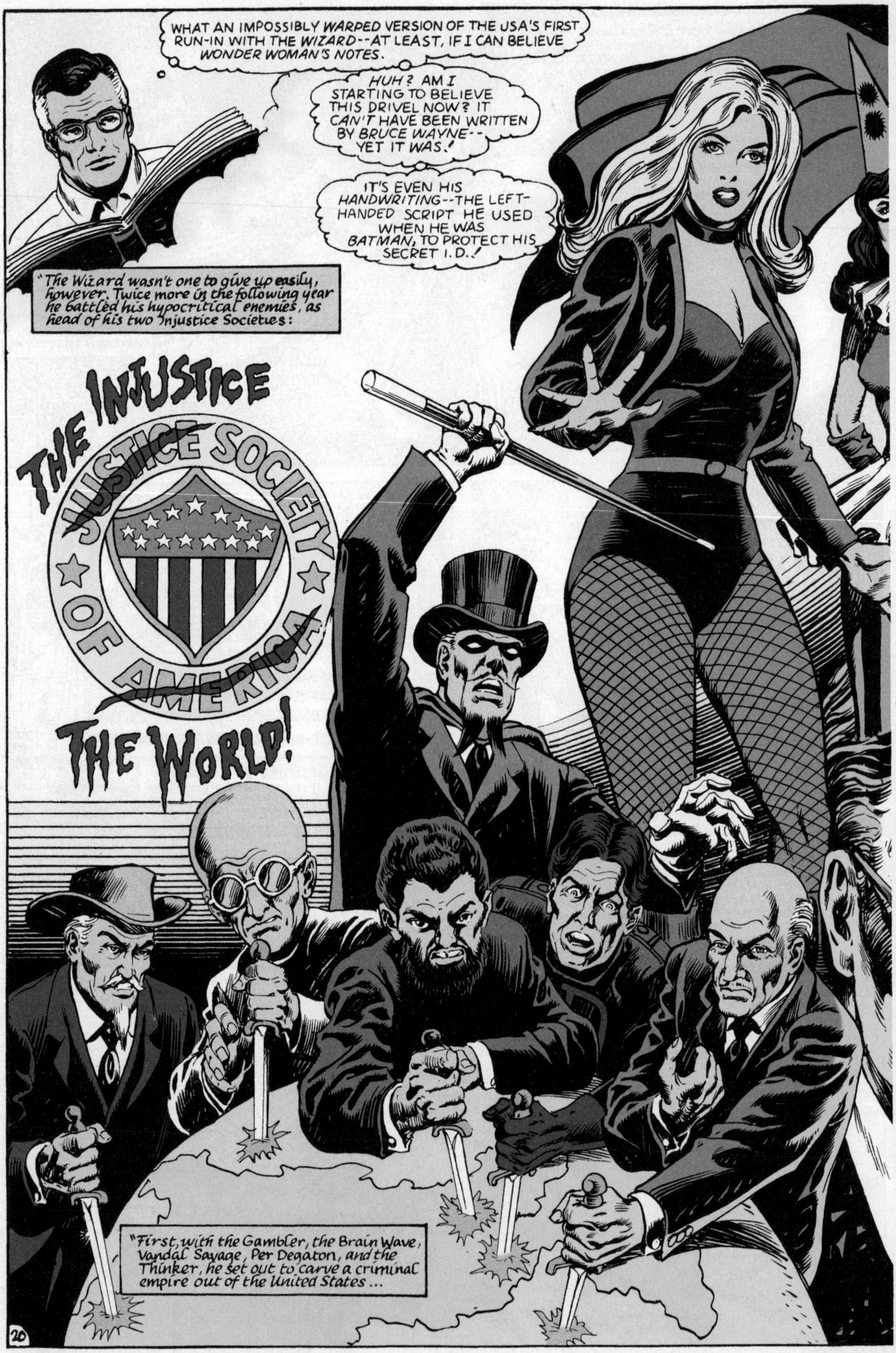
WHAT AN IMPOSSIBLY WARPED VERSION OF THE USA'S FIRST RUN-IN WITH THE WIZARD--AT LEAST, IF I CAN BELIEVE WONDER WOMAN'S NOTES.
HUH? AM I STARTING TO BELIEVE THIS DRIVEL NOW? IT CAN'T HAVE BEEN WRITTEN BY BRUCE WAYNE--YET IT WAS!
IT'S EVEN HIS HANDWRITING--THE LEFT-HANDED SCRIPT HE USED WHEN HE WAS BATMAN, TO PROTECT HIS SECRET I.D.!
"The Wizard wasn't one to give up easily, however. Twice more in the following year he battled his hypocritical enemies, as head of his two Injustice Societies:
THE INJUSTICE SOCIETY OF THE WORLD!
JUSTICE SOCIETY OF AMERICA
"First, with the Gambler, the Brain Wave, Vandal Savage, Per Degaton, and the Thinker, he set out to carve a criminal empire out of the United States...
20

"Later, with Sportsmaster, Icicle, the Fiddler, and the Huntress, he briefly made mindless slaves of the JSA --

"-- till Green Lantern's old friend/foe The Harlequin teamed up with newcomer Black Canary to put the lid back on things.

"And so the JSA's sinister secret was safe again, from the one man who might have exposed it.

"If more proof of JSA perfidy is needed, consider their longtime friendship with Prof. Elwood P. Napier, which lasted at least as late as 1950 --

"-- despite the fact that Napier had designed the deadly Flying Eye which terrorized the East Coast in January, 1942 !

21

"Then came Senator O'Fallon."

I WAS WONDERING WHEN HE'D GET AROUND TO THAT GUY!

"It was early 1951. After the fatal car accident of Sen. Joseph McCarthy of Wisconsin, O'Fallon took over special JSA-related hearings conducted by the Combined Congressional Un-Americans Activities Committee; and...

THE DAY OF HIDING BEHIND MASKS IN THIS COUNTRY IS OVER!

WE KNOW NOTHING ABOUT YOU JSAers BUT THE FEW FACTS YOU HAVE GIVEN REPORTERS--AND THAT IS NOT ENOUGH!

"I myself was there, in my other identity... as were many reporters... including Clark Kent of the Daily Star...

IF YOU ARE GOOD AMERICANS, YOU WILL SHOW THIS COMMITTEE YOUR FACES--AND THEN WE MAY BEGIN THE PROCESS OF CLEARING YOU.

WELL?

WHAT IS YOUR DECISION?

WE RESPECTFULLY DECLINE, SENATOR.

OUR FACES-- OUR NAMES-- OUR LIVES-- ARE OUR OWN BUSINESS.

BUT DON'T WORRY--

--BECAUSE YOU WON'T BE HEARING FROM US AGAIN!

HOLY--!

POOF!

"A nice exit staged by the Green Lantern-- grandstanding to the end!

"Unfortunately, Sen. O'Fallon himself died mysteriously soon afterward...

"...too soon to follow up on his investigations, and learn the JSA's startling wartime secret.

"A few masked heroes survived those days, of course:

"Myself, because of my special relationship with the Gotham City Police Commissioner...

"Wonder Woman, who had been cleared by Military Intelligence...

"...and Superman, who'd been given special status by the U.N.

22

"And so a decade went by--a decade whose menaces were a more easily recognizable lot:

"The Reds--youthful rebellion--and rock'n'roll.

"Its heroes were a different sort. They smiled or they brooded... but very few of them wore masks.

"Yet the time came--in 1963, to be exact--when the Justice Society ended its voluntary retirement--

"--to deal with another erst-while foe, Vandal Savage.

"As Savage has since vanished from the face of the earth, precisely what crimes he com-mitted--if indeed any--has never been determined.

"Over the years, I more or less retired as Batman--but Robin grew up and, because I did not tell him the true reasons for my objections, became a full fledged member of the JSA.

"The Star-Spangled Kid, not a JSAer in the 40's came out of a time warp to join--

"--as, in a sense, did Power Girl, who is rumored to be Superman's cousin.

23

29

"But if I'd given up trying to find cold, hard proof of JSA perfidy... another man had only begun.

--BRUCE WAYNE! HE'S BECOME GOTHAM'S POLICE COMMISSIONER SINCE JIM GORDON DIED, AND HE'S--

FORGET HIM FOR NOW! I'M CALLING THE WIFE AND ARRANGING A LITTLE VACATION.

YOU'LL HAVE THAT VACATION, FLASH-- AT THE STATE'S EXPENSE!

WH--? WAYNE!

RIGHT! YOU PEOPLE HAVE BEEN CAUSING CHAOS IN THIS CITY FOR WEEKS NOW--

--AND I'M TAKING YOU IN!

"Wayne spoke too quickly, though. He may have learned, somehow, how to infiltrate the group's headquarters...

"...but nothing could help mere policemen overcome super-powered devils like the Justice Society!"

"Since that day, I have felt that both Bruce Wayne and I are marked men... marked for death."

AND THAT'S JUST ABOUT IT!

IT WAS ONLY A FEW WEEKS LATER--IN EARLY '79--

"--THAT BATMAN CAME OUT OF RETIREMENT LONG ENOUGH TO BATTLE AN ESCAPED CONVICT NAMED BILL JENSEN.

"THEY BOTH DIED ON A GOTHAM ROOFTOP THAT DAY--VICTIMS OF A THIRD MAN NEITHER OF THEM KNEW--

"--BEFORE THE ANGUISHED EYES OF A NEW JSAer CALLED THE HUNTRESS.

"BATMAN--BRUCE--NEVER LIVED TO KNOW SHE WAS ALSO--HIS DAUGHTER.

24

30

"SURE, THE JUSTICE SOCIETY CAUGHT THE *REAL KILLER* LATER--ONE *FREDRIC VAUX,* WHO'D SOLD HIS SOUL TO SOME *NETHER GODS*--

"--BUT THAT COULDN'T BRING *BATMAN* BACK TO LIFE.

*d.1979*

"THE MOST THAT COULD BE DONE WAS FOR *DR. FATE* TO USE HIS *MAGIC*--

BUT NOW, MAYBE DR. FATE'S WORK-- MUST BE *UNDONE.*

"--TO MAKE EVERY-ONE BELIEVE THAT *BRUCE WAYNE* AND *BATMAN* DIED *SEPARATE DEATHS* THAT DAY.

*BRUCE WAYNE*
*1915-1979*

"THAT PROTECTED *DICK'S* AND *HELENA'S* ALTER EGOS...

YET-- IT'S NOT FOR *ME* TO DECIDE.

OLSEN!

YOU CALLED ME, CHIEF?

I TOLD YOU-- DON'T CALL ME "CHIEF"!

I WANT YOU TO *VERIFY* THE AUTHENTICITY OF THIS *DOCUMENT* SOMEONE TURNED OVER TO ME--

--THEN DECIDE IF ITS CONTENTS SHOULD BE *PUBLISHED* OR *NOT!*

TRUTH WILL OUT, MAN OF STEEL--NOR SHALL THIS *TIME* PROVE AN EXCEPTION.

I GUESS THEY CHECKED OUT *BATMAN'S HANDWRITING* EVEN FASTER THAN I'D FIGURED.

CAN YOU EVER *FORGIVE* ME, MY FRIENDS-- FOR LETTING THAT *TISSUE OF LIES* BE PRINTED?

IF ONLY WE KNEW *WHY* BATMAN WROTE ALL THOSE LIES --

--SO THAT NO *INNOCENT PERSONS* ARE HURT IN THE STRUGGLE TO *CAPTURE* YOU!

WE ASK YOU TO GIVE YOURSELVES UP, PENDING A *CONGRESSIONAL INVESTIGATION*--

--AND HOW TO *DEFEND* OUR-SELVES, WITHOUT *SLANDERING* THE MEMORY OF--

ATTENTION, JUSTICE SOCIETY!--

THEY'RE HERE!

WE HAD EVEN LESS TIME TO PLOT STRATEGY THAN WE'D THOUGHT!

SUPERMAN IS *NOT* ACCUSED-- NOR ROBIN OR THE YOUNGER MEMBERS--SO IF THEY ARE WITH YOU--!

HERE THEY COME!

25

POWER GIRL AND THE OTHER YOUNGSTERS AREN'T HERE, SOLDIER--

--BUT IF YOU WANT THE JUSTICE SOCIETY--

--THEN YOU'VE GOT TO TAKE IN SUPERMAN, AS WELL!

NOW WHAT?

WE BROUGHT ALONG KRYPTONITE MANACLES-- JUST IN CASE.

UP WITH 'EM, SUPERMAN!

THEN I'M GOING, T--

NO, ROBIN! ONE OF US MUST REMAIN FREE, TO GET TO THE BOTTOM OF ALL THIS--

--ONE WHO WAS TOO YOUNG IN THE EARLY 1940'S TO BE ACCUSED OF TREASON.

I'LL...DO THE BEST I CAN, FOR YOUR SAKE--AND FOR BATMAN'S.

UH--KEEP MOVING, JSA!

WHILE, NEARBY...

SO! IT BEGINS...

...AND THERE WAS NOTHING I COULD DO, BUT WATCH.

WELL, THE HUNTRESS IS ALL DONE WITH WATCHING!

I'M GOING TO FIND OUT IF MY FELLOW JSAers ARE GUILTY OR INNOCENT.

AND IF THEY'RE INNOCENT, I'LL GO THROUGH HELL TO DEFEND THEM--AS HELENA WAYNE, ATTORNEY-AT-LAW--

--EVEN IF IT MEANS I MUST CALL MY FATHER A LIAR-- IN HIS VERY GRAVE!

26

WHILE, IN THE SHADOW OF THE HUGE WAITING 'COPTER, THE HUNTRESS' VIRTUAL STEP-BROTHER-- THE MAN WHO WAS ONCE BRUCE WAYNE'S WARD-- SEETHES WITH AN IMPOTENT RAGE WHICH THREATENS TO TEAR HIM APART FROM WITHIN.

BUT HE SAYS NOTHING MORE...

ART THIS CHAPTER BY RAFAEL KAYANAN & ALFREDO ALCALA

CHAPTER TWO

# WITNESS FOR THE PERSECUTION!

27

... AS, NEXT MOMENT, THE JSAers ARE HERDED UNCEREMONIOUSLY ABOARD, BY SOLDIERS AND POLICEMEN WHOSE FACES BETRAY AN EERIE MIXTURE OF TENSION AND RELIEF.

WHATEVER THEIR PRIVATE OPINIONS AS TO THE FALLEN HEROES' GUILT OR INNOCENCE, THE UNIFORMED MEN SUSPECT (CORRECTLY) THAT A GOODLY NUMBER OF THEM COULD BREAK FREE AT ANY INSTANT, SHOULD THEY SO DESIRE.

POLICE

28

YET THEY GO QUIETLY, THESE LONGTIME DEFENDERS OF AMERICAN JUSTICE, BECAUSE THEY HAVE ELECTED TO HEED THE ADVICE OF ONE SOCRATES, CONDEMNED TO DEATH BY ATHENS IN 399 B.C. AND REFUSING TO FLEE THE CITY FOR HIS LIFE:

"DO YOU IMAGINE THAT A STATE CAN SUBSIST AND NOT BE OVERTHROWN, IN WHICH THE DECISIONS OF LAW HAVE NO POWER, BUT ARE SET ASIDE AND TRAMPLED UPON BY INDIVIDUALS?"

IF ANY AMONG THEM HAS NAGGING DOUBTS ABOUT THE COURSE OF ACTION DECIDED UPON, HE DOES NOT REVEAL IT.

THE JUSTICE SOCIETY HAS EVER BEEN A GROUP WHICH HAS ACTED BY CONSENSUS; THIS HAS BEEN ITS ROCK, ITS STRENGTH, IN DAYS AND DECADES PAST.

IS IT JUST BARELY POSSIBLE THAT, TODAY, IT MAY PROVE TO BE THE JSA'S TRAGIC WEAKNESS, AS WELL?

29

DICK...

WH--? OH-- HELENA! I WONDERED IF MAYBE YOU WERE LURKING AROUND SOMEWHERE.

I WAS-- AGAINST "UNCLE CLARK'S" ADVICE.

WELL, NOW, WHAT DO WE DO?

I--I JUST DON'T KNOW! HELL, I'M NOT EVEN SURE I SHOULD DO ANYTHING.

HUH? YOU DON'T MEAN YOU THINK THEY MIGHT BE GUILTY!?

NO! AND YET-- THAT DIARY WAS WRITTEN BY BATMAN-- BY BRUCE. IT'S NOT A FORGERY.

I KNOW WHAT YOU'RE GOING TO SAY: THAT JUST MEANS HE MUST'VE HAD A GOOD REASON TO WRITE IT, AND WE'VE JUST GOT TO FIGURE OUT WHAT IT WAS.

AND LORD, DON'T I WISH IT WAS THAT SIMPLE!

AND WHY ISN'T IT?

MAYBE MORE, 'CAUSE I'VE BEEN ONE OF 'EM A LOT LONGER.

LOOK, I WANT TO ASSUME THE JSAers ARE INNOCENT, AS MUCH AS YOU DO.

BUT?

BUT BATMAN'S WORD ALWAYS CARRIED A LOT OF WEIGHT WITH ME--STILL DOES.

OR MAYBE THAT'S JUST BECAUSE I KNEW HIM A LOT BETTER THAN YOU EVER DID!

30

BULL! IF YOU WANT TO BELIEVE DAD COULD EVER HAVE BEEN A *NAZI SPY,* EVEN FOR ONE MINUTE, THAT JUST PROVES YOU NEVER KNEW HIM AS WELL AS YOU *THINK* YOU DID!

OKAY, GO PLAY *HAMLET* ALL YOU WANT--FUTZING AROUND THE EDGES OF THE ACTION, DOING NOTHING--BUT NOT *ME!*

BRUCE WAYNE WAS MY *FATHER,* DICK--BUT I STILL SAY THAT DIARY'S A DAMNED *LIE,* FROM START TO FINISH!

WHAT'S MORE, I INTEND TO *PROVE* IT-- AND NOW THAT YOU'RE BACK TO PLAYING *LAWYER* AGAIN YOURSELF, I'D THINK YOU'D BUST YOUR BUNS *HELPING* ME!

I'D LIKE TO, AND YOU *KNOW* I WANT TO SEE THE USAERS *ACQUITTED...*

DO I?

...BUT I JUST CAN'T BE A PARTY TO ANY-THING THAT MIGHT *DEFAME BATMAN*-- EVEN IN *DEATH!*

PUT IT DOWN TO MY NOT HAVING *HAD* A REAL FATHER A LOT OF THE TIME WHEN I WAS GROWING UP; MAYBE I JUST NEED THE MEMORIES I *DO* HAVE A LOT WORSE THAN YOU DO.

THINK ANY DAMN THING YOU *WANT*--BUT I'M GONNA HAVE TO SIT THIS ONE OUT!

DICK, I...

I DIDN'T REALIZE YOU WERE IN... SUCH *PAIN.*

I'M SO SORRY.

ME, TOO, HELENA. ME, TOO.

GOD.

LOOK, YOU DO WHAT YOU'VE GOT TO DO. ME, I'M STILL FEELING GUILTY AS HELL FOR SITTING AROUND IN THERE--AND NEVER *TELLING* THE OTHERS HOW I FELT.

WHATEVER HAPPENS--LET'S NOT LET ANYTHING PUT UP *BARRIERS* BETWEEN US, OKAY? LET'S ALWAYS BE ABLE TO *TALK.*

I PRAY WE WILL, DICK.

GOODBYE... FOR NOW.

31

...AND THIS TAPE, JUST IN, SHOWS THE JSA SURRENDERING TO ARMY TROOPS, ONLY MINUTES AGO....!

IS THIS SOME KIND OF JOKE!??

I KNOW THOSE MANACLES ARE A LEGAL REQUIREMENT-- SINCE THEY'RE ACCUSED OF A FELONY-- BUT--

EASY, FURY--LYTA! YOU MAY BE WONDER WOMAN'S KID AND ALL, BUT I'M STILL AN AUXILIARY JSAer MYSELF...

AND I'M POSITIVE THEY'LL BEAT THIS THING, WHEN THE TRUTH COMES OUT.

IF THAT'S THE KIND OF "JUSTICE" THE SOCIETY'S BEEN FIGHTING FOR ALL THESE YEARS--MAYBE WE'RE LUCKY THEY DIDN'T VOTE TO LET US IN, LAST CHRISTMAS EVE.

YEAH. LUCKY US.

IF IT COMES OUT! GUESS YOU 1940'S TYPES JUST HAVE A WEE BIT MORE FAITH IN JUSTICE TRIUMPHANT THAN LYTA AND I DO.

SYLVESTER PEMBERTON

BUT I STILL THINK MAYBE WE SHOULD HEAD BACK EAST AND HAVE A TALK WITH THEM-- OFFER TO HELP.

WHAT DO YOU SAY, JADE?

32

HELP? WHAT HELP'S *INFINITY, INC.* GONNA BE--IF THE *JUSTICE SOCIETY* CAN'T HELP *THEM*-SELVES?

*CHECK,* SIS. BESIDES, EVEN IF THE *GREEN LANTERN* IS OUR OLD MAN--WE DON'T KNOW FOR *SURE* WHAT THE SCORE IS, RIGHT?

WHO KNOWS? MAYBE THAT CRAZY *RIVER* A WHILE BACK JUST REVEALED A RUTHLESS SIDE OF THEM THAT'S BEEN AROUND *ALL ALONG!*

THAT KIND OF TALK'LL GET YOU A *FAT LIP,* SHADOW-MAN! YOU *HEAR* ME?

THIS IS *HAWKMAN'S* NUMBER-ONE SON TALKIN' AT YOU!

WHOA, *HEC!* OBSIDIAN'S NOT YOUR ENEMY. STILL, IF HE CAN SAY THAT, WHAT HOPE IS THERE FOR THE REST OF THE COUNTRY?

MAYBE WE *WILL* HAVE TO GO BUST THEM OUT OF JAIL, AT THAT!

*I'M READY!*

LOOK, *NORTHWIND* AND I ARE JUST A COUPLE OF *HONORARY GODSONS*--BUT WE VOTE TO *COOL* IT FOR A WHILE, TILL THE *DUST* SETTLES.

WELL SAID, *NUKLON.*

AFTER ALL *HAWKMAN* AND THE OTHERS *SURRENDERED* --SO PERHAPS THEY HAVE A *PLAN* ALL THEIR OWN.

MAKES SENSE. WHAT SAY *YOU,* SYL? YOU KNOW 'EM BETTER THAN MOST OF *US* DO.

IF YOU'LL ALL JUST STAY PUT A DAY OR TWO, I'LL *CONTACT* THEM, SEE WHAT THEY'VE GOT TO SAY--AND MAKE SURE THEY'VE GOT THE BEST *LAWYER* THE PEMBERTON FORTUNE CAN BUY.

IF THE JSA WERE EVER *NAZIS,* THEN THE *STAR-SPANGLED KID* WAS A CHARTER MEMBER OF THE *HITLER YOUTH!*

33

MEANWHILE, ACROSS THE COUNTRY, FEELINGS OF EVERY SORT RUN HIGH:

HEY, DAD--SEE THIS? THEY'VE ARRESTED THOSE OLD FOGEYS YOU'RE ALWAYS TALKING ABOUT-- YOU KNOW, THE JUSTICE SOCIETY!?

I'M STILL TRYING TO DIGEST THESE HEADLINES ABOUT THE BATMAN DIARY! IF ANYBODY BUT HIM HAD ACCUSED THEM--!

THEM GUYS WAS MY HEROES! GUESS YOU CAN'T TRUST NOBODY NO MORE.!

IT SEEMS IMPOSSIBLE--YET THEY DO SAY FDR KNEW ABOUT PEARL HARBOR IN ADVANCE, SO MAYBE--!

HELL, I COULD'VE TOLD YOU THAT!

HEY, JILL, YOU READ THIS ABOUT THE USA?

WHAT'S THAT? SOME AIRLINE GOING BANKRUPT?

DAMN! DINNER'S BURNED AGAIN.!

AS, IN WASHINGTON, D.C.:

CAPITAL GLO[BE]

12 JUSTICE SOCIETY MEMB[ERS] SURRENDER TO AUTHOR[ITIES]

CONGRESS[IONAL] COMMITTE[E] SET UP TO[O] INVESTIG[ATE] CHARGES [OF] TREASO[N]

NOW THAT'S MORE LIKE IT!

BROUGHT TO CAPITAL IN CHAINS--INTERRED PENDING EARLY INVESTIGATION

THAT'S THE KIND OF HEADLINE I WANT TO SEE ON THIS NEWSPAPER--NOT SOME NAMBY-PAMBY CRUD ABOUT PEACE OFFENSES IN THE MIDDLE EAST AND WARGAMES IN CENTRAL AMERICA!

DON'T YOU THINK YOU WERE TOO SOFT ON THE JSA, THOUGH, WILKINS? I'D HAVE SAID "TWELVE TRAITORS SURRENDERED".!

DO YOU REALLY NEED YOUR EDITOR TO REMIND YOU, A.K. THAT THEY'RE PRESUMED INNOCENT UNTIL PROVEN GUILTY?

I'M JUST SORRY CONGRESS IS WASTING TIME WITH THIS COMMITTEE NONSENSE!

NOT BY MY PAPER, THEY'RE NOT!

34

THEY'RE GUILTY, ALL RIGHT! WHY ELSE'VE THEY BEEN *HIDING BEHIND MASKS* ALL THESE YEARS, LIKE A BUNCH OF *BANK ROBBERS?*

THAT *"LONE RANGER"* STUFF WENT DOWN THE DRAIN A LONG *TIME* AGO--YOU *HEAR* ME, WILKINS?

LOUD AND CLEAR MR. O'FALLON.

MY *FATHER* KNEW HOW TO DEAL WITH THOSE *COSTUMED FIFTH-COLUMNISTS,* BY HEAVEN!

HE PUT 'EM OUT OF BUSINESS BACK IN '51 WITH HIS *JOINT CONGRESSIONAL COMMITTEE*--EVEN IF HE COULDN'T QUITE *PROVE* THEY WERE NAZIS OR REDS OR ANYTHING!

**CAPITAL GLOBE**

## JUSTICE SOCIETY DISBANDS FOR GOOD

VANISHES BEFORE EYES OF JCUAC

"COULDN'T FACE THE MUSIC!" DECLARES SEN. O'FALLON

HE'D HAVE BEEN RIGHT THERE TO HOUND 'EM BACK OUT OF EXISTENCE WHEN THEY RE-FORMED IN THE *EARLY 60'S,* TOO--

--IF THEY HADN'T *GOT HIM EARLIER* WITH THAT *MYSTERIOUS FIRE!*

MR. O'FALLON, NOBODY EVER *SUGGESTED* THAT THE JSA HAD ANYTHING TO DO WITH THAT--

NOBODY EXCEPT THE *GLOBE!* THAT'S WHY I WORKED ALL MY LIFE JUST FOR THE DAY I COULD *OWN* THIS PAPER--USE IT TO *GET BACK* AT THOSE MURDERING TRAITORS!

NOW GET YOUR SO-CALLED *REPORTERS* TO WORK DIGGING UP MORE *DIRT* ON THEM--IF YOU WANT TO KEEP YOUR *JOB!*

Y-YES, SIR.

HE'S A MAN *POSSESSED!* I'D ALMOST THINK HE'S *PERSONALLY ENGINEERED* THIS BATMAN-DIARY THING.

BUT THAT'S *IMPOSSIBLE*-- ISN'T IT?

SLAMM

GOOD RIDDANCE! I JUST GOT AN IDEA TO *REALLY* PUT THE SCREWS TO THOSE CAPED FASCISTS!

SHELLY-- GET ME THE ATTORNEY-GENERAL'S OFFICE-- NOW!

BZZZ

YES, MR. O'FALLON!

35

AS, ELSEWHERE IN THE NATION'S CAPITAL, A TALL YOUNG WOMAN STRIDES UP THE STAIRS OF AN IMPOSING STRUCTURE.

HER NAME IS HELENA WAYNE; AND FOR SEVERAL YEARS NOW SHE HAS BEEN A RISING ATTORNEY WITH THE FIRM OF CRANSTON, WAYNE, & GRAYSON.

UNKNOWN TO MOST OF THE WORLD, SHE IS ALSO THE HUNTRESS-- AND BATMAN'S DAUGHTER.

OH YEAH... YOU'RE EXPECTED, MS. WAYNE.

I SORT-OF THOUGHT I MIGHT BE.

THEY'RE IN THERE. PERSONALLY, I HOPE YOU GET 'EM OFF. SOMETIMES I THINK THERE'S A CONSPIRACY AGAINST LAW-AND-ORDER TYPES.

IF IT WAS ANYBODY BUT BATMAN ACCUSIN' 'EM-- EVEN FROM THE GRAVE--!

THE FACTS IN THE CASE STILL AREN'T DECIDED, GUARD.

MAYBE NOT-- BUT IF THEY TURN OUT TO BE GUILTY, I SAY LET 'EM FRY.

MY OLD MAN WAS KILLED AT NORMANDY IN '44.

HELLO, HAWKMAN... ALL OF YOU. I'M HELENA WAYNE, AND I'VE COME TO OFFER YOU LEGAL COUNSEL.

HOW ARE THEY TREATING YOU?

TO TELL THE TRUTH, MS. WAYNE, THE, uh, HUNTRESS CLUED US IN WE MIGHT EXPECT YOU.

AS YOU PROBABLY KNOW, THE LAW PROTECTS OUR COSTUMED IDENTITIES-- UNTIL AND UNLESS WE'RE CONVICTED OF A FELONY.

YEAH-- WHICH TREASON IS DEFINITELY ONE OF!

SLOW DOWN, WILDCAT! WE'RE NOT EXACTLY SPLINTERING ROCKS AT LEAVENWORTH YET, ARE WE?

MAYBE NOT, MID-NITE... BUT IF SOME OF THE NEWS COMMENTATORS I'VE HEARD HAVE THEIR WAY--!

THEY *WON'T!* NOW LET'S GET DOWN TO CASES, SHALL WE?

I MEAN, WE'VE *HAD* OUR VISITS WITH OUR WIVES AND LOVED ONES...AND THE *INFINITORS* WON'T BE HERE TILL TOMORROW...

GOD, I *HATE* GETTING THOSE *KIDS* MIXED UP IN THIS! THEY'RE JUST *STARTING* OUT...!

*THEY* DO A PRETTY GOOD JOB OF TAKING CARE OF *THEMSELVES,* HAWK...OF *US,* TOO, SOMETIMES.

HE *KNOWS,* LANTERN, THAT *KOEHAHA* BUSINESS WASN'T THAT LONG AGO.

IN ANY EVENT--CAN WE BEGIN *NOW?* I LEFT MY *HUSBAND* IN DIRE STRAITS TO JOIN YOU ALL--

WE AP-PRECIATE THAT, DIANA.

--BUT I WANT TO GET BACK TO AMAZON COUNTRY AS SOON AS POSSIBLE!

BY THE WAY, HELENA--THE HAWKMAN'S *COYNESS* TO THE CONTRARY, WE MADE SURE THIS ROOM *ISN'T BUGGED.*

SO YOU CAN *RELAX,* AND TELL US--HOW COME *DICK GRAYSON* DIDN'T COME WITH YOU? ISN'T HE PRACTICING LAW AGAIN?

HE--HE *WOULD'VE* COME, BUT HE'S--WELL, HE'S FEELING PRETTY *CONFUSED,* RIGHT ABOUT NOW.

AREN'T WE *ALL!*

I...SEE.

WELL, BE THAT AS IT MAY--HAVE YOU THOUGHT OF ANY *DEFENSE* WE CAN USE AGAINST YOUR FATHER'S CHARGES?

IF HE'S THE ONE WHO MADE THEM! WELL--

HOW ABOUT THE FACT THAT, AS POLICE COMMISSIONER, BRUCE WAYNE WAS OBVIOUSLY-- *TROUBLED* IN HIS LAST DAYS?

YES, I'M *PREPARED* TO GO THAT FAR-- IF I MUST.

37

ARE YOU CERTAIN, HELENA? IT WOULD SEEM A PITY TO REVEAL YOUR LATE FATHER'S SECRET--UNDO WHAT I DID TO PRESERVE IT--!

AS A LAST RESORT, ATOM--WHATEVER THE REST OF YOU MAY DECIDE--I DO NOT INTEND TO SPEND THE REST OF MY ALLOTTED DAYS IN PRISON IN MAN'S WORLD. MAKE OF THAT-- WHAT YOU MAY!

YEAH, FATE, BUT AS A LAST RESORT--!

WHAT'S WRONG, LANTERN?

THERE WENT THE LAST OF MY RING-POWER! IT'S BEEN 24 HOURS SINCE I CHARGED IT.

IS THAT ALL? MY MIRACLO WORE OFF HOURS AGO.

SURE! THAT'S IT! THEY'LL STRIP US OF OUR POWERS, ONE BY ONE--WEAR US DOWN--THEN LOCK US UP AND VAPORIZE THE KEY!

WHAM!

WILDCAT, FOR PITY'S SAKE--!

DON'T BREAK YOUR FIST ON THAT WALL, FRIEND. LORD KNOWS, I FEEL AS LOW AS ANY OF YOU.

AW, YOU JUST DID WHAT YA HAD TO DO!

BUT OKAY, LADY--LET'S HEAR YOUR ANGLE!

WILDCAT'S RIGHT: AS CLARK KENT, SUPERMAN ONLY DID WHAT ANY OF US, OR ANY RESPONSIBLE JOURNALIST, WOULD HAVE DONE IF GIVEN THAT DIARY.

NOW, THE WAY I SEE IT, THERE ARE TWO CHARGES WHICH, IF PROVEN TO THE COMMITTEE'S SATISFACTION, WILL LEAD TO YOUR BEING TRIED FOR TREASON.

AND THEY ARE?

FIRST: THAT ALL OF YOU, EXCEPT MAYBE SUPERMAN, WORKED FOR HITLER DURING THE WAR...

...AND SECOND: THE SABOTAGE OF THAT BOMB DEFENSE RAY IN '41.

EVERYTHING ELSE IS JUST COVER-UP. BAD ENOUGH, BUT...

38

WHAT YOU'RE SAYING, THEN, IS THAT WE'D BETTER TELL YOU ALL WE KNOW ABOUT THOSE TWO LITTLE EPISODES--

--AND HOPE WE CAN COME UP WITH PROOF THAT WE'RE TELLING THE TRUTH, RIGHT?

ESSENTIALLY. OF COURSE, THIS ISN'T A TRIAL-- JUST A CONGRESSIONAL INQUIRY TO SEE IF THERE ARE GROUNDS TO TRY YOU ALL FOR TREASON, BUT--

OKAY. WELL, ALAN AND I ARE THE ONLY TWO STILL ALIVE WHO WERE IN ON THE HITLER THING FROM THE VERY START...

...SO I GUESS THE BALL'S IN MY COURT.

PLEASE TELL ME WHAT REALLY HAPPENED BACK THERE IN NOVEMBER 1940--AND LET ME TAKE IT FROM THERE.

WELL, LET'S SEE-- FDR HAD JUST GOT HIMSELF ELECTED TO A THIRD TERM--

"--HITLER HAD ALREADY GOBBLED UP MOST OF WESTERN EUROPE, JAPAN WAS NIBBLING AWAY AT CHIANG KAI-SHEK'S CHINA--

"--AND IN KEYSTONE CITY, I WAS USING MY SUPER-SPEED FOR REALLY IMPORTANT THINGS LIKE TACKLING CHEAP HOODS WHO'D CONFUSED A SAVINGS-AND-LOAN COMPANY WITH THEIR PERSONAL PIGGY-BANKS, WHEN--

FLASH! GLAD I LOCATED YOU! I'LL TAKE THOSE TWO.

GOTHAM CITY'S POLICE COMMISSIONER ASKED IF YOU COULD SCOOT OVER TO HIS BURG FOR A LITTLE WHILE.

HMMM... WONDER WHAT GOTHAM'S TOP COP WANTS WITH ME!?

"IT'S A HUNDRED MILES OR SO FROM KEYSTONE TO GOTHAM. SO, A COUPLE OF MINUTES LATER...

HELLO, COMMISSIONER GORDON. I'M--HEY! ISN'T THAT THE GREEN LANTERN BESIDE YOU?

FLATTERED YOU'VE HEARD OF ME, FLASH.

I'VE SIGNALED THE BATMAN TO COME HERE AS SOON AS POSSIBLE, ALSO; GENTLEMEN.

I'LL AWAIT HIM IN MY OTHER OFFICE -- THEN TURN YOU ALL OVER TO "MR. SMYTHE" HERE FOR A BRIEFING ON WHY I CONTACTED YOU.

"'SMYTHE'--LIKE THAT 'DIARY' SAID, HE WAS A BRITISH SECRET AGENT WHO WORKED FOR 'THE MAN CALLED INTREPID.'

"IT WASN'T LONG BEFORE BATMAN JOINED US, AND --

39

"WELL, AT LEAST, THE 'DIARY' GOT HIS PART STRAIGHT:

GENTLEMEN, YOUR *PRESIDENT* HAS AUTHORIZED ME TO ASK THE THREE OF YOU--

--TO UNDERTAKE A *SECRET MISSION* WHICH MAY WELL DECIDE THE SURVIVAL OF THE *BRITISH NATION*--AND YOUR OWN."

"I DON'T GUESS ANY OF US HAD *MET* ROOSEVELT...AT THAT POINT--BUT ANYWAY, OFF WE WENT--"

"--FIRST TO *SCOTLAND*, WHERE A NAZI NAMED *HELMUT STREICHER* HAD SET UP A HIDDEN BASE TO BACKSTOP AN *INVASION* FROM THE *CONTINENT.*"

"WHEN THINGS TIPPED OUR WAY, HE UN-LEASHED HIS APTLY-NAMED 'MURDER MACHINE' AT US--A *ROBOT,* PRETTY ADVANCED FOR THOSE DAYS--"

"--AND, LET'S FACE IT--IT *CLOBBERED* US!"

"WHEN WE WOKE FROM A SEDATED SLEEP, WE WERE IN *BERLIN,* OF ALL PLACES--LISTENING TO *DER FÜHRER* HIMSELF IN THE MIDDLE OF ONE OF HIS PATENTED *RANT-AND-RAVE* SPEECHES..."

WE, THE GERMAN RACE, HAVE ALWAYS KNOWN WE *ARYANS* WERE THE BORN MASTERS OF THE WORLD-- BUT NOW I SHALL *PROVE* IT --

--BY *KILLING* THESE THREE *AMERIKANER "HEROES"*--WITH THE ANCIENT *SPEAR OF DESTINY* THAT A ROMAN SOLDIER ONCE USED ON *CHRIST* HIMSELF!

"THIS WAS THE *FIRST* WE SAW OF THAT ODD SPEAR WHICH GAVE US SO MUCH TROUBLE DURING THE WAR--AND I GUESS IT WOULD'VE BEEN THE *LAST,* TOO--"

"--EXCEPT THAT, JUST THEN, *HERR HITLER* HAD COMPANY:

"DR. FATE AND THE HOURMAN, WHO'D ANSWERED THE PRESIDENT'S CALL A WEE BIT LATE.

"WELL, BETTER LATE THAN NEVER, I ALWAYS SAY.

"UNCLE ADOLF PROBABLY HAD OTHER IDEAS."

"WHEN HE SAW FATE SCATTERING HIS TROOPS LIKE SO MANY SAUSAGES, *DER FÜHRER* USED THE *SPEAR OF DESTINY* TO CALL UP A COUPLE OF FIST-FULS OF *VALKYRIES,* NO LESS.

"I'LL LEAVE IT TO *CONGRESS* TO DEBATE WHETHER THEY WERE THE REAL VALHALLA McCOY--OR WHETHER HITLER JUST CALLED THEM INTO EXISTENCE WITH *MAGIC* ADDED TO HIS WELL-DOCUMENTED *WILL POWER.*

"THEY CAME, ANY-WAY--AND EVEN *HE* PROBABLY HAD NO IDEA OF THE FANTASTICALLY POWERFUL *FORCES* HE'D JUST UN-LEASHED ON THE WORLD.

"THE *SWORD-SISTERS*--THE *'CHOOSERS OF THE SLAIN'*--TOOK OFF TOWARD *GREAT BRITAIN*--

"--LEAVING US NO CHOICE BUT TO BREAK OFF FIGHTING AND *PURSUE* THEM--

"--WHILE HITLER CONTINUED TO *RAVE:*

*THE GODS THEMSELVES HAVE SHOWN THAT I AM RIGHT--AND GERMANY IS DESTINED TO RULE!*

*ORDER THE SHIPS TO SEA! WE INVADE ENGLAND-- TONIGHT!*

"SO WHILE *WE* FOUGHT THE VALKYRIES OVER-HEAD, IT'S VIRTUALLY UNKNOWN TODAY THAT--MORE THAN 3½ YEARS BEFORE OUR *D-DAY*--AN INVASION FLEET SET SAIL *FROM* OCCUPIED FRANCE FOR BRITAIN.

"*DR. FATE* HAD SENT OUT A FOUR-PRONGED MYSTIC TENTACLE TO *AMERICA,* THOUGH--

"--AND THAT'S WHY *HAWKMAN, SANDMAN,* AND THE *ATOM* WERE ON HAND TO GIVE THE NAZIS A *WELCOME* THEY'D NEVER FORGET.

"BUT I SAID 'FOUR-PRONGED,' NOT THREE.

"THE FOURTH PART OF FATE'S TENTACLE HAD REACHED A BEING EVEN MORE POWERFUL THAN HIMSELF--THE SPECTRE!

"SCRATCH ONE INVASION FLEET.

"THE SPECTRE ISN'T LIKELY TO VOUCH FOR HIS PART IN THINGS, OF COURSE, SINCE HE CROSSED OVER TO DWELL ON EARTH-ONE A FEW YEARS BACK...

"OH YEAH, I ALMOST FORGOT-- HITLER'D SENT A PROTOTYPE SUPER-BOMBER TO ATTACK THE CAPITAL, TOO.

"EVEN WITH THE SPECTRE ON OUR SIDE, WE WERE HARD-PRESSED FIGHTING THE VALKYRIES--

"BUT THAT MADE NINE OF US WHO COULD NOW CHASE THE VALKYRIES, WHO'D FLOWN OFF NOW FOR WASHINGTON, D.C.

"--WHEN A GENT NAMED SUPERMAN CAME ROCKETING UP FROM A PHONE BOOTH SOMEWHERE IN THE PRESS BUILDING, BLESS HIS HEART!

SMAASH!

"SINCE EYE-WITNESSES COULD VERIFY THAT HE ONLY CAME IN ON ACT THREE, HE'S NOT NAMED AS A TRAITOR IN THAT DIARY BATMAN'S SUPPOSED TO HAVE WRITTEN.

"AS FOR US, WE COULD USE ALL THE HELP WE COULD GET...

42

"...SINCE WE WERE BARELY *HOLDING OUR OWN* AGAINST THE WARRIOR WOMEN."

"THE *ATOM* WAS ONE OF THOSE WHO FELL..."

"BUT YOU KNOW *AL,* HERE; HE'S A SCRAPPER, AND YOU'D HAVE TO *KILL* HIM TO STOP HIM."

"SO, WHEN THE *FOREMOST* OF THE VALKYRIES MADE IT TO THE *WHITE HOUSE*--TO FULFILL HER MISSION BY KILLING *PRESIDENT ROOSEVELT* HIMSELF--"

"--IT WAS THE *MIGHTY MITE* WHO TOOK THE BLOW INSTEAD!"

"*ONLY* A MADMAN OR A LIAR WOULD TRY CONVINCING THE WORLD HE JUST *STUMBLED* INTO HER PATH--OR THAT HE WAS REALLY THERE TO ASSASSINATE FDR."

"ANYWAY, NEXT MOMENT, *SUPERMAN* WAS THERE--"

"--WITH A GRIP EVEN A *VALKYRIE* COULDN'T BREAK."

"THAT'S WHY SHE WAS SUMMONED BACK TO *VALHALLA,* HER MISSION A FAILURE."

"SO *FATE* AND THE *SPECTRE* SAID, ANYWAY."

"THE OTHER VALKYRIES VANISHED, TOO, SO--"

HOW'S THE *LITTLE FELLOW?* THE ONE WHO TOOK THE SPEAR MEANT FOR ME?

F-FINE, SIR, DON'T YOU KNOW-- YOU CAN'T SPLIT AN ATOM?

HA HA HA! VERY GOOD!

HERE YOU STAND-- THE *GREATEST HEROES* OUR GREAT NATION HAS KNOWN. IT'S A SHAME YOU CAN'T STAY TOGETHER THAT WAY.

"WHEN FDR TALKED THAT WAY, YOU KNEW HE WAS *AFTER* SOMETHING--AND OF COURSE HE GOT IT."

"IT WAS SUPERMAN WHO GAVE US OUR *NAME*--"

43

--BUT THE *REAL* FOUNDER OF THE *JUSTICE SOCIETY OF AMERICA* WAS NONE OTHER THAN *FRANKLIN DELANO ROOSEVELT.*

INTERESTING. HE SORT-OF CALLED THE WARTIME *ALL-STAR SQUADRON* INTO EXISTENCE ABOUT A YEAR LATER, TOO, DIDN'T HE?

YES-- RIGHT AFTER *PEARL HARBOR.*

NOW, ABOUT THAT *SECOND* MAIN POINT YOU RAISED --THE *BOMB DEFENSE FORMULA* THING--

"--THAT DIARY'S *RIGHT* IN TELLING HOW SOME JSAers SAVED A BUNCH OF PROMINENT SCIENTISTS FROM ARMED *SPIES*--

"--THOUGH IT DOESN'T OFFER A SHRED OF *PROOF* THAT THEY WERE REALLY *SOVIET* ONES, NOT *NAZIS.*

"THE BOYS WENT INTO THE *FAR FUTURE,* MORE OR LESS LIKE IT SAYS, TO GET THE FORMULA--

"--AND CAME BACK TO THE SAME *SECOND* THEY'D *LEFT.*

I DON'T KNOW *WHY* IT WORKED THE FIRST TIME IT WAS TRIED--PROTECTING A HUGE FIELD FROM THE BIGGEST *BOMBS* THE ARMY AIR FORCE COULD HURL AT IT--

--OR WHY IT *FAILED* A SECOND TEST, LEAVING A CRATER BIG ENOUGH TO PLAY *FOOTBALL* IN.

THAT WASN'T OUR *DEPARTMENT.*

"IF GENIUSES LIKE *EVERSON* AND *ZEE* WERE AT A LOSS TO EXPLAIN IT--

"--HOW ARE *WE* SUPPOSED TO KNOW WHAT HAPPENED?

"THE DIARY CLAIMS THE FORMULA-DEVICE WAS TAMPERED WITH; I WOULDN'T KNOW ABOUT THAT, EITHER.

"BUT IT IS TRUE THAT BECAUSE OF THAT FAILURE, IT WAS NEVER TESTED AGAIN--AND EVENTUALLY WOUND UP ON THE SCRAP HEAP BEFORE WAR'S END.

"SOON AFTERWARD, THAT BRAIN TRUST BROKE UP, EACH MAN GOING HIS OWN WAY TO WORK ON TIME-RELATED INVENTIONS...

...END OF ALIBI.

HAWKMAN, YOU LOOK LIKE YOU'D LIKE TO ADD SOMETHING TO THAT.

I WAS JUST THINKING HOW, IN LATER YEARS, OUR PATHS CROSSED THOSE OF SO MANY OF THOSE SCIENTISTS AGAIN...

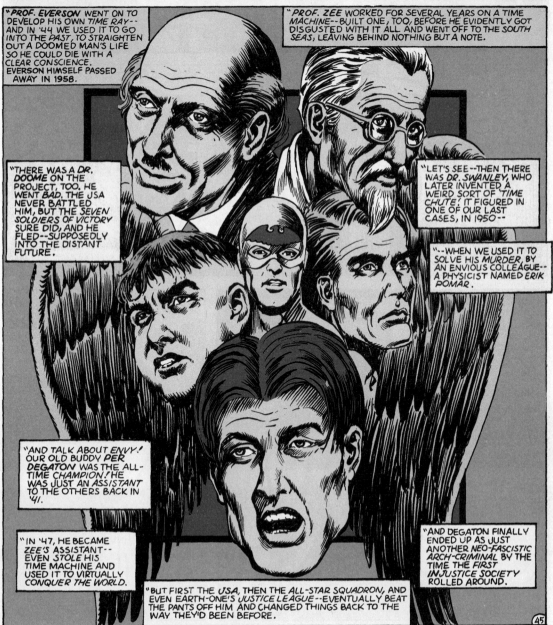

"PROF. EVERSON WENT ON TO DEVELOP HIS OWN TIME RAY--AND IN '44 WE USED IT TO GO INTO THE PAST, TO STRAIGHTEN OUT A DOOMED MAN'S LIFE SO HE COULD DIE WITH A CLEAR CONSCIENCE. EVERSON HIMSELF PASSED AWAY IN 1958.

"PROF. ZEE WORKED FOR SEVERAL YEARS ON A TIME MACHINE--BUILT ONE, TOO, BEFORE HE EVIDENTLY GOT DISGUSTED WITH IT ALL AND WENT OFF TO THE SOUTH SEAS, LEAVING BEHIND NOTHING BUT A NOTE.

"THERE WAS A DR. DOOME ON THE PROJECT, TOO. HE WENT BAD. THE JSA NEVER BATTLED HIM, BUT THE SEVEN SOLDIERS OF VICTORY SURE DID, AND HE FLED--SUPPOSEDLY INTO THE DISTANT FUTURE.

"LET'S SEE--THEN THERE WAS DR. SWANLEY, WHO LATER INVENTED A WEIRD SORT OF 'TIME CHUTE.' IT FIGURED IN ONE OF OUR LAST CASES, IN 1950 --

"--WHEN WE USED IT TO SOLVE HIS MURDER, BY AN ENVIOUS COLLEAGUE-- A PHYSICIST NAMED ERIK POMAR.

"AND TALK ABOUT ENVY! OUR OLD BUDDY PER DEGATON WAS THE ALL-TIME CHAMPION! HE WAS JUST AN ASSISTANT TO THE OTHERS BACK IN '41.

"IN '47, HE BECAME ZEE'S ASSISTANT-- EVEN STOLE HIS TIME MACHINE AND USED IT TO VIRTUALLY CONQUER THE WORLD.

"AND DEGATON FINALLY ENDED UP AS JUST ANOTHER NEO-FASCISTIC ARCH-CRIMINAL BY THE TIME THE FIRST INJUSTICE SOCIETY ROLLED AROUND.

"BUT FIRST THE USA, THEN THE ALL-STAR SQUADRON, AND EVEN EARTH-ONE'S JUSTICE LEAGUE--EVENTUALLY BEAT THE PANTS OFF HIM AND CHANGED THINGS BACK TO THE WAY THEY'D BEEN BEFORE.

45

HE WAS OUT ON *PAROLE*, LAST I HEARD--A BROKEN OLD MAN, BUT--

SAY, I WAS JUST WONDERING-- WHY WASN'T *PROF. NICHOLS* IN THAT WARTIME *BRAIN TRUST?* THINK IT WAS BECAUSE THAT TIME TRAVEL WAS ALL DONE BY *HYPNOSIS?*

*PLEASE!* MY HEAD'S STILL SPINNING FROM ALL THAT TIME- TRAVEL --!

UH-- PARDON ME, MS. WAYNE...

YES?

JUST CAUGHT THIS ON THE *TUBE* DURING MY *BREAK*-- FIGURED ANOTHER CHANNEL'D BE SHOWING IT BY NOW.

SHOWING *WHAT?*

YOU'LL SEE.

ANDREW VINSON HERE, IN WASHINGTON--

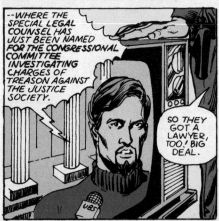

--WHERE THE SPECIAL LEGAL COUNSEL HAS JUST BEEN NAMED FOR THE CONGRESSIONAL COMMITTEE INVESTIGATING CHARGES OF *TREASON* AGAINST THE JUSTICE SOCIETY.

SO THEY GOT A *LAWYER*, TOO! *BIG DEAL.*

THE ANNOUNCEMENT CAME AS A *BLOCKBUSTER*, SINCE IT'S A MAN WHO HAS TIES TO ONE OF THE STERNEST *CRITICS* OF THE *JSA* --

*CRITICS?* WHO THE --?

*NO!* IT CAN'T BE HIM! IT *CAN'T!*

--NAMELY, *RICHARD M. GRAYSON*, FORMER AMBASSADOR TO THE UNION OF SOUTH AFRICA!

NOT ONLY IS GRAYSON THE FORMER WARD OF THE LATE POLICE COMMISSIONER *BRUCE WAYNE*, WHO HAD LED A DRIVE TO *OUTLAW* THE JSA BEFORE HIS UNTIMELY DEATH IN 1979...

...BUT RUMOR HAS IT THAT WAYNE'S DAUGHTER *HELENA* IS EVEN NOW BEING RETAINED AS COUNSEL BY THE JUSTICE SOCIETY ITSELF.

SHOULD MAKE FOR SOME *INTERESTING* HEARINGS, EH, FOLKS?

OH MY GOD...!

46

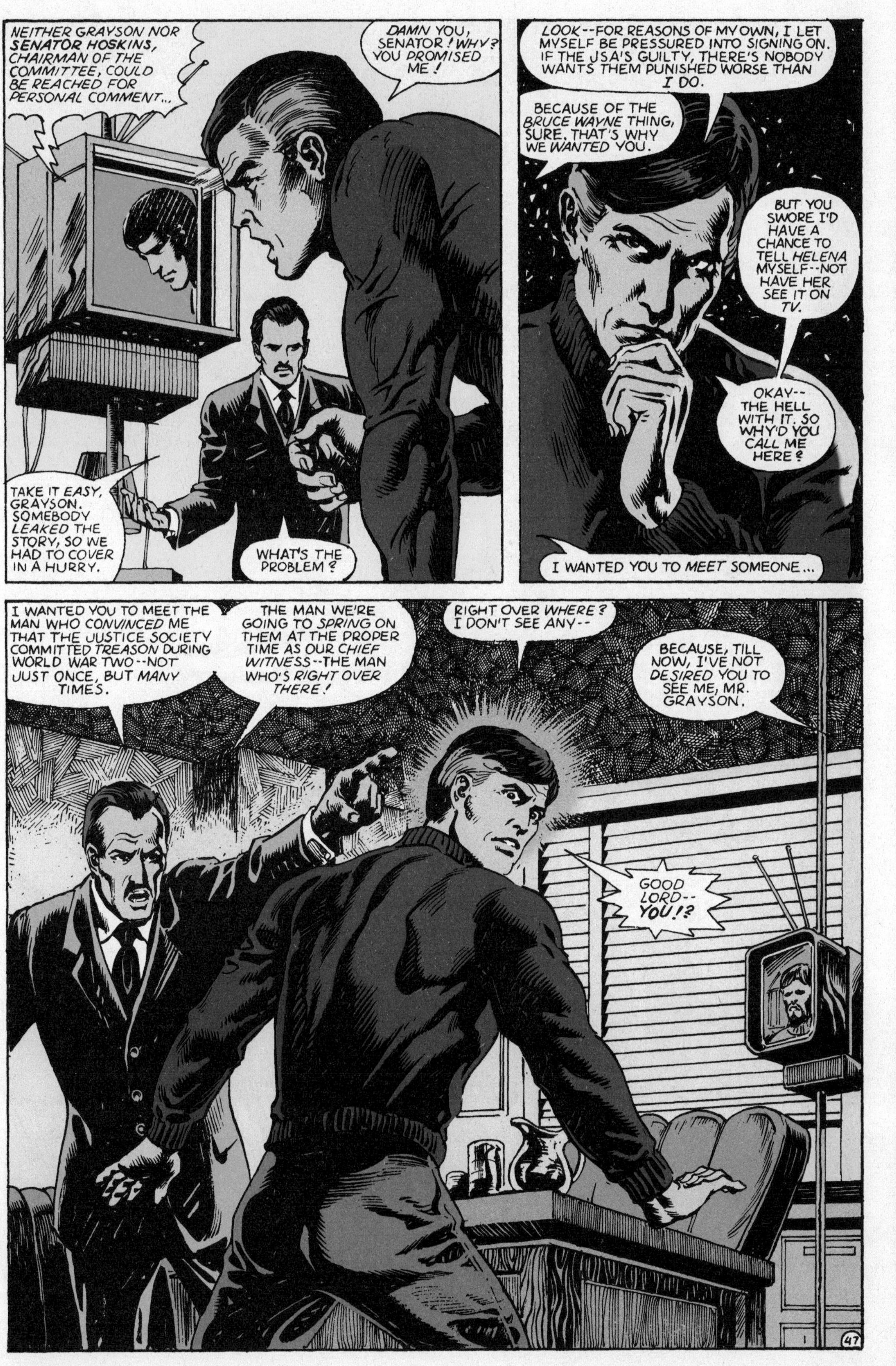
NEITHER GRAYSON NOR SENATOR HOSKINS, CHAIRMAN OF THE COMMITTEE, COULD BE REACHED FOR PERSONAL COMMENT...
DAMN YOU, SENATOR! WHY? YOU PROMISED ME!
TAKE IT EASY, GRAYSON. SOMEBODY LEAKED THE STORY, SO WE HAD TO COVER IN A HURRY.
WHAT'S THE PROBLEM?
LOOK--FOR REASONS OF MY OWN, I LET MYSELF BE PRESSURED INTO SIGNING ON. IF THE JSA'S GUILTY, THERE'S NOBODY WANTS THEM PUNISHED WORSE THAN I DO.
BECAUSE OF THE BRUCE WAYNE THING, SURE. THAT'S WHY WE WANTED YOU.
BUT YOU SWORE I'D HAVE A CHANCE TO TELL HELENA MYSELF--NOT HAVE HER SEE IT ON TV.
OKAY-- THE HELL WITH IT. SO WHY'D YOU CALL ME HERE?
I WANTED YOU TO MEET SOMEONE...
I WANTED YOU TO MEET THE MAN WHO CONVINCED ME THAT THE JUSTICE SOCIETY COMMITTED TREASON DURING WORLD WAR TWO--NOT JUST ONCE, BUT MANY TIMES.
THE MAN WE'RE GOING TO SPRING ON THEM AT THE PROPER TIME AS OUR CHIEF WITNESS--THE MAN WHO'S RIGHT OVER THERE!
RIGHT OVER WHERE? I DON'T SEE ANY--
BECAUSE, TILL NOW, I'VE NOT DESIRED YOU TO SEE ME, MR. GRAYSON.
GOOD LORD-- YOU!?
47

NEXT ISSUE:
# TRIAL BY CONGRESS!

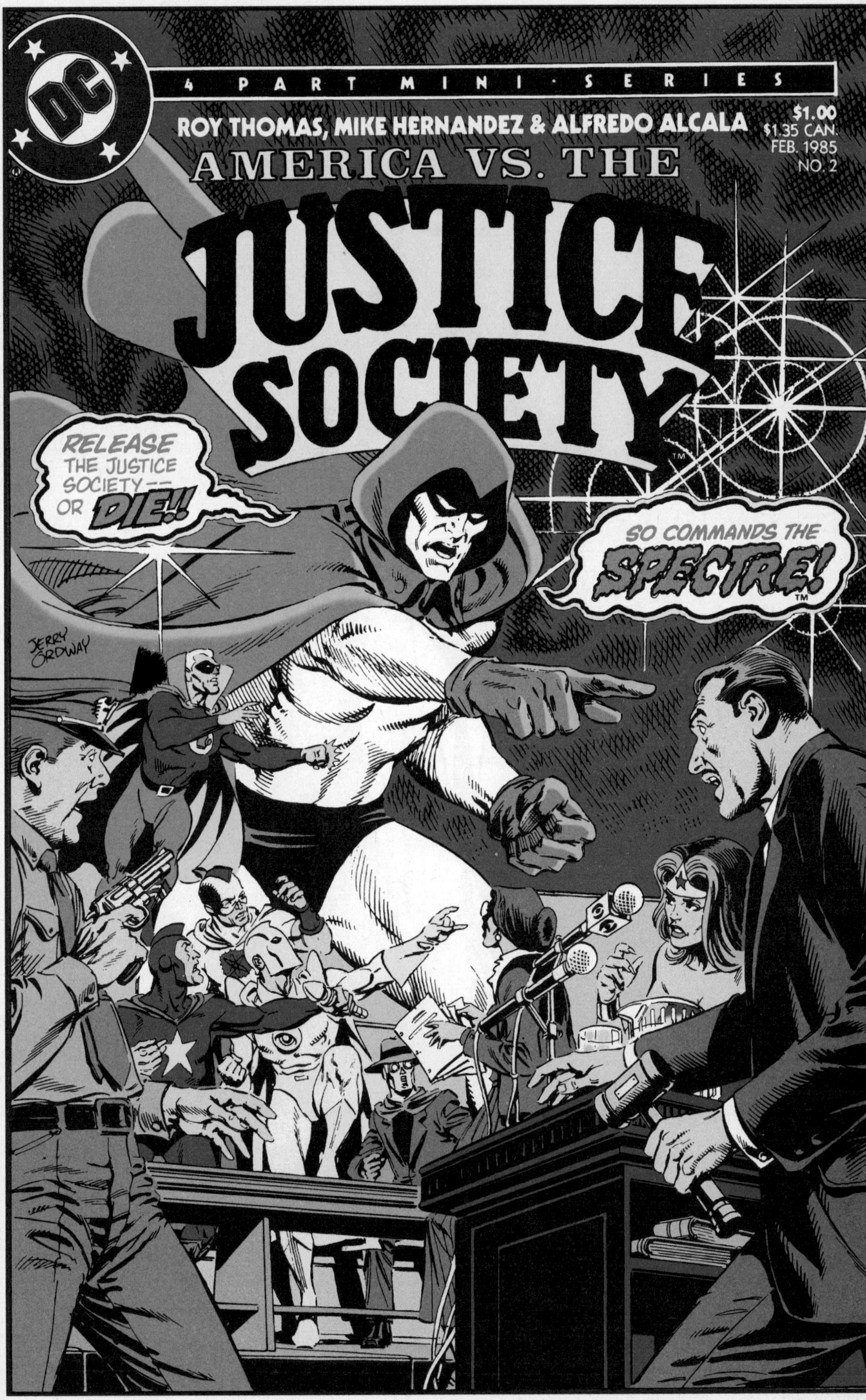

4 PART MINI-SERIES
ROY THOMAS, MIKE HERNANDEZ & ALFREDO ALCALA
$1.00
$1.35 CAN.
FEB. 1985
NO. 2
AMERICA VS. THE
JUSTICE SOCIETY
RELEASE THE JUSTICE SOCIETY -- OR DIE!!
SO COMMANDS THE SPECTRE!
JERRY ORDWAY

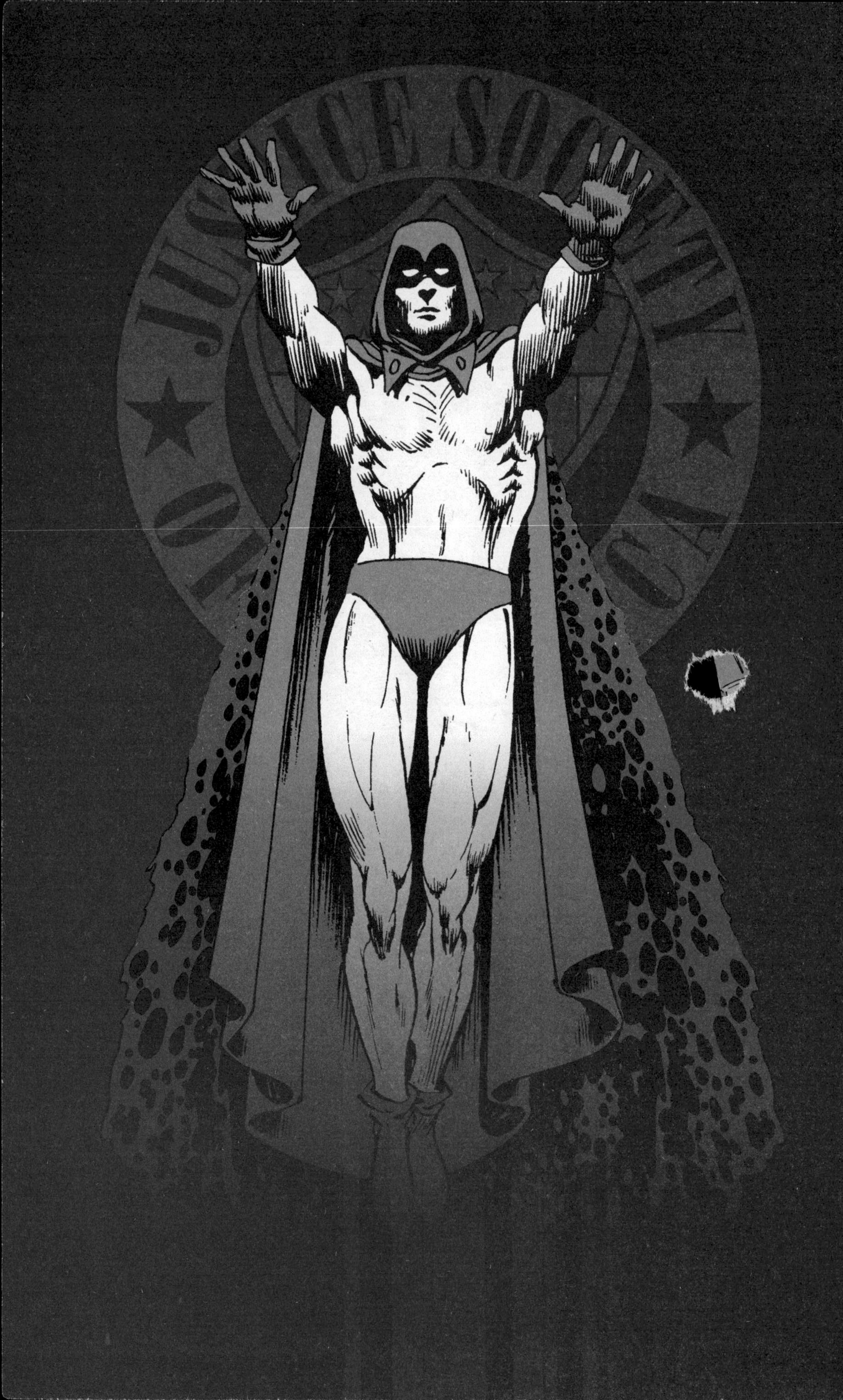

# TRIAL BY CONGRESS!

| ROY THOMAS * | MIKE HERNANDEZ * | ALFREDO ALCALA | * | DANN THOMAS..........CO-PLOTTER<br>CARL GAFFORD.:........COLORIST<br>CODY................LETTERER |
|---|---|---|---|---|
| WRITER/EDITOR | ILLUSTRATORS-IN-TANDEM | | | |

MANY A TIME SINCE THE AUTUMN OF 1940 HAS THIS LEGENDARY ROLL BEEN CALLED. YET TODAY, AMID THE MOCKING ECHOES OF A RENTED HALL IN THE NATION'S CAPITAL, THE LONG-ILLUSTRIOUS NAMES ARE THOSE OF MEN -- AND A WOMAN -- WHO STAND ACCUSED OF THE CRIME OF *TREASON* AGAINST THE LAND THEY HAVE PROUDLY SERVED FOR DECADES...

HAWKMAN... THE FLASH... GREEN LANTERN... SUPERMAN... DR. MID-NITE... DR. FATE... STARMAN... SANDMAN... WILDCAT... HOURMAN... THE ATOM... JOHNNY THUNDER... WONDER WOMAN...

THIS IS A *CONGRESSIONAL COMMITTEE HEARING,* NOT A *TRIAL*... AND YET WE ARE ALL AWARE THAT THE *MEDIA* AND THE *PUBLIC* ARE ALREADY REFERRING TO IT AS IF IT WERE A TRIAL... AS IF IT WERE THE CASE OF--

AMERICA VS. THE JUSTICE SOCIETY ™

"Treason doth not prosper: What's the reason? For if it prosper, none dare call it treason." --Sir John Harington (1561-1612)

THIS INVESTIGATION MAY, OF COURSE, *LEAD* TO *CRIMINAL CHARGES* BEING LEVIED BY THE *JUSTICE DEPARTMENT* AT A LATER DATE. BUT UNTIL SUCH TIME, WE HAVE HONORED YOUR LONG-STANDING OFFICIAL STATUS AS *LAW ENFORCERS*, AND HAVE NOT DEMANDED TO KNOW YOUR *TRUE NAMES* BEHIND YOUR MASKS AND, *ER*, OTHER MEANS OF CONCEALING YOUR ACTUAL IDENTITIES.

DESPITE THE SOMEWHAT, SHALL WE SAY, *HYSTERICAL* METHOD OF YOUR *SUMMONS* BY THIS COMMITTEE, YOU ARE EACH HERE OF YOUR *OWN FREE WILL*, IS THAT NOT TRUE?

SPEAKING FOR MY FELLOW JUSTICE SOCIETY MEMBERS, SENATOR... IT *IS.*

WE'RE GRATEFUL FOR THIS *PUBLIC FORUM*... FOR THE OPPORTUNITY TO *CLEAR OUR GOOD NAMES*, ONCE AND FOR ALL.

THEN LET US HOPE, SUPERMAN, THAT *THAT* IS WHAT *EMERGES* FROM THESE HEARINGS--EVEN THOUGH YOU YOURSELF ARE *NOT* ACCUSED IN THE SAME MANNER AS THESE OTHERS.

IS THERE ANYTHING *ELSE* ANY OF YOU WISH TO *SAY*, BEFORE THE *GENERAL PUBLIC* AND *MEDIA PEOPLE* ARE ADMITTED?

ON ADVICE OF *COUNSEL*, SENATOR--NAMELY *MYSELF*-- NONE OF THE *JSA* HAS ANYTHING FURTHER TO ADD UNTIL THE HEARINGS *OFFICIALLY* BEGIN.

THEN, GUARDS... WILL YOU PLEASE ADMIT THOSE WAITING OUTSIDE.

MEMBERS OF THE *JOINT COMMITTEE*-- THESE THIRTEEN STAND ACCUSED OF *TREASON* BY THE WRITTEN WORD OF A *DEAD MAN.*

SOON, TO THE RELATIVELY SMALL HANDFUL OF SPECTATORS SEATED AT ONE SIDE OF THE CHAMBER, *HELENA WAYNE* SPEAKS AGAIN... WELL AWARE OF THE FUROR WHICH WOULD ERUPT IF IT WERE KNOWN THAT SHE IS ALSO *THE HUNTRESS*, HERSELF A RECENT RECRUIT TO THE *JUSTICE SOCIETY*:

TRUE, THAT MAN IS *THE BATMAN*--BEFORE HIS DEATH IN 1979, A *JSAer* HIMSELF. STILL--

PLEASE, MS. WAYNE... WE KNOW IT'S BEEN AGREED IN ADVANCE THAT THESE HEARINGS WILL BE CONDUCTED IN A HIGHLY *INFORMAL* MANNER.

STILL, I BELIEVE IT ONLY *RIGHT* AND *PROPER* THAT WE THREE *COMMITTEE MEMBERS* IDENTIFY OURSELVES AT THIS JUNCTURE.

OF COURSE, SENATOR.

②

I'M CONGRESSWOMAN LINDA VALDEZ OF CALIFORNIA. LET ME SAY AT THE OUTSET THAT, FOR VARIOUS REASONS, I'VE NOT BEEN AN ADMIRER OF THE SO-CALLED JUSTICE SOCIETY OVER THE YEARS.

BUT THAT WILL NOT, IN ANY WAY, STAND IN THE PATH OF A FAIR AND IMPARTIAL HEARING.

CONGRESSMAN JASON PHILIPS HERE... AND MY' HARLEM CONSTITUENCY HAS HAD RELATIVELY FEW DEALINGS WITH THE JSA, WHICH IS WHY I CONSENTED TO TAKE PART.

I'M SENATOR WILLIAM HOPKINS OF MISSOURI. AS ONE FROM THE SHOW-ME STATE, I PLAN TO CHAIR THESE SESSIONS WITH AN OPEN MIND.

OH, AND SEATED BEHIND US IS RICHARD GRAYSON, OUR OWN COUNSEL.

SO DICK'S REALLY GOING THROUGH WITH IT!

IT'S EVEN HARDER FOR HIM THAN FOR US TO BELIEVE THAT BATMAN WAS LYING VIRTUALLY ON HIS DEATHBED, DOC... BUT AT LEAST HE'LL BE FAIR, RIGHT, HELENA?

I... WANT TO BELIEVE THAT, HAWKMAN.

GOD, HOW I WANT TO BELIEVE!

MR. CHAIRMAN, I'M PROBABLY OUT OF ORDER, BUT I WANTED TO NOTE RIGHT OFF THE BAT THAT ONE OF OUR NUMBER HAS SUFFERED A STROKE IN RECENT MONTHS, AND WE'D HOPED THAT --

STARMAN MEANS ME, MR. CHAIRMAN -- BUT THE SANDMAN ASKS NO SPECIAL FAVORS OF ANYONE.

I AM NO MORE GUILTY OR INNOCENT OF TREASON THAN ANY OF MY FELLOW J.S.A.ers.

DULY NOTED, BOTH OF YOU.

THIS SETUP MAKES ME WANNA BARF! EVERYBODY'S SO NICE AND POLITE -- BUT MEANTIME, I GOT THE FEELIN' SOMEBODY SOMEWHERE IS KNITTIN' US A NICE TIGHT NOOSE.

AT EASE, WILDCAT.

AT LEAST WE'VE GOT OUR ROOTERS, RIGHT?...

"LIKE, THERE'S LOIS KENT... SUPES' WIFE. SHE DOES LOOK A LITTLE HAGGARD, THOUGH... PROBABLY BEEN CRYING A LOT, LIKE MY OWN WIFE MARY."

"LEAST SHE'S HERE. MARY COULDN'T TAKE BEING HERE TODAY -- AND I CAN'T SAY I BLAME HER."

"I SEE A COUPLE OF *OTHER* WIVES MADE IT, THOUGH--LIKE *JOAN GARRICK*, THE FLASH'S BETTER HALF--

THERE'S HAWKMAN'S WIFE *SHIERA*--

"OH, YEAH, AND THERE'S *INZA NELSON*, GIVING THE HIGH SIGN TO *DR. FATE.*

"I KNOW THOSE *INFINITY, INC.* KIDS WANTED TO BE HERE, TOO--BUT AFTER THAT PRESS CONFERENCE IN HOLLYWOOD, WE ALL DECIDED IT'D BE MORE PRUDENT IF THEY STAYED AWAY.

"IT'S WONDER WOMAN I'M REALLY WORRIED ABOUT, THOUGH--SHE'S VERY CONCERNED ABOUT HUBBIE *STEVE*, WHO'S STILL LAID UP ON AN ISLAND BACK IN *AMAZON TERRITORY.*

"IF THIS BROUHAHA LASTS *TOO* LONG--SHE MIGHT DECIDE NOT TO STICK AROUND FOR THE OUTCOME.

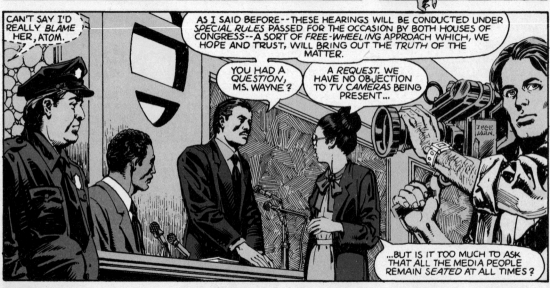

CAN'T SAY I'D REALLY BLAME HER, ATOM.

AS I SAID BEFORE--THESE HEARINGS WILL BE CONDUCTED UNDER *SPECIAL RULES* PASSED FOR THE OCCASION BY BOTH HOUSES OF CONGRESS--A SORT OF *FREE-WHEELING* APPROACH WHICH, WE HOPE AND TRUST, WILL BRING OUT THE *TRUTH* OF THE MATTER.

YOU HAD A *QUESTION*, MS. WAYNE?

A *REQUEST.* WE HAVE NO OBJECTION TO *TV CAMERAS* BEING PRESENT...

...BUT IS IT TOO MUCH TO ASK THAT ALL THE MEDIA PEOPLE REMAIN *SEATED* AT ALL TIMES?

I CONCUR, MR. CHAIRMAN. THIS IS A *JOINT* CONGRESSIONAL HEARING, NOT A *CIRCUS.*

I'M AFRAID THAT INCLUDES *YOU*, MR. VINSON.

I THINK THE AMERICAN PUBLIC HAS A *RIGHT* TO *KNOW* WHAT'S GOING ON HERE, CONGRESS-WOMAN... BUT I'LL KEEP *MY* PEOPLE UNDER CONTROL.

PLEASE *DO*. NOW, MS. WAYNE... *HAPPY*?

I'LL BE HAPPY WHEN MY CLIENTS ARE FULLY *VINDICATED*, SENATOR, AND NOT BEFORE.

BUT THANK YOU, ALL THE SAME.

NOW, IF WE MAY PROCEED:

VARIOUS NEWSPAPERS AND MAGAZINES HAVE PRINTED THE FULL TEXT OF WHAT IS POPULARLY CALLED THE "BATMAN DIARY," SO ITS CONTENTS, AT LEAST, ARE NOT AT ISSUE HERE.

ONE OF ITS MAJOR ACCUSATIONS TO BE EXAMINED HERE IS WHETHER OR NOT, IN FACT, THE ORIGINAL JSAers WERE CONVINCED BY ADOLF HITLER HIMSELF, IN 1940, TO BECOME SECRET AGENTS OF NAZI GERMANY.

MR. PHILIPS?

OF NEARLY AS MUCH CONCERN TO THIS COMMITTEE IS THE ALLEGED SABOTAGING BY THE JSA OF WORK ON THE TOP-SECRET BOMB-DEFENSE FORMULA IN MID-1941--A FORMULA WHICH MIGHT HAVE PREVENTED THE SUCCESSFUL JAPANESE ATTACK ON PEARL HARBOR THAT DECEMBER.

THE MASSIVE ALLEGED JSA COVER-UP SINCE THAT TIME WILL BE INVESTIGATED, ALSO...

BUT THESE TWO ITEMS ARE, AS WE SEE IT, THE MAJOR REVELATIONS OF BATMAN'S SECRET JOURNAL.

JUST THE SAME, IT SURE LOOKS LIKE WE HIRED OURSELVES THE RIGHT LAWYER.

WELL, OLD FRIENDS? DID YOUR LEGAL EAGLE FIGURE RIGHT WHEN SHE GUESSED WHAT THE MAIN POINTS OF ATTACK WOULD BE?

NOBODY'S EXACTLY ATTACKING YET, HELENA.

RIGHT?! BUT I THOUGHT HELENA WAS A LIBERAL!

AS YOU WERE, JOHNNY.

MEMBERS OF THE COMMITTEE--WE ACKNOWLEDGE THAT THE DOCUMENT IN QUESTION WAS INDEED WRITTEN BY THE BATMAN SHORTLY BEFORE HIS DEATH, FOR MY CLIENTS HAD REASON TO KNOW HIS HANDWRITING WELL.

STILL, MANY OF HIS PURPORTED "FACTS" THEREIN WE WILL SHOW TO BE UNTRUTHS BORDERING ON THE RIDICULOUS...

...WHATEVER THE BATMAN'S MOTIVES MAY HAVE BEEN.

HELENA CAN SCARCELY MISS SEEING DICK GRAYSON BRISTLE AT HER WORDS.

IS IT BECAUSE THE PERSON ACCUSING BATMAN OF LYING--IS THE CAPED CRUSADER'S OWN DAUGHTER?

YOU DID GOOD, HELENA.

THE BELL'S SCARCELY SOUNDED FOR THE FIRST ROUND TO BEGIN YET, HAWK.

I HOPE YOU CAN SAY THE SAME THING WHEN WE'VE GONE THE DISTANCE.

5

ALL RIGHT, THEN LET US DEAL WITH THE *EARLIEST* OF THE *ALLEGEDLY TREASONOUS* ACTS RECORDED IN *BATMAN'S DIARY*--THE JSA'S SUPPOSED ENCOUNTER WITH *ADOLF HITLER* IN NOVEMBER 1940--

--AND *WHY*, IF THEY DID NOT THEN BECOME *NAZI* AGENTS, THEY DID NOT *CAPTURE* HIM RIGHT THERE, PERHAPS BRINGING AN EARLY END TO *WORLD WAR TWO!*

MS. WAYNE? AS PREVIOUSLY AGREED, WE WILL HEAR FIRST FROM *WHICHEVER* OF YOUR CLIENTS' NUMBER THEY DESIRE...

THEY HAVE ALREADY CHOSEN *THE FLASH,* SENATOR--FIRST CHAIRMAN OF THE GROUP.

WADE *INTO 'EM,* FLASHER!

MEMBERS OF THE COMMITTEE--THOUGH *GREEN LANTERN* AND I MET THE BATMAN FIRST AND CONSIDERED HIM A FRIEND--I SUSPECT NONE OF US *KNEW* HIM AS WELL AS WE'D HAVE HOPED.

LIKE SUPERMAN, HE WAS A *CHARTER MEMBER* OF OUR SOCIETY-- YET CHOSE, UNTIL THE 1960'S, TO BE A GENERALLY *INACTIVE* ONE.

STILL, FOR REASONS YET *UNKNOWN,* BATMAN CHOSE TO LEAVE US AS HIS FINAL LEGACY THE *JOURNAL* YOU HOLD IN YOUR HAND--

--A JOURNAL WHICH IS LITTLE MORE THAN A THINLY-DISGUISED *TISSUE OF LIES!*

WELL, *THAT* OUGHT TO STIR THINGS UP, EH, FATE?

*AYE, DIANA.*

I UNDERSTAND YOUR FEELINGS, MR. GARRICK. HOWEVER, I MUST ASK THAT YOU SIMPLY *RELATE* THE EVENTS IN QUESTION-- NOT CAST ASPERSIONS ON A DECEASED BUT VERY GREAT AMERICAN.

*SORRY, CONGRESSMAN...*

AND NOW, HIS VOICE HEAVY WITH EMOTION--HIS MIND GROPING FOR THE EXACT WORDS, THE PRECISE ORDER, OF EVENTS MORE THAN FOUR DECADES PAST--

--JAY GARRICK TELLS PUBLICLY, FOR THE FIRST TIME EVER, THE LONG-SECRET STORY OF HOW HE, BATMAN, GREEN LANTERN, HOURMAN, AND DR. FATE HAD FOUND THEMSELVES FACE TO FACE WITH THE NAZI FÜHRER IN NOVEMBER, 1940.

IT IS A TALE OF A BATTLE IN BERLIN-- A BATTLE DOOMED TO END IN FRUS-TRATION FOR THE COSTUMED YANKS, PERHAPS BECAUSE OF THE FABLED SPEAR OF DESTINY THEN IN HITLER'S POSSESSION--AN ARTIFACT OF SORCERY MOST UNHOLY.

FOR, WITH IT, HAD HE NOT CONJURED UP POWERFUL VÁLKYRIES OUT OF PAGAN LEGEND?

EVEN WHEN JOINED BY HAWKMAN, THE ATOM, SANDMAN, AND THE GRIM SPECTRE, THE HEROES COULD NOT PREVENT THE EERIE WARRIOR-WOMEN FROM REACHING THE SKIES ABOVE WASHINGTON, D.C. ...

... AND ONLY THE SUDDEN APPEAR-ANCE OF THE MAN OF STEEL FROM BELOW HAD TIPPED THE SCALES AT THE LAST MOMENT, BY SMASHING THE MODIFIED SUPER-BOMBER SENT TO RAIN TERROR ON THE CAPITAL.

YET, CAN ANY MAN BLAME THOSE WHO MAY FEEL SKEPTICAL AT THE TALE TOLD BY THE FASTEST MAN ALIVE?

AFTER ALL, NO FRAGMENTS OF THE FALLEN NAZI BOMBER WERE EVER REVEALED TO THE AMERICAN PEOPLE--

--AND THOSE GAZING SKYWARD THAT DAY HAD SEEN ONLY TEN COLOR-SPLASHED FIGURES, DARTING TO AND FRO AMID A SUDDEN THUNDERSTORM WHICH HAD ASSAULTED THE CITY.

STILL, IN THE END, THOSE TEN HAD TRIUMPHED OVER THE SWORD-WIELDING BATTLE-MAIDENS FROM SOME NORDIC VALHALLA--

AND, THOUGH CHOOSING NOT TO REVEAL THE DAY'S HAPPENINGS TO THE PUBLIC--FOR WHO MIGHT HAVE BELIEVED HIM?--

--PRESIDENT FRANKLIN DELANO ROOSEVELT HAD SEEN TO IT THAT, FROM THAT DAY FORWARD, THERE WAS A NEW FORCE TO BE RECKONED WITH BY THE DICTATORS AND DESPOTS OF THE OLD WORLD.

A FORCE KNOWN AS-- THE JUSTICE SOCIETY OF AMERICA!

NOW, AS THE FLASH COMPLETES HIS NARRATION:

INTERESTING-- IF TRUE.

I WAS THERE, TOO, MA'AM... AND WE WORKED WITH WHOEVER SHOWED UP.

WE NEVER TURNED AWAY ANYBODY BECAUSE OF RACE... OR SEX.

BUT IF YOU PEOPLE WERE REALLY OPPOSED TO THE NAZI RACISTS--WHY WERE THERE NO BLACKS, NO HISPANICS, NOT EVEN ANY WOMEN IN YOUR SOCIETY?

MAY I SPEAK, MR. CHAIRMAN?

THIS WAS STILL NEARLY A YEAR BEFORE I CAME TO MAN'S WORLD, OF COURSE.

BUT IT SEEMS OBVIOUS THAT, EXCEPT ON PARADISE ISLAND, CONDITIONS JUST WEREN'T RIGHT YET FOR THE EMERGENCE OF A FEMALE SUPER-HERO.

AS THE GROUP'S *PERMANENT CHAIRMAN* SINCE 1941, SIR, I CAN VOUCH FOR WHAT GREEN LANTERN AND WONDER WOMAN SAY.

AT ANY RATE, *SUPERMAN* AND *BATMAN*--CLAIMING THEY WERE SO BUSY WITH THEIR OWN CASES, THEY COULD ONLY BECOME *HONORARY MEMBERS*-- DIDN'T ATTEND OUR FIRST MEETING, HELD ON *NOVEMBER 22, 1940.*

WE FIGURED THE *EIGHT* OF US OUGHT TO BE ABLE TO HANDLE ANYTHING THAT CAME UP.

WHAT DID *WE* KNOW? WE WERE ALL *YOUNG* THEN...

...THE *OLDEST* OF US NOT BEING OUT OF HIS *MIDDLE 20'S.*

WE SEE ALL EIGHT OF THOSE *HERE* TODAY--EXCEPT FOR THE SO-CALLED *SPECTRE.*

AND YOU *WON'T* SEE HIM HERE, SIR, BECAUSE HE'S--WELL, ER--HE'S--

MAY AS WELL JUST SPIT IT OUT, FLASH.

YEAH, GUESS SO...

"THE SPECTRE IS AN ACTUAL *GHOST,* SIR--AND FOR SEVERAL YEARS NOW, HE HAS MADE HIS HOME IN *WORLDS BEYOND OUR KEN*--

--DIMENSIONS BEYOND EVEN THE REACH OF *SUPERMAN.*

NICE SAVE, JAY! IF WE ALSO TRIED TO EXPLAIN HE'S *ALSO* POPPED UP FROM TIME TO TIME AS THE *JIM CORRIGAN* OF AN *ALTERNATE EARTH*-- WE'D BE HERE TILL BOTH EARTHS *FREEZE OVER!*

HMMM...SO MUCH FOR OUR CHANCES OF *SUBPOENAING* THE SPECTRE, I SUPPOSE.

EVEN IF WE *BELIEVED* IN GHOSTS!

NOW, USAers, ABOUT YOUR FIRST *REAL* CASE...

I'LL FIELD THAT ONE: WHILE THE OTHERS SWAPPED STORIES AT OUR DINNER MEETING IN NEW YORK--

"--I HOTFOOTED IT DOWN TO *WASHINGTON* TO MEET FBI CHIEF *J. EDGAR HOOVER,* WHO ASKED THAT THE JUSTICE SOCIETY--

--SEARCH OUT THE *MAIN NAZI SPYMASTER* CURRENTLY OPERATING IN THE UNITED STATES.

WE'LL FLUSH HIM OUT FOR YOU--*NEVER FEAR.*

9

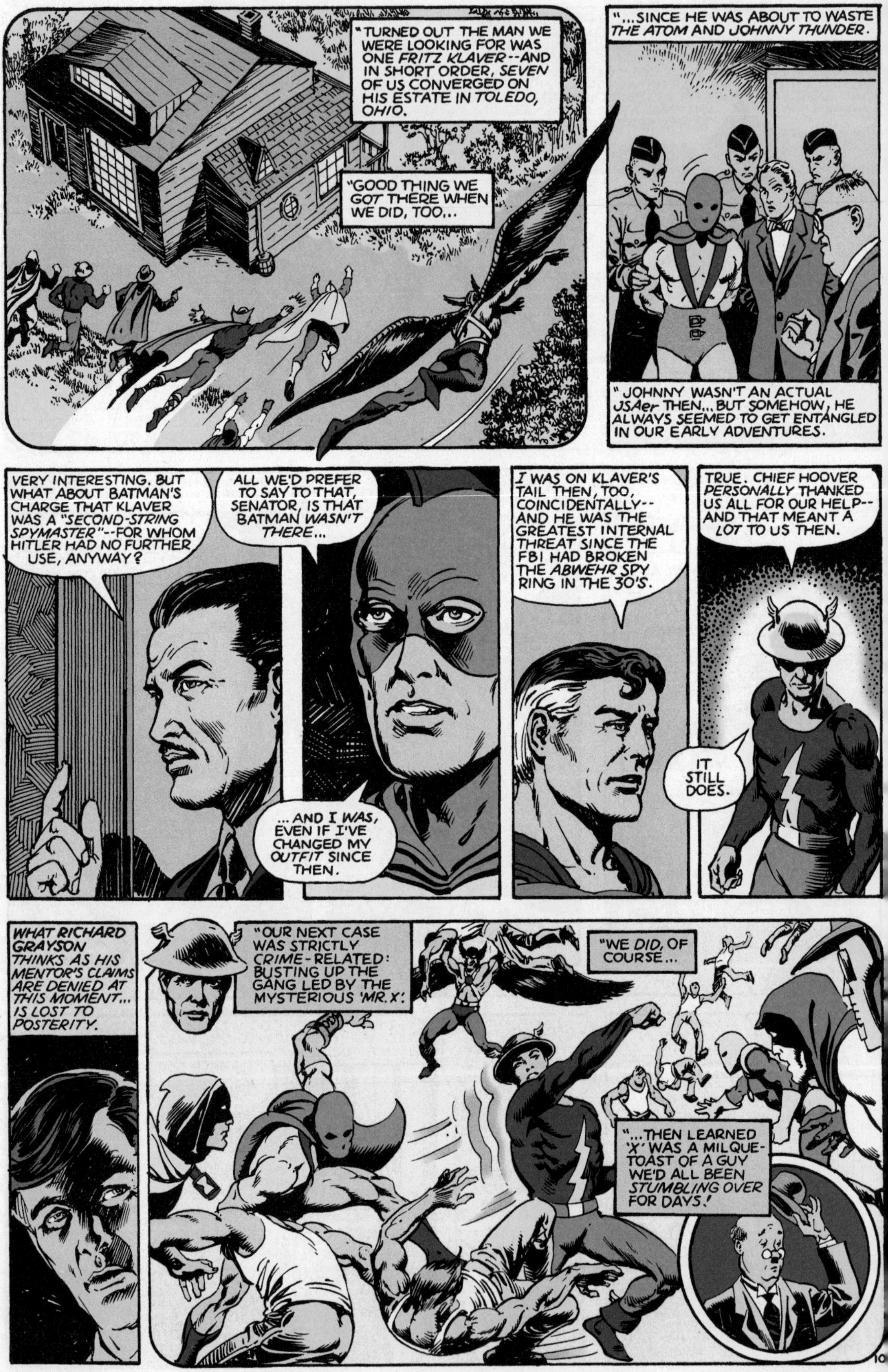
"TURNED OUT THE MAN WE WERE LOOKING FOR WAS ONE FRITZ KLAVER--AND IN SHORT ORDER, SEVEN OF US CONVERGED ON HIS ESTATE IN TOLEDO, OHIO.
"GOOD THING WE GOT THERE WHEN WE DID, TOO...
"...SINCE HE WAS ABOUT TO WASTE THE ATOM AND JOHNNY THUNDER.
"JOHNNY WASN'T AN ACTUAL JSAer THEN... BUT SOMEHOW, HE ALWAYS SEEMED TO GET ENTANGLED IN OUR EARLY ADVENTURES.
VERY INTERESTING. BUT WHAT ABOUT BATMAN'S CHARGE THAT KLAVER WAS A "SECOND-STRING SPYMASTER"--FOR WHOM HITLER HAD NO FURTHER USE, ANYWAY?
ALL WE'D PREFER TO SAY TO THAT, SENATOR, IS THAT BATMAN WASN'T THERE...
...AND I WAS, EVEN IF I'VE CHANGED MY OUTFIT SINCE THEN.
I WAS ON KLAVER'S TAIL THEN, TOO, COINCIDENTALLY--AND HE WAS THE GREATEST INTERNAL THREAT SINCE THE FBI HAD BROKEN THE ABWEHR SPY RING IN THE 30'S.
TRUE. CHIEF HOOVER PERSONALLY THANKED US ALL FOR OUR HELP--AND THAT MEANT A LOT TO US THEN.
IT STILL DOES.
WHAT RICHARD GRAYSON THINKS AS HIS MENTOR'S CLAIMS ARE DENIED AT THIS MOMENT... IS LOST TO POSTERITY.
"OUR NEXT CASE WAS STRICTLY CRIME-RELATED: BUSTING UP THE GANG LED BY THE MYSTERIOUS 'MR. X'.
"WE DID, OF COURSE...
"...THEN LEARNED 'X' WAS A MILQUETOAST OF A GUY WE'D ALL BEEN STUMBLING OVER FOR DAYS!
10

"ABOUT THIS TIME, *I*, TOO, GOT SO BUSY WITH OUTSIDE ASSIGNMENTS THAT I HAD TO *STEP DOWN* AS JSA CHAIRMAN... AND BECOME ITS THIRD *HONORARY*."

"NATURALLY, THE GUYS CHOSE *JOHNNY THUNDER* TO TAKE MY PLACE... THOUGH NOT UNTIL HE'D TAKEN A LOT OF GOOD-NATURED RAZZING, AND EVEN BEEN SENT ON WHAT AMOUNTED TO A *SNIPE HUNT*."

YOU REALLY EXPECT THIS COMMITTEE TO BELIEVE THAT THE JSA PUT A NEW RECRUIT THROUGH ITS OWN VERSION OF A COLLEGE FRATERNITY HELL WEEK?

AW, IT WASN'T *THAT BAD*, SENATOR-- AND *HEY*-- WE CAUGHT A FEW CROOKS ALONG THE WAY, AT THE SAME TIME!

MEANWHILE, *SHIERA HALL*, WATCHING GRIMLY FROM THE SIDELINES, CANNOT RESIST A WRY SMILE...

*HMMPH!* NOTHING AGAINST JOHNNY-- BUT I'D HELPED CARTER OUT ON THAT "MR. X" CASE-- AS *HAWKGIRL*.

WONDER WOMAN'S KIND-OF *FORGOTTEN* ABOUT THAT-- BUT THEN, SO HAVE THE OTHERS!

"THAT WOULD HAVE BEEN IN *MID-1941*, CORRECT? ABOUT THE TIME *YOU* STEPPED DOWN AS CHAIRMAN, GREEN LANTERN-- YOUR SPOT TAKEN BY *DR. MID-NITE*--

"--WHILE *HOURMAN'S* PLACE WAS TAKEN BY A NEW MYSTERY-TYPE CALLED *STARMAN*, AM I RIGHT?

YOU *ARE*, CONGRESSMAN. I GOT SO BUSY, I HAD TO BECOME THE JSA'S *FOURTH* HONORARY-- AND HAWKMAN'S BEEN WIELDING THE GAVEL EVER SINCE.

BUT I'M AWARE THAT THE "BATMAN DIARY" CHARGES THAT NO WAR ORPHAN EVER BENEFITED FROM THAT MILLION.

I SEEM TO RECALL READING, JSA, THAT YOUR *NEXT* JOB INVOLVED RAISING $1,000,000 FOR *WAR ORPHANS*.

AND THAT'S A BALD-FACED *LIE!*

11

IN FACT, *DR. FATE* AND I DELIVERED THE MONEY PERSONALLY TO *PRESIDENT ROOSEVELT*-- JUST IN TIME TO RESCUE HIM FROM A COUPLE OF ATTACKING *SHADOW-MEN*...

...AND TO SAVE A *CHARRED LIST* FEATURING THE NAMES OF *TEN AMERICANS* MARKED FOR *DEATH*, STARTING WITH *FOR HIMSELF.*

ALL MY *JSA* COMRADES *SUCCEEDED* IN THEIR MISSIONS--EVERYBODY BUT *ME.*

FOR, THOUGH I MANAGED TO FIGHT *DR. FATE'S* OLD ENEMY *WOTAN* TO A STAND-STILL, HE LASHED OUT WITH A--A FORM OF ASSAULT I *COULDN'T COUNTER*--

...AND A *CHILD DIED.*

EVEN AFTER MORE THAN FORTY YEARS, THAT'S STILL THE *FAILURE* IN MY LIFE... I FIND THE *HARDEST* TO LIVE WITH.

IN FACT, THAT'S WHEN I *RESIGNED* FOR SEVERAL YEARS FROM THE *JSA*... CHAIRMANSHIP AND ALL.

THAT PARTICULAR CASE HAS BEEN A *SECRET* ALL THESE DECADES--BECAUSE WE DIDN'T THINK THE WORLD WAS *READY* TO LEARN ABOUT IT-- AND ITS *IMPLICATIONS.*

I'M SURE WE ALL-- *APPRECIATE* THE GRIEF YOU FEEL, GREEN LANTERN.

BUT MAY WE ASK *WHY* THAT PARTICULAR CASE HAS BEEN KEPT *UNDER WRAPS* EVER SINCE 1941?

I... *PREFER* NOT TO *ANSWER* THAT, CONGRESSWOMAN.

I ONLY *HEARD* ABOUT IT *LATER*--BUT IF I *MUST*--

I'LL DO IT, WONDER WOMAN.

AFTER ALL THESE YEARS, I THINK IT'S TIME THE *TRUTH* WERE KNOWN--TO ONE AND ALL.

PLEASE PROCEED, SUPERMAN.

12

THIS MAY BE A BIT HARD TO *FOLLOW*-- BUT THE SHADOW-MEN AND OTHER ARCHVILLAINS HAD BEEN MASTERMINDED BY ANOTHER OLD FOE OF DR. FATE'S--ONE *IAN KARKULL*--

--A MASTER OF *PERVERTED SCIENCE,* WHO HATED AMERICA FOR NOT RECOGNIZING HIS *GENIUS.*

AN OLD STORY, EVEN THEN.

HAVING STUMBLED ON A WAY TO PEER INTO *AMERICA'S FUTURE,* KARKULL LEARNED WHO THE *NEXT NINE PRESIDENTS* AFTER FDR WOULD BE--AND HE TRIED TO HAVE EACH OF THEM *ASSASSINATED* ON JUNE 28, 1941.

IN THAT WAY, HE HOPED TO *ALTER* THIS COUNTRY'S FORTUNES--HE HOPED FOR THE *WORSE.*

IRONICALLY, EVEN *NOW,* WE HAVE NO REAL WAY OF JUDGING WHETHER HE *SUCCEEDED* OR NOT.

BUT WE DID MANAGE TO *SAVE* EVERY FUTURE PRESIDENT FROM *TRUMAN* THROUGH *REAGAN.*

DUE TO CIRCUMSTANCES BEYOND *ANYONE'S* CONTROL, HOWEVER, GREEN LANTERN WAS UNABLE TO SAVE *HIS* MAN--THEN A *BOY,* OF COURSE.

*Chicago Daily Tribune*
DEWEY DEFEATS TRUMAN

1948

THE HISTORY OF *AMERICA*-- PERHAPS EVEN OF *MANKIND!*

HOPE YOU CAN SEE WHY WE'VE KEPT THIS CASE *SECRET* FOR SO LONG. EVEN THE MEREST *PUBLIC AWARENESS* OF IT WOULD DOUBTLESS HAVE AFFECTED HISTORY, ONE WAY OR ANOTHER.

1960

A HUSH FALLS OVER THE CHAMBER...

*IS ANYBODY GONNA BELIEVE THIS*-- EVEN *NOW?*

AND *LOST--WHO?*

UH-- *HOURMAN?*

I'M UP FOR IT, OLD FRIEND.

THEY SAVED JFK BACK IN '41?!

UBS UBS

*NIXON?*

*REAGAN?*

WE'LL ALL HAVE TO *DIGEST* THAT PARTICULAR REVELATION A MOMENT.

MEANWHILE, MY NOTES SAY *HOURMAN* LEFT THE JSA ABOUT THAT TIME. WOULD HE CARE TO TELL US *WHY?*

13

"IT'S FAIRLY WELL KNOWN I GET MY SPECIAL POWERS FROM A CONCOCTION OF MY OWN-- CALLED *MIRACLO.*

"IT GIVES ME THE STRENGTH, THE STAMINA, THE SPEED OF *SEVERAL* MEN, FOR SIXTY MINUTES AT A TIME.

I WON'T GO INTO THE *DETAILS,* BUT WHILE I WAS ON THAT PARTICULAR ASSIGNMENT, I CAME TO A *REALIZATION* I'D BEEN FIGHTING FOR A LONG TIME--

--NAMELY, THAT I WAS A *MIRACLO* ADDICT.

THAT'S WHEN I TOSSED THOSE EARLY PILLS--FOR GOOD--

--AND, SOME TIME LATER, I WORKED OUT A *RAY-MACHINE* THAT GAVE ME MIRACLO POWERS *WITHOUT ANY* SIDE-EFFECTS.

AT LEAST WITHOUT *THOSE* SIDE-EFFECTS.

I SEE. AND THAT, I ASSUME, IS WHEN YOU RETURNED TO THE PUBLIC EYE AS HOURMAN--BUT THIS TIME IN THE NEWER *ALL-STAR SQUADRON,* RATHER THAN THE *JSA?*

YES. I WASN'T A JSAer AGAIN TILL THE 1960'S-- AND I WAS *NEVER* A TRAITOR!

*THAT,* OF COURSE, IS WHAT THIS HEARING IS TO *DETERMINE,* ISN'T IT? THANK YOU. YOU MAY STEP DOWN.

IS THERE ANYTHING *ELSE* ABOUT THAT LONG-CONCEALED CASE ANYONE WISHES TO SAY, BEFORE WE PRESS ON TO THE EXPLOITS YOU *DID* TELL THE WORLD ABOUT?

YES, *STARMAN?*

ONLY THAT, IN APPARENTLY *DESTROYING KARKULL,* EVERYONE PRESENT WAS BATHED IN--I GUESS YOU'D CALL THEM *WAVES OF TIME*--CHRONAL ENERGY TRAPPED WITHIN KARKULL'S BODY.

THAT'S WHY SO MANY OF US--EVEN IN OUR 60'S--STILL RETAIN OUR POWERS, AND THE VITALITY OF MEN AND WOMEN FAR *YOUNGER.*

MYSELF, I *WASN'T* A JSAer THEN--BUT I'D HELPED HOURMAN ON HIS ASSIGNMENT, BECAUSE I *WANTED* TO BECOME ONE.

SOON AFTERWARD, THEY VOTED TO ADMIT ME TO *REPLACE* HIM-- AND I'VE NEVER BEEN *PROUDER* OF ANYTHING IN MY LIFE.

NOT EVEN *NOW,* WHEN WE ALL STAND ACCUSED OF *TREASON* BY--IT SEEMS--THE LATE *BATMAN* HIMSELF!

14

ANDREW VINSON HERE, FOR *UBS.* THE USAers ARE SURE SCORING SOME POINTS--AND THEY SURE DON'T *TALK* LIKE PEOPLE WHO EVER SHILLED FOR ADOLF HITLER!

MR. CHAIRMAN--YOU'LL HAVE TO *PARDON* HOURMAN AND STARMAN IF THEY'VE TENDED TO MAKE *SPEECHES.*

BUT AFTER ALL, THEY'VE SERVED THIS COUNTRY FOR DECADES, ONLY TO FIND THEMSELVES TREATED AS *PUBLIC ENEMIES*--JUST AS *DR. J. ROBERT OPPENHEIMER* AND OTHERS WERE, DURING THE *1950'S.* THEY--

WELL, HAWKMAN--WE CAN CERTAINLY BE GLAD YOU'RE NOT GOING TO MAKE A SPEECH, CAN'T WE?

HA HA HA HA HA

WHILE, ELSEWHERE IN THE NATION'S CAPITAL...

THE CHAIR RECOGNIZES MS. *HELENA WAYNE,* COUNSEL TO THE JUSTICE SOCIETY...

DON'T LET THEM *OFF THE HOOK,* SENATOR HOPKINS! JUST DIG IT IN TIGHTER--EVER TIGHTER!

I MUST OBJECT TO THE SENATOR'S ATTEMPTS TO MAKE MY CLIENTS THE OBJECT OF *RIDICULE...*

I ONLY HOPE THE COMMITTEE AND THEIR WITNESSES DO THE JOB OF *DESTROYING THE JSA*--

CAT PERFUME
Kitty

--OR ELSE, I'LL HAVE TO STEP IN AND DO IT *PERSONALLY*--

--AND THAT DEFINITELY WON'T BE PRETTY!

MS. WAYNE, THIS HAS BEEN, UNDERSTANDABLY, A *TRYING* MORNING FOR US ALL, AND I'M SORRY IF I OFFENDED ANYONE. I DID NOT MEAN TO.

IF YOU OR THE JUSTICE SOCIETY WOULD LIKE A SHORT RECESS...?

THE JSA WANT NO SPECIAL FAVORS, SENATOR-- JUST A CHANCE TO TELL THE *TRUTH,* AS THEY SEE IT.

THEY FEEL THAT, ONLY BY KNOWING THE *FULL STORY* OF THE JUSTICE SOCIETY'S CAREER ALL THESE YEARS, CAN THE COMMITTEE--AND THE *AMERICAN PEOPLE*--MAKE AN INTELLIGENT DECISION.

IF THEN!

WILDCAT...!

15

MAY I SPEAK, MR. CHAIRMAN?

SURELY, DR. MID-NITE.

ACTUALLY, THOUGH I REPLACED GREEN LANTERN IN THE JSA, HE'D *LEFT* SOME WEEKS BEFORE I HAPPENED ALONG.

"WITH MY OWL MASCOT *HOOTY*, I'D BEEN FIGHTING CRIME ON MY OWN--AND RUN INTO A MADNESS-INDUCING BADDIE KNOWN ONLY AS '*DR. ELBA*.' I ENLISTED THE JSA'S HELP JUST AFTER STARMAN JOINED--

"--SO THAT THE TWO OF US *WON OUR SPURS*, SO TO SPEAK, ON THE VERY SAME ADVENTURE.

"SOON AFTERWARD, CHIEF HOOVER SENT US TO *MEXICO* AND *CENTRAL AND SOUTH AMERICA*, WHERE IT WAS WELL KNOWN THE NAZIS WERE TRYING TO MAKE INROADS.

"WE PUT 'EM ON THE ROAD, ALL RIGHT--RIGHT BACK TO *BERLIN*!"

VERY IMPRESSIVE, DOCTOR--BUT IT WAS RIGHT AFTER THAT, WASN'T IT, THAT YOUR SOCIETY MUFFED ITS CHANCE TO GET THE *BOMB-DEFENSE FORMULA* FOR THE U.S. UNDER VERY *SUSPICIOUS* CIRCUMSTANCES?

HAWK--*I* WAS IN ON THE START OF THAT CASE, TOO-- BACK WHEN I WAS DOING MY *PURPLE-AND-GOLD* SHTICK.

MAYBE I SHOULD--

LET DOC TAKE CARE OF IT, WES. WE APPRECIATE YOUR BEING HERE--BUT YOU'RE STILL TOO *WEAK* TO--

YEAH.

"TO *CONTINUE*, SENATOR HOPKINS: THE FIRST PART OF WHAT BATMAN SAYS IN HIS JOURNAL IS CORRECT. NOT LONG BEFORE PEARL HARBOR, HAWKMAN, SANDMAN, AND I INTERVENED TO SAVE SOME *THREATENED SCIENTISTS* FROM ARMED GUNMEN--THOUGH ALL EVIDENCE SUGGESTS THEY WERE *AXIS SPIES*, NOT RUSSIANS, AS BATMAN CLAIMS.

"HE'S *RIGHT*, THOUGH, IN SAYING THOSE SCIENTISTS HAD FOUND A WAY TO PROJECT MEN--AT LEAST THOSE POSSESSING STAMINA ENOUGH TO SURVIVE THE TRIP-- INTO THE *FAR FUTURE* AND BACK--

16

"--SO *WE EIGHT* MADE THE JOURNEY TO *2941 A.D.* WHILE FLASH AND GREEN LANTERN VOLUNTEERED TO GUARD THE SCIENTISTS TILL OUR RETURN.

"BELIEVE ME WHEN I SAY--GETTING THERE WAS DEFINITELY *NOT* HALF THE FUN!

"STILL, WE *LIVED* THROUGH IT, SOMEHOW--

"--AND BROUGHT BACK ENOUGH DATA FOR THE SCIENTISTS TO CONSTRUCT A *WORKING MODEL* OF A DEVICE WHICH WOULD, WE ALL PRAYED, MAKE AMERICA VIRTUALLY *BOMBPROOF* BY MEANS OF AN *INDESTRUCTIBLE FORCE FIELD.*

"OTHER SCIENTISTS HAD PROPOSED SIMILAR THINGS--INCLUDING THE FAMOUS GENIUS *NIKOLA TESLA,* WHO DIED LATER IN THE WAR.

"A *PLANELOAD* OF POWERFUL *BOMBS* WERE DROPPED ON THE FORCE FIELD FORMED BY THE MODEL--AND THE AREA AROUND IT WASN'T EVEN *MUSSED.*

WHRROOOM!

"I SUPPOSE *SABOTAGE* IS A POSSIBLE, EVEN PROBABLE, ANSWER TO *WHY* IT DIDN'T WORK A *SECOND* TIME--AND WAS SOON *SCRAPPED*--

"--BUT SABOTAGE BY *SOMEONE ELSE,* NOT THE *USA!*

"MAYBE THE *SCIENTISTS* THEM-SELVES--WHAT WE'VE OFTEN CALLED *'THE TIME TRUST'* BECAUSE OF THEIR CHRONO-STUDIES-- COULD TELL YOU MORE. BUT OF COURSE THEY'RE MOSTLY *DECEASED* BY NOW, THEIR RECORDS LOST:

"ONLY *DR. NICHOLS*--WHOSE METHODS OF HYPNOSIS SENT BATMAN AND SUPERMAN BACK IN TIME ON MORE THAN ONE OCCASION YEARS AGO--IS ALIVE *AND* ACCESSIBLE. AND HE IS TOO OLD, TOO INFIRM, TO BE HERE TODAY.

"PROF. *DAMON EVERSON...* PROF. *MALACHI ZEE...* DR. *JAMES SWANLEY...* DR. *WILFRED DOOME...* AND EVEN *PER DEGATON,* FOR ALL WE KNOW...

"NOR WAS HE A *MEMBER* OF THE *TIME TRUST.*

17

DR. NICHOLS WILL BE SUMMONED IN DUE COURSE-- SINCE IT WAS TO HIM THAT THE BATMAN GAVE HIS "DIARY" SEVERAL YEARS AGO, JUST BEFORE HIS MURDER.

IS THERE ANYTHING ELSE?

I'D JUST LIKE TO SUGGEST YOU PUT OUT AN ALL-POINTS BULLETIN FOR THE OTHER SCIENTISTS -- SO THEY THEMSELVES CAN TESTIFY, IF THEY'RE STILL ALIVE.

ONLY SWANLEY AND EVERSON ARE DEFINITELY DEAD, SO--

THANK YOU, DOCTOR. WE'LL, ER, TAKE THAT UNDER ADVISEMENT.

THAT BRINGS US TO THE NEXT--AND ONE OF THE MOST IMPORTANT ITEMS ON OUR AGENDA--THE WHERE-ABOUTS OF THE JSA DURING THE JAPANESE ATTACK ON PEARL HARBOR--

--AND WHY THEY, WITH THEIR EXTRAORDINARY ABILITIES, DIDN'T PREVENT IT.

PEARL HARBOR? WAS THAT IN WORLD WAR ONE OR TWO?

HOW SHOULD I KNOW? I NEVER WAS ANY GOOD AT ANCIENT HISTORY.

QUIET, PLEASE! HERE WE HAVE THE ORIGINAL SPOOLS FROM A WIRE RECORDING MADE IN THE OVAL OFFICE BY PRESIDENT ROOSEVELT AND HIS ADVISOR HARRY HOPKINS LATE IN THE EVENING OF DECEMBER 6th, 1941...

FDR 12·6·41

It seems time has run out on us, Harry, old friend. I'd hoped to have the powerful Justice Society, with their formidable powers, standing by -- forming some sort of All-Star Squadron to help out in the present emergency, but --

Are you really certain they'll be needed so soon, Mr President?

You've read the decoded message which we've learned the Japanese will deliver to our Secretary of State tomorrow, Harry. It's complete enough for me to know -- this means war!

MAY I SPEAK, MR. CHAIRMAN?

FORGIVE ME IF I SEEM TO BE RUSHING MATTERS HERE--

PLEASE DO, MRS. TREVOR.

--BUT AS YOU MAY KNOW--MY HUSBAND--RETIRED GENERAL STEVE TREVOR--WAS BADLY INJURED DURING A DONNY-BROOK BETWEEN ME AND INFINITY, INC.--WHILE I WAS UNDER THE INFLUENCE OF THE STREAM OF RUTHLESSNESS.

HE'S RESPONDING SLOWLY--AND I HOPE SURELY--TO TREATMENT NEAR MY AMAZON HOMELAND. AND NATURALLY, I HOPE TO RETURN TO HIS SIDE AS SOON AS POSSIBLE.

THUS, I CAN ONLY HOPE YOU WILL BELIEVE WHAT I'M ABOUT TO TELL YOU ABOUT EVENTS ON DECEMBER 6-7, 1941...

18

...THAT NOT ONLY ARE WE USAers CONVINCED THAT THE PRESIDENT DIDN'T KNOW THE PRECISE NATURE OF THE IMPENDING JAPANESE ASSAULT...

...BUT THAT THE JUSTICE SOCIETY AND EVERYBODY ELSE ON EARTH HAS FORGOTTEN CERTAIN EVENTS THAT OCCURRED THEN -- AND WHICH CAN BE RE-CONSTRUCTED NOW ONLY WITH THE AID OF MY MAGIC SPHERE!

UH-OH! HERE'S WHERE IT ALL HITS THE FAN!

YEAH -- AND THAT'S ABOUT THE ONLY TIME ANYBODY, INCLUDING US, COULD MAKE ANY SENSE OUT OF IT, EITHER!

LET'S FACE IT, GUYS -- IF IT'S HARD FOR US CHARTER MEMBERS OF INFINITY, INC. TO COMPREHEND -- THINK HOW IMPOSSIBLE IT'S GONNA BE FOR A BUNCH OF LEGISLATORS WHOSE MAIN WORRIES ARE USUALLY PORK-BARRELING AND GETTING RE-ELECTED!

IF YOU WERE "USA BRATS" LIKE LYTA AND ME, OBSIDIAN -- YOU COULD RECITE THIS STORY IN YOUR SLEEP.

WHAT'S YOUR MOM TALKING ABOUT, FURY?

NOW WHO'S BEING CYNICAL, LYTA?

I JUST WISH DAD * AND THE OTHERS DIDN'T FEEL OUR BEING THERE WOULD TURN THAT HEARING INTO MORE OF A CIRCUS THAN IT ALREADY IS!

HE'S PROBABLY RIGHT -- AND ANYWAY, MOM'S THERE -- BUT STILL --

*HAWKMAN. --R.

HEY, WE'VE GOT A STAKE IN THIS, TOO, SCARAB -- REMEMBER?

CHECK! ESPECIALLY IF IT TURNS OUT THE GREEN LANTERN REALLY IS OUR LONG-LOST OLD MAN.

HEY -- LISTEN --!

...SO YOU SAY THAT ONLY YOUR MAGIC SPHERE CAN SHOW US THE TRUE STORY -- AND YOU'D HAVE TO BRING IT HERE FROM PARADISE ISLAND?

FROM WHAT I'VE READ ABOUT YOUR SO-CALLED "MAGIC SPHERE," WONDER WOMAN, IT MERELY SIMULATES EVENTS THAT HAVE ALREADY HAPPENED IN THE PAST -- IT DOESN'T PHOTOGRAPH THEM.

AND IF CAMERAS CAN LIE -- I'D THINK A MAGIC SPHERE COULD MAKE UP A WHOLE MYTHOLOGY ON CUE!

WHAT!?

19

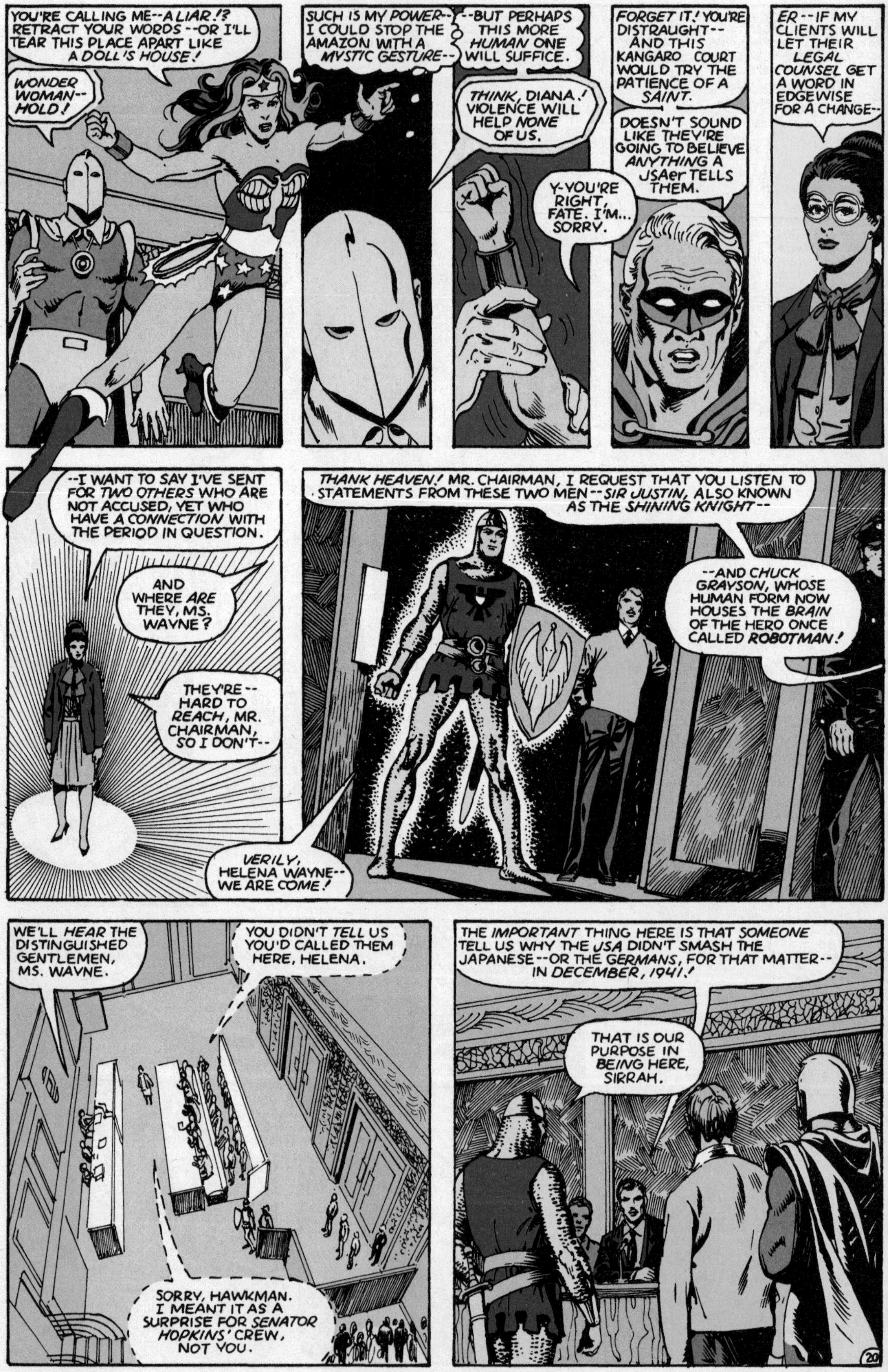
YOU'RE CALLING ME--A LIAR!? RETRACT YOUR WORDS--OR I'LL TEAR THIS PLACE APART LIKE A DOLL'S HOUSE!
WONDER WOMAN--HOLD!
SUCH IS MY POWER--I COULD STOP THE AMAZON WITH A MYSTIC GESTURE--
--BUT PERHAPS THIS MORE HUMAN ONE WILL SUFFICE.
THINK, DIANA! VIOLENCE WILL HELP NONE OF US.
Y-YOU'RE RIGHT, FATE. I'M... SORRY.
FORGET IT! YOU'RE DISTRAUGHT--AND THIS KANGARO COURT WOULD TRY THE PATIENCE OF A SAINT.
DOESN'T SOUND LIKE THEY'RE GOING TO BELIEVE ANYTHING A JSAer TELLS THEM.
ER--IF MY CLIENTS WILL LET THEIR LEGAL COUNSEL GET A WORD IN EDGEWISE FOR A CHANGE--
--I WANT TO SAY I'VE SENT FOR TWO OTHERS WHO ARE NOT ACCUSED, YET WHO HAVE A CONNECTION WITH THE PERIOD IN QUESTION.
AND WHERE ARE THEY, MS. WAYNE?
THEY'RE--HARD TO REACH, MR. CHAIRMAN, SO I DON'T--
VERILY, HELENA WAYNE--WE ARE COME!
THANK HEAVEN! MR. CHAIRMAN, I REQUEST THAT YOU LISTEN TO STATEMENTS FROM THESE TWO MEN--SIR JUSTIN, ALSO KNOWN AS THE SHINING KNIGHT--
--AND CHUCK GRAYSON, WHOSE HUMAN FORM NOW HOUSES THE BRAIN OF THE HERO ONCE CALLED ROBOTMAN!
WE'LL HEAR THE DISTINGUISHED GENTLEMEN, MS. WAYNE.
YOU DIDN'T TELL US YOU'D CALLED THEM HERE, HELENA.
SORRY, HAWKMAN. I MEANT IT AS A SURPRISE FOR SENATOR HOPKINS' CREW, NOT YOU.
THE IMPORTANT THING HERE IS THAT SOMEONE TELL US WHY THE USA DIDN'T SMASH THE JAPANESE--OR THE GERMANS, FOR THAT MATTER--IN DECEMBER, 1941!
THAT IS OUR PURPOSE IN BEING HERE, SIRRAH.
20

UH, *RICHARD*, ISN'T THIS *GRAYSON* FELLOW SOME SORT OF *RELATIVE* OF YOURS?

HIS BODY IS, I GUESS-- BUT CHUCK GRAYSON *DIED* YEARS AGO, AND ROBOTMAN'S HUMAN BRAIN WAS PUT INSIDE IT.

HMMM... CONFUSING *LEGALLY*, BUT WE MAY AS WELL SEE WHAT HE'S GOT TO SAY.

'TIS GOOD TO SEE YOU AGAIN, MY FRIENDS.

AND YOU! JUST HOPE THESE *CHARACTERS* BELIEVE *YOU* MORE THAN THEY HAVE US, SO FAR!

WHEN THE NEW ARRIVALS HAVE BEEN DULY SWORN IN...

...NOW THAT YOU KNOW *MY* TANGLED ORIGINS, LET ME TELL YOU HOW I--AS ROBOTMAN-- HAPPENED TO BECOME INVOLVED WITH THE *JSA* IN DECEMBER OF '41.

"I WAS FEELING SORRY FOR MYSELF AROUND THE *LINCOLN MEMORIAL* IN WASHINGTON--WHEN I SPOTTED *HAWKMAN*, *DR. MID-NITE*, AND THE *ATOM* TAKING ON A *JEKYLL-AND-HYDE* TYPE CALLED 'THE MONSTER.'

"THEY *BEAT* HIM--AND BEFORE OUR VERY EYES, HE TURNED BACK INTO A *MEEK* LITTLE GUY--

"--THEN *VANISHED* TOTALLY, JUST TO MAKE THINGS EVEN MORE CONFUSING!

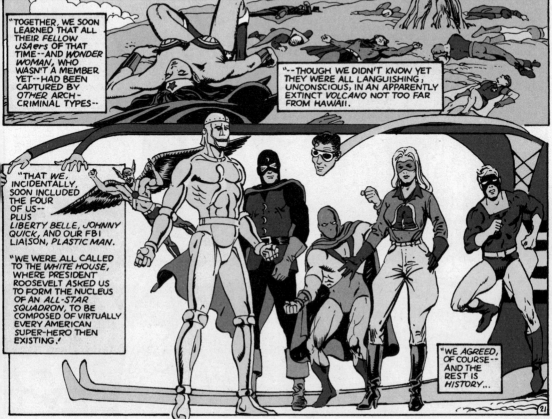

"TOGETHER, WE SOON LEARNED THAT ALL THEIR *FELLOW* JSA ers OF THAT TIME--AND *WONDER WOMAN*, WHO WASN'T A MEMBER YET--HAD BEEN CAPTURED BY OTHER ARCH-CRIMINAL TYPES--

"--THOUGH WE DIDN'T KNOW YET THEY WERE ALL LANGUISHING, UNCONSCIOUS, IN AN APPARENTLY EXTINCT *VOLCANO* NOT TOO FAR FROM HAWAII.

"THAT *WE*, INCIDENTALLY, SOON INCLUDED THE *FOUR* OF US-- PLUS *LIBERTY BELLE*, *JOHNNY QUICK*, AND OUR FBI LIAISON, *PLASTIC MAN*.

"WE WERE ALL CALLED TO THE *WHITE HOUSE*, WHERE PRESIDENT *ROOSEVELT* ASKED US TO FORM THE NUCLEUS OF AN *ALL-STAR SQUADRON*, TO BE COMPOSED OF VIRTUALLY EVERY AMERICAN SUPER-HERO THEN EXISTING!

"WE AGREED, OF COURSE--AND THE REST IS *HISTORY*...

...OR AT LEAST IT *WOULD'VE* BEEN, IF NOT FOR ALL THE *TIME PARADOXES* AT WORK.

UH-OH! THAT SOUNDS LIKE MORE OF WHAT *WONDER WOMAN* WAS SAYING.

IF SO, SIRRAH, 'TIS ONLY BECAUSE SHE DID SPEAK THE *TRUTH*--WHICH IS WHAT IS SORELY *DESIRED* AT SUCH A CONCLAVE AS THIS, IS'T NOT?

I MYSELF HAVE APPEARED BUT LITTLE IN PUBLIC SINCE I RETURNED TO THIS WORLD-- I, AND OTHERS OF THE *SEVEN SOLDIERS OF VICTORY*, AS WE WERE CALLED DURING THE *HITLERIAN* WAR.

*The Seven Soldiers of Victory!*

ER--WE KNOW YOU WERE A *KNIGHT* OF KING ARTHUR'S *ROUND TABLE*, SIR JUSTIN, BEFORE YOU JOURNEYED TO OUR TIME--HARD AS THAT IS TO *BELIEVE*--

'TIS NO MORE INCREDIBLE THAN THE *EVENTS* I AM ABOUT TO UNFOLD, SENATOR--EVENTS WHICH BOTH *DID* AND, IN ANOTHER SENSE, *DID NOT* HAPPEN DURING THOSE FATEFUL HOURS NOW MORE THAN FOUR DECADES GONE...

...FOR, BY THE OATH JUST TAKEN, I VOW THAT THE *JUSTICE SOCIETY* WERE INDEED HELD *CAPTIVE* BY CERTAIN *VARLETS* WHILE *PEARL HARBOR* WAS UNDER ATTACK.

'WAY TO TELL THEM, SIR JUSTIN!

GOD! IN SOME WAYS, IT'S NEARLY AS TOUGH FOR ME TO BE BACK HERE IN *CALIFORNIA* TODAY-- INSTEAD OF BACK IN *WASHINGTON*-- AS IT MUST BE FOR THE *OTHER* INFINITORS.

AFTER ALL, THE ONE PERSON WHO'S *EVER* BEEN A MEMBER OF THE SEVEN SOLDIERS--INFINITY, INC.-- AND THE JUSTICE SOCIETY OF AMERICA--

--IS THE *STAR-SPANGLED KID!*

IN THE DAWNING HOURS OF DECEMBER 7, 1941, I ARRIVED UPON THAT VOLCANIC *ISLE* OF WHICH *CHUCK GRAYSON* HAS SPOKEN-- TO DISCOVER A *YOUNG WOMAN* ALREADY THERE.

AT THE TIME, SHE WAS BUT PURSUING A *SCIENTIFIC* CALLING--NOR DID I *SUSPECT* THAT, ERE THE ADVENTURE WAS OVER, SHE WOULD RECEIVE POWERS WHICH WOULD MAKE HER A *PALADIN* IN HER OWN RIGHT.

I SPEAK OF THE ONE LATER KNOWN AS-- *FIREBRAND*.

22

WE BOTH WERE HELD CAPTIVE FOR A TIME ALSO, THAT DAY, BY THE ARCH-CRIMINAL NAMED *PER DEGATON.* PERHAPS YOU HAVE HEARD OF HIM?

AYE! AND INDEED, 'TWAS FROM THAT SELFSAME YEAR HE HAD COME *BACK-WARD IN TIME*--TO TRY TO INFLUENCE THE *OUTCOME* OF THE WAR--AND IN SO DOING, TO CARVE HIMSELF AN *EMPIRE!*

NOW *WAIT!* I'VE DONE MY HOMEWORK HERE--AND I KNOW THERE'S *NO* CRIMINAL RECORD FOR DEGATON TILL *1947!*

YOU KNOW, PEOPLE, I'VE *TRAVELED* IN TIME--AND EVEN *I'M* STARTING TO FEEL *SORRY* FOR THE COMMITTEE, TRYING TO SIFT THROUGH ALL THIS!

BUT THE *QUESTION* IS-- WILL THEY *BELIEVE* IT?

SIR JUSTIN CONTINUES: "THE MAIDEN AND I--I CANNOT REVEAL HER TRUE NAME-- WANDERED INTO THE NOW-SMOLDER-ING VOLCANO, TO DISCOVER--

'TIS THE HERO OF HEROES CALLED-- *SUPERMAN!*

AND NEAR HIM-- ALL THOSE *OTHERS!*

"ERE LONG, A COMBINATION OF CIRCUMSTANCES OVER-CAME THE STRANGE AURAS WHICH HELD THE JUSTICE SOCIETY *PRISONER*--

"--LEAVING *DEGATON* NO CHOICE BUT TO RETURN TO *1947*--

"--THOUGH HE KNEW THAT, IN SO DOING, HE WOULD *FORGET* ALL THAT HAD OCCURRED--AND RETURN TO HIS *MENIAL* LIFE AS ASSISTANT TO PROFESSOR *ZEE.*

"THEN, THE FORMIDABLE *SPECTRE* DID GATHER UP ALL THE HEROES--ALL WHO HAVE BEEN NAMED TODAY--

"--AND TRANSPORT US ALL TO *SAN FRANCISCO,* WHERE WE VOWED TO BECOME THE *ALL-STAR SQUADRON,* IN ACCORDANCE WITH A PRESIDENT'S MOST FERVENT HOPE.'"

23

I... SEE, SIR JUSTIN.

AND THE *REST* OF THE COUNTRY--DID *IT* EVER KNOW ANYTHING OF THIS DEGATON PERSON'S PLOT--WHATEVER IT MIGHT ALLEGEDLY HAVE BEEN?

NAY, MR. CHAIRMAN. FOR THE VERY ACTS DEGATON HAD PERPETRATED WERE *WIPED OUT*--FORGOTTEN BY ALL--THE MOMENT HE ELECTED TO RETURN TO 1947.

THEN YOU'VE REALLY NO MORE *PROOF* OF WHAT YOU SAY THAN WONDER WOMAN'S SO-CALLED *MAGIC SPHERE?!*

ALAS--I SUPPOSE NOT, SINCE WE TOO LEARNED OF THAT ENCOUNTER, SOMEWHAT LATER, ONLY FROM THE *SPHERE* ITSELF.

YET, IS NOT *MINE* EXISTENCE IN THIS CENTURY PROOF ENOW THAT TIME AND SPACE ARE BUT *FRAGILE THINGS?*

--YOU'D FIND IT HARD TO BE SURE OF *ANYTHING*--OR *ANYONE*--THAT EVER EXISTED, FOR IT'S ALL JUST *WORDS ON PAPER*--A FEW FOSSIL FRAGMENTS--A HANDFUL OF *ARTIFACTS*--!

PERHAPS. THEN IN *DECEMBER '41*, RATHER THAN WITH THE *INJUSTICE SOCIETY*, WAS THE FIRST TIME YOUR GROUP ENCOUNTERED PER DEGATON?

IF YOU INSIST ON *HARD PROOF,* SENATOR--

RIGHT NOW--YOU ASKED US *WHY* WE DIDN'T *SMASH THE AXIS* IN THE HOURS AND DAYS THAT FOLLOWED. CERTAINLY A FAIR ENOUGH QUESTION.

TO TELL THE TRUTH, THAT'S JUST WHAT WAS ON THE MINDS OF *TEN* MEMBERS OF THE NEW *ALL-STAR SQUADRON* ON THE MORNING OF *DECEMBER 8, 1941*--

--AFTER WE, AND VARIOUS OTHERS, HAD SEEN THE DAMAGE THE JAPANESE *SNEAK ATTACK* HAD WROUGHT ON *PEARL HARBOR.*

YES... AND NO, MR. PHILIPS. BUT WE'LL CLARIFY THAT *LATER,* IF YOU DON'T MIND.

"WE ONLY LEARNED *LATER* WHAT STOPPED US, ON A TINY ATOLL:

"*ADOLF HITLER* OF NAZI GERMANY AND *ADMIRAL TOJO* OF JAPAN HAD POOLED THEIR RESOURCES AND COME UP WITH THE *PERFECT DEFENSE* OF THE GAINS THEY'D WON THUS FAR IN THE WAR.

"THE *SPEAR OF DESTINY* IN HITLER'S HANDS -- AND A *STONE* IN TOJO'S, WHICH MAY HAVE BEEN THE PROTOTYPE FOR THE LEGENDARY *HOLY GRAIL*--

"--THEY WERE *AUGMENTED* BY MECHANICAL MEANS THAT DAY, TO CREATE A WORLDWIDE *MAGICAL SHIELD.*

"FROM THEN ON, FOR MUCH OF THE WAR, ANYONE WHO WAS ESPECIALLY IN TUNE WITH *MAGIC* -- AND WHO PASSED INTO *AXIS*-HELD TERRITORY-- WOULD BE ALMOST INSTANTLY TRANSFORMED INTO A FIERCE *FIGHTER* FOR THEIR CAUSE!

"THAT'S HOW THE SPECTRE, DR. FATE, GREEN LANTERN, WONDER WOMAN--AND *SUPERMAN*, AS IT TURNED OUT -- WOUND UP GOING OVER MOMENTARILY TO THE *AXIS* SIDE--

"--THOUGH THE *REST* OF US MANAGED TO *LURE* THEM *OUT* OF THE DANGER ZONE, AND THUS RESTORE THEM TO THEIR *SENSES.* THEY--"

*HOLD IT!* YOU MEAN TO SAY *THAT'S* THE REASON THE AXIS WASN'T DEFEATED BY *AMERICAN* SUPER-HEROES INSTEAD OF *ALLIED* ARMIES?

IF THAT'S TRUE, WHY DIDN'T ANYONE EVER *MENTION* IT TILL NOW?

WE DEAL IN *RESULTS,* SENATOR, NOT *EXCUSES.*

AND NOW, IF IT PLEASE YOU, SIRRAH -- I MUST TAKE MY LEAVE.

UH--SO DO I, IF IT'S --

WE'LL ALL GET TOGETHER WHEN THIS IS *OVER,* ROBO--ER, CHUCK-- I MEAN --

MAKE IT *BOB* NOW, OKAY?

WHAT *NOW,* LAWYER-LADY? THINK WE'RE GETTING THROUGH TO 'EM?

WITH *THOSE* THREE, ATOM, WE WON'T KNOW TILL AFTER THE *AUTOPSY.*

25

81

COULD WE HAVE A LITTLE *SILENCE*, PLEASE?

THANK YOU. NOW, IF ONE OF YOU COULD EXPLAIN TO US HOW AND WHY THE *JSA* ITSELF DECIDED TO *BREAK UP* ONLY A FEW DAYS LATER-- JUST WHEN THEIR NATION *NEEDED* THEM MOST?

WITH AMERICA FINALLY IN THE WAR, EACH OF US WANTED TO DO HIS FIGHTING AS *SOLDIERS*-- NOT AS HOME-FRONT *"MYSTERY-MEN,"* AS THE TERM WAS THEN.

THEN WHY DIDN'T YOU *GIVE UP* YOUR SECRET IDENTITIES-- SO YOU COULD'VE DONE THE *MAXIMUM* TO HELP THE WAR EFFORT?

THAT'S EXACTLY *WHY* WE DID IT, SENATOR HOPKINS.

*WHAM!*

**Washington World**

BUY WAR BONDS

EARLY BIRD EXTRA

**JSA DISBANDS!**

DECISION RUMORED SINCE DEC. 9 CONFIRMED

STATEMENT REVEALS EIGHT CURRENT MEMBERS HAVE ENLISTED IN ARMED SERVICES UNDER REAL NAMES!

MAYBE WE WERE JUST *MISGUIDED PATRIOTS*... I DON'T KNOW. BUT FDR DIDN'T WANT THAT, OBVIOUSLY.

THEN *ALL EIGHT* OF YOU SHOWN IN THIS OLD PAPER JOINED THE SERVICE?

ALL EXCEPT THE *SPECTRE*, MA'AM.

AND *HE* WAS...?

TECHNICALLY *DEAD*-- SINCE *LATE '39!*

*HMMMF!*

TO MAKE A LONG STORY *SHORT*-- AND I'M JUST THE GUY TO DO IT--

--WE WERE IN THE *ARMY* AND ITS AIR FORCES ONLY A COUPLE OF MONTHS, TOPS-- WHEN ALL OF US, MINUS THE SPECTRE, WERE *LURED* INTO A STATESIDE TRAP AND *CAPTURED* BY A NEW FOE--THE *BRAIN WAVE!*

OH YES, HE SNAGGED *WONDER WOMAN*, TOO. IN FACT, THAT'S WHAT LED TO HER *JOINING* THE JSA.

WHEN WE WERE *FREED*, MOSTLY BY THE EFFORTS OF THE *GREEN LANTERN*, WE DECIDED TO RE-GROUP FOR THE DURATION AS THE *JUSTICE BATTALION*, UNDER THE DIRECT ORDERS OF THE *WAR DEPARTMENT*.

*"SO THAT'S* WHY WE JSAers SPENT ONLY A RELATIVELY FEW WEEKS IN THIS MAN'S ARMY!*"

26

AND THE NAVY! DON'T FORGET THE--

--navy.

ULP! DIDN'T MEAN TO PLUG MY OWN OLD BRANCH, GUYS.

YOU HAVE DONE NOTHING AMISS, JOHNNY THUNDER.

AND YOU BECAME SECRETARY AT THIS TIME, WONDER WOMAN?

PERHAPS YOU CAN RECOUNT WHAT HAPPENED NEXT.

GLADLY, SENATOR. AFTER GATHERING UP THE SPECTRE, OUR FIRST FORAY AS THE JUSTICE BATTALION WAS TO SMASH THE JAPANESE SABOTEUR GANG KNOWN AS THE BLACK DRAGONS--WHICH WE DID.

SOON AFTERWARD, SOME OF HITLER'S BOYS MANAGED SOMEHOW TO SEND EIGHT OF US INTO HYPER-DIMENSIONAL SPACE--AS MUCH BY ACCIDENT AS BY DESIGN.

WE SURVIVED, OF COURSE.

NEXT, THE GUYS WENT ABROAD BRIEFLY--TO DELIVER SOME SPECIALLY-DEVELOPED EMERGENCY FOOD PELLETS TO HUNGRY MEMBERS OF THE EUROPEAN UNDERGROUND--SO THEY COULD GO ON FIGHTING THE NAZIS.

NATURALLY, OVERCOMING THE SPEAR OF DESTINY'S AURA POSED PROBLEMS FOR DR. FATE AND THE SPECTRE--BUT THEY OBVIOUSLY MANAGED.

OCCUPIED EUROPE

27

THAT LAST MISSION'S *WELL-DOCUMENTED*, SENATOR--AND BATMAN OR *NO* BATMAN, MAN'S WORLD MUST BE *MAD* TO BELIEVE THE JUSTICE SOCIETY COULD *EVER* HAVE BEEN GUILTY OF COLLABORATING WITH HITLER!

NOR DO I BELIEVE THE *BATMAN* HIMSELF EVER DID SO!

UNDER THE CIRCUMSTANCES-- I CAN'T LET YOU DO THAT, MRS. TREVOR.

I'VE HAD *ENOUGH* OF THIS MOCKERY! I'M LEAVING-- *NOW!*

SO STAY RIGHT WHERE YOU *ARE*, LADY!

YOUR *JSA* BUDDIES, TOO, IF THEY KNOW WHAT'S GOOD FOR THEM!

I WANT *NO* HELP.

I'LL NOT *FIGHT* YOU-- BUT IF YOU WON'T LET ME LEAVE BY THE *DOOR*--

--I'LL MAKE MY *OWN* PATH OUT!

*K-I-C-K*

*JUSTICE SOCIETY!* IF YOU WON'T HELP HER-- CAN'T YOU TRY TO *STOP* HER??

I WOULDN'T SUGGEST YOU TRY IT, OLD FRIENDS!

A MOMENT'S INDECISION, AMONG A WORLD'S MIGHTIEST HEROES--

THEN SUDDENLY--

YOU ARE ALONE NO LONGER, PRINCESS DIANA!

GREAT *HERA!* WHO--?

FROM WORLDS BEYOND WORLDS HAVE I OBSERVED THESE OBSCENE PROCEEDINGS-- THIS TRAVESTY IN THE NAME OF JUSTICE!

THE *SPECTRE!?*

AT LAST HAVE I SAID, *HOLD!* *ENOUGH!* THIS INSANITY MUST END!

28

SAY BUT THE WORD, JUSTICE SOCIETY-- AND I SHALL SHRIVEL THIS PLANET LIKE AN OVERRIDE APPLE--OR SEND IT SPINNING WILDLY INTO THE SUN!

YOURSELVES I SHALL TAKE TO NEWER WORLDS, OTHER EARTHS, WHERE YOU ARE NOW BUT HONORED LEGENDS.

UH-- MY THANKS, SPECTRE-- BUT WHEN YOU PUT IT THAT WAY--

--IT REMINDS ME THIS IS MY PLANET, IF NOT MY HERITAGE.

THE WAY THIS COMMITTEE SEES IT, SPECTRE--YOU SHOULD BE HERE BEFORE US, JUST AS MUCH AS ANY OF THESE OTHERS--

--MAYBE MORE, TO JUDGE BY THE THREATS YOU'VE BEEN MAKING!

GUARDS-- YOU'D BETTER--

SILENCE, MORTAL! JUST BE GLAD I DO NOT DRAW THE SOUL FROM YOUR BODY, WITH A WAVE OF MY HAND!

WELL, OLD COMRADES? WILL YOU COME WITH ME?

'FRAID NOT, SPECTRE-- THANKS JUST THE SAME.

MAYBE THIS ISN'T KRYPTON--BUT THAT'S SOMETHING EVEN YOU CAN'T GIVE ME.

TEMPT HIM NOT, SUPERMAN!

BEGONE, SPECTRE! YOU MEAN WELL--BUT YOU ARE TOO FAR REMOVED NOW FROM YOUR HUMAN PAST... BECOME, AT LAST, ALL GHOST, LEAVING NO PART MAN.

NOR SHOULD YOU SEEK TO DESTROY THIS WORLD, OR ALL THE JSA SHALL MARCH AGAINST YOU--

--AND IN THEIR FOREFRONT SHALL BE DOCTOR FATE!

29

BRAVE WORDS, FATE--SINCE YOU KNOW THAT, POWERFUL AS YOU ARE, MY STRENGTH IS GREATER THAN THINE.

GOOD LORD! WHAT'S THE HUNTRESS DOING IN THE SAME CLUB A GUY LIKE THAT ONCE BELONGED TO!? HE'S LIKE SOME-- BLINDING ANGEL OF JUDGMENT.

OR, IF YOU PREFER..., TO SPHERES WHERE NO MORTALS HAVE EVER TROD.

GUYS--MAYBE WE SHOULD--

NO, LANTERN. WE CAN SPEAK FOR OURSELVES-- BUT NOT FOR DIANA.

WHAT'S IT TO BE, WONDER WOMAN?

WHAT OF YOU ALONE, THEN, DIANA TREVOR? IN AN INSTANT, I CAN TAKE YOU TO A GLEAMING STAR-FLUNG PARADISE...

...YOU, AND YOUR MAN WITH YOU.

BUT I MUST KNOW... NOW.

MY HUSBAND AND I WERE BORN ON THIS EARTH-- AND ITS DESTINY, NO MATTER HOW STAR-CROSSED, IS OURS AS WELL!

I'M SORRY, SPECTRE... BUT I CAN'T.

VERY WELL. I AM STILL JUST HUMAN ENOUGH... TO UNDERSTAND.

NOW, FARE YOU WELL, JUSTICE SOCIETY. MAY YOU EMERGE FROM THE SHADOWS OF SUSPICION INTO THE LIGHT OF VINDICATION!

WHATEVER THAT MEANS, FELLA-- YOU'RE GOING NOWHERE! HANDS UP!

AMUSING.

QUITE AMUSING.

THEN, IT SEEMS AS IF A DIFFERENT UNIVERSE OPENS UP BENEATH THE FEET OF ONE WHO HAS BEEN JIM CORRIGAN ON AT LEAST TWO EARTHS...

...AND THE SPECTRE IS SEEN NO MORE AMONG MEN.

I CAN'T *BELIEVE* THIS! WHERE'D HE GO??

*TRUST* ME, MR. CHAIRMAN-- YOU DON'T *WANT* TO KNOW!

WOULD IT BE TOO *BRAZEN* OF ME TO SUGGEST-- A RECESS?

UNDER THE *CIRCUMSTANCES*, MS. WAYNE-- ALL RIGHT--

THIS HEARING IS RECESSED UNTIL *TOMORROW* MORNING, SAME TIME.

STUNNED, UNSPEAKING AT WHAT THEY'VE SEEN-- AT YAWNING ABYSSES DIMLY GLIMPSED-- THE SPEC-TATORS FILE SLOWLY OUT.

I DON'T GUESS ANY OF US REALLY *KNOW* THE SPECTRE--NOT ANYMORE.

WHAT DO YOU THINK, HELENA? WERE WE *HURT* BY THE SPECTRE POPPING UP AND OFFERING TO *DESTROY* THE EARTH FOR US?

I'M HOPING YOUR *DISCLAIMERS* NEGATED THAT-- BUT I STILL FEEL SENATOR HOPKINS HAD SOMETHING UP HIS *SLEEVE!*

LET HIM *COME!* EVEN IF THE WHOLE WORLD TURNS AGAINST US, AT LEAST *WE'LL* STILL KNOW THAT-- OH, HELLO, SON.

CAN I HAVE YOUR *AUTOGRAPH*, SUPERMAN?

WELL, WELL! MAYBE THERE'S *HOPE* FOR US, YET!

AS, IN THE CHAMBER...

HELENA?

HELLO, DICK.

YOU'RE TRYING TO MAKE *BRUCE*--THE *BATMAN*--LOOK LIKE A *FOOL*, HELENA...A MAN WHO OUGHT TO MEAN MORE TO YOU THAN *ANYBODY.*

HE *DID*, DICK, HE *DOES*. BUT I ALSO KNOW BRUCE WAYNE TURNED *AGAINST* THE JSA BEFORE HE DIED--

--AND I CAN'T LET HIM *SMEAR* INNOCENT FRIENDS, EVEN FROM THE *GRAVE.*

BUT THE *COMMITTEE* DON'T KNOW COMMISSIONER BRUCE WAYNE WAS THE *BATMAN*-- AND THEY *WON'T*, UNLESS YOU TELL THEM!

THEN ... I MAY JUST HAVE TO DO THAT.

GOODBYE, DICK, AND... I'M SORRY.

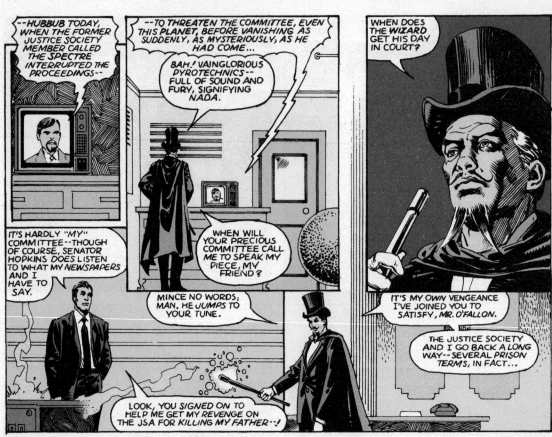

--HUBBUB TODAY, WHEN THE FORMER JUSTICE SOCIETY MEMBER CALLED THE SPECTRE INTERRUPTED THE PROCEEDINGS--

--TO THREATEN THE COMMITTEE, EVEN THIS PLANET, BEFORE VANISHING AS SUDDENLY, AS MYSTERIOUSLY, AS HE HAD COME...

BAH! VAINGLORIOUS PYROTECHNICS-- FULL OF SOUND AND FURY, SIGNIFYING NADA.

WHEN DOES THE WIZARD GET HIS DAY IN COURT?

IT'S HARDLY "MY" COMMITTEE--THOUGH OF COURSE, SENATOR HOPKINS DOES LISTEN TO WHAT MY NEWSPAPERS AND I HAVE TO SAY.

WHEN WILL YOUR PRECIOUS COMMITTEE CALL ME TO SPEAK MY PIECE, MY FRIEND?

MINCE NO WORDS, MAN. HE JUMPS TO YOUR TUNE.

IT'S MY OWN VENGEANCE I'VE JOINED YOU TO SATISFY, MR. O'FALLON.

THE JUSTICE SOCIETY AND I GO BACK A LONG WAY-- SEVERAL PRISON TERMS, IN FACT...

LOOK, YOU SIGNED ON TO HELP ME GET MY REVENGE ON THE JSA FOR KILLING MY FATHER--!

...AND IF THEY THINK THEY'RE GOING TO WALK AWAY FROM THIS ONE SCOTT FREE, AS FROM OUR PREVIOUS ENCOUNTERS--

BOOGA BOOGA

--THEY'VE GOT A SURPRISE IN STORE FOR THEM TOMORROW--

--A VERY GREAT SURPRISE.

I'LL SQUASH THEM--

--LIKE A BUG.

AND THE SAME FATE IS RESERVED FOR ANYONE WHO TRIES TO KEEP ME FROM GAINING THAT VENGEANCE.

DO I MAKE MYSELF CLEAR?

VERY CLEAR.

NEXT ISSUE:
# HOSTILE WITNESS!
(AND BOY, DO WE MEAN HOSTILE!)

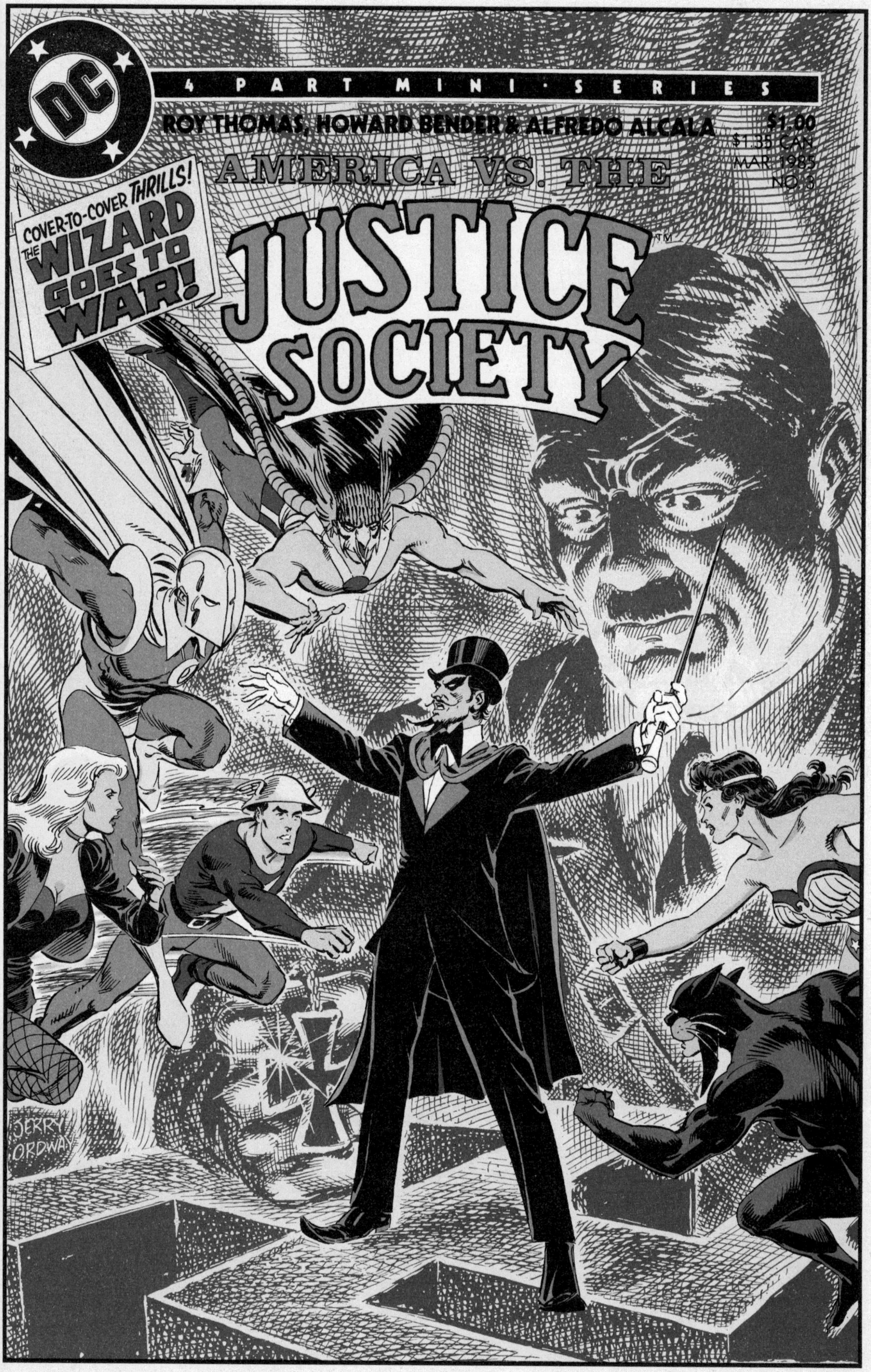

4 PART MINI·SERIES
ROY THOMAS, HOWARD BENDER & ALFREDO ALCALA
$1.00
$1.35 CAN.
MAR 1985
NO.3
AMERICA VS. THE
JUSTICE SOCIETY
COVER-TO-COVER THRILLS!
THE WIZARD GOES TO WAR!
JERRY ORDWAY

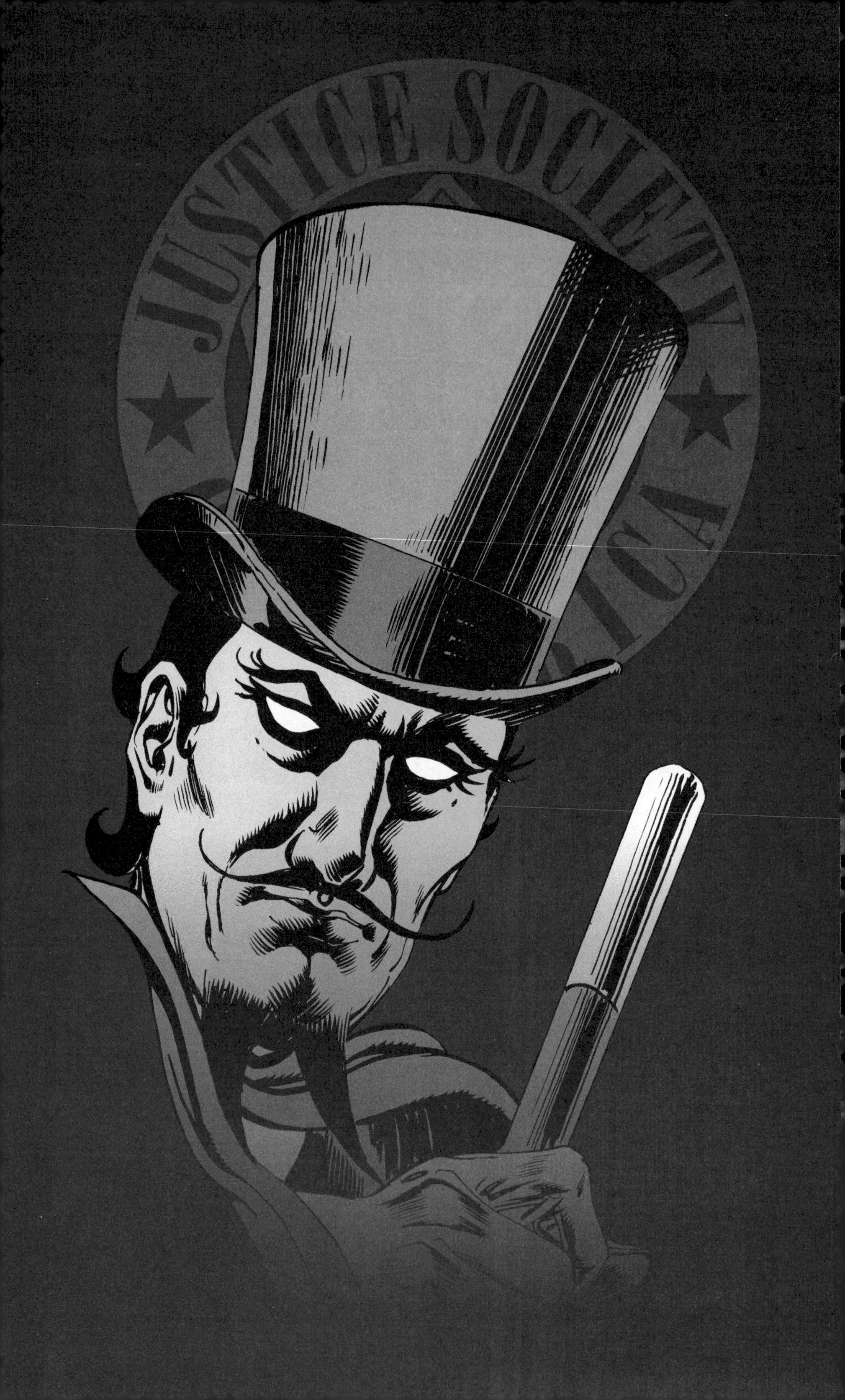
JUSTICE SOCIETY

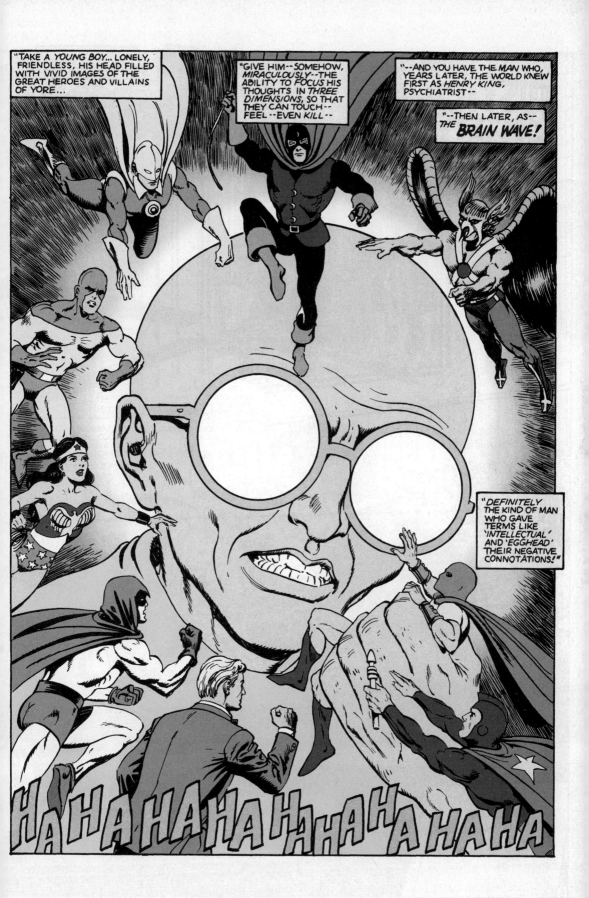

"TAKE A *YOUNG BOY*... LONELY, FRIENDLESS, HIS HEAD FILLED WITH *VIVID* IMAGES OF THE *GREAT HEROES* AND *VILLAINS* OF *YORE*..."

"GIVE HIM--SOMEHOW, MIRACULOUSLY--THE ABILITY TO *FOCUS* HIS THOUGHTS IN *THREE DIMENSIONS*, SO THAT THEY CAN *TOUCH*-- FEEL--EVEN *KILL*--"

"--AND YOU HAVE THE *MAN* WHO, YEARS LATER, THE WORLD KNEW FIRST AS *HENRY KING*, PSYCHIATRIST--"

"--THEN LATER, AS-- *THE BRAIN WAVE!*"

"*DEFINITELY* THE KIND OF MAN WHO GAVE TERMS LIKE 'INTELLECTUAL' AND 'EGGHEAD' THEIR *NEGATIVE* CONNOTATIONS!"

HAHAHAHAHAHAHAHAHAHA

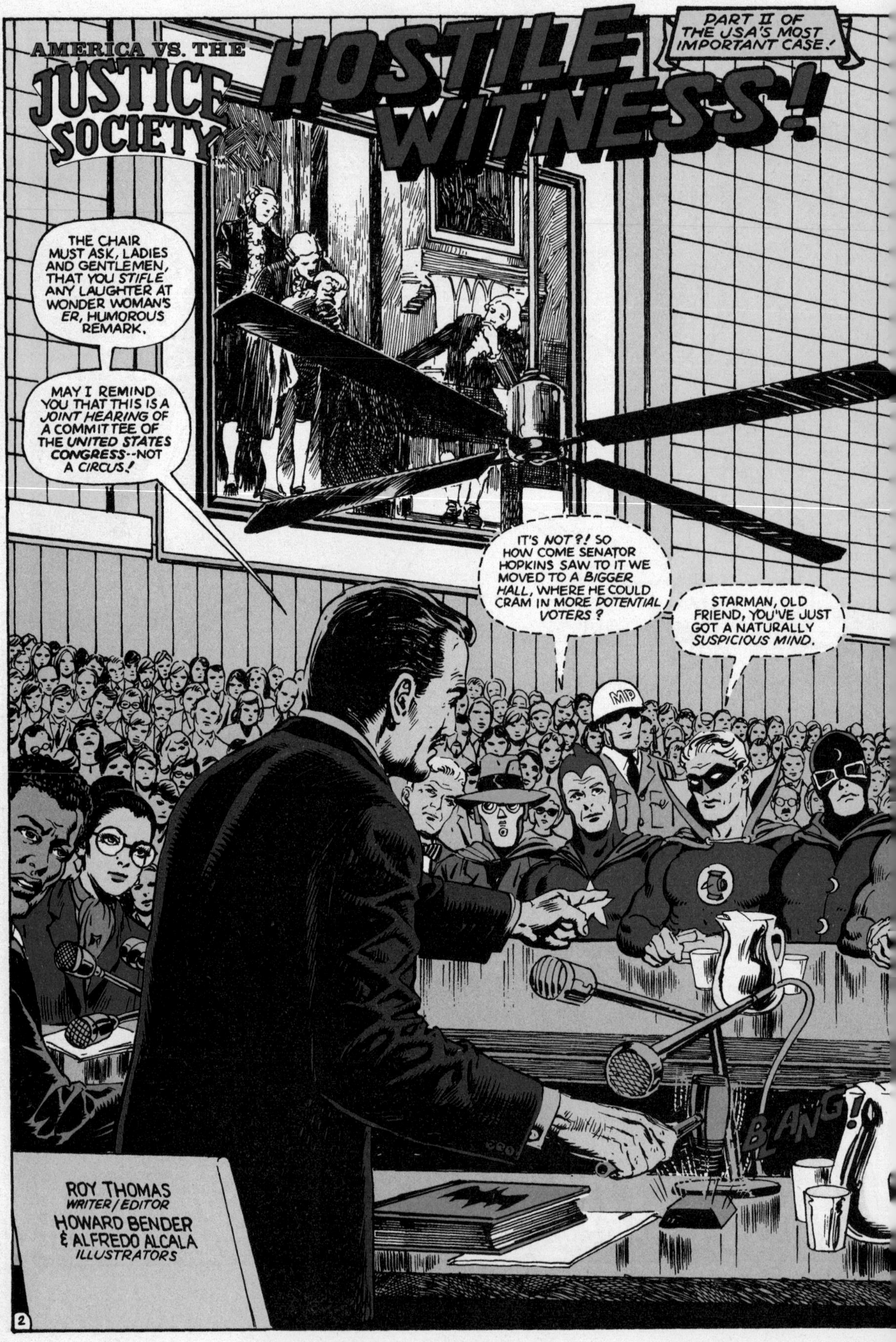

AMERICA VS. THE JUSTICE SOCIETY
HOSTILE WITNESS!
PART II OF THE USA'S MOST IMPORTANT CASE!
THE CHAIR MUST ASK, LADIES AND GENTLEMEN, THAT YOU STIFLE ANY LAUGHTER AT WONDER WOMAN'S ER, HUMOROUS REMARK.
MAY I REMIND YOU THAT THIS IS A JOINT HEARING OF A COMMITTEE OF THE UNITED STATES CONGRESS--NOT A CIRCUS!
IT'S NOT?! SO HOW COME SENATOR HOPKINS SAW TO IT WE MOVED TO A BIGGER HALL, WHERE HE COULD CRAM IN MORE POTENTIAL VOTERS?
STARMAN, OLD FRIEND, YOU'VE JUST GOT A NATURALLY SUSPICIOUS MIND.
MP
BLANG!
ROY THOMAS WRITER/EDITOR
HOWARD BENDER & ALFREDO ALCALA ILLUSTRATORS
2

SORRY, SENATOR. ZEUS KNOWS, THESE PROCEEDINGS COULD USE A BIT OF LEVITY.

STILL, I DIDN'T *MEAN* TO MAKE A JOKE, REALLY. I'M QUITE AWARE THAT THE JUSTICE SOCIETY IS ON *TRIAL* HERE--IN *FACT* IF NOT IN *NAME*--

--AND THAT IF WE *DON'T* DISPROVE THE ALLEGATIONS OF THE SO-CALLED *BATMAN DIARY*-- THE JSA IS *FINISHED!*

YOU MAY PROCEED WITH YOUR TESTIMONY, MRS. TREVOR.

DANN THOMAS
*CO-PLOTTER*
CARL GAFFORD
*COLORIST*
CODY
*LETTERER*
RICH MORRISEY
*CONSULTANT*

THANK YOU, CONGRESSWOMAN VALDEZ. I HOPE THIS COMMITTEE'S LEARNING MORE ABOUT OUR 1943 ENCOUNTERS WITH THE BRAIN WAVE WILL SHOW THAT, FAR FROM BEING TRAITORS AND SECRET SABOTEURS, AS BATMAN'S JOURNAL SUGGESTS--

--WE WERE WORKING FOR AMERICA'S WAR EFFORT, RIGHT ALONG!

THE RECORD SHOWS THAT THE BRAIN WAVE WAS CREATING MENTAL IMAGES TO DO HIS PLUNDERING FOR HIM...

"FIRST, I LED THE COSTUMED *GIRLFRIENDS* OF SEVERAL OF THE *JSAers* AGAINST HIM--

"--AND THE BOYS THEMSELVES ARRIVED TO COMPLETE THE JOB.

CRASH

STAY AWAY! I--HELP!

WE'VE GOT TO--TOO LATE! BUT IT'S PROBABLY *BETTER* THIS WAY.

AAAGGHHH

YOU'RE TELLING US?!

"OUR NEXT MISSION DIDN'T RECEIVE MUCH *FANFARE*: SMASHING NAZI AGENTS WHO WERE TRYING TO *DIVIDE* AMERICA, TURNING RACE AGAINST RACE, EMPLOYEE AGAINST EMPLOYER.

"LITTLE DID WE REALIZE, MEANWHILE, THAT THE BRAIN WAVE HAD *ESCAPED DEATH*...

MY LONG SMOCK *SAVED* ME! NOW TO MAKE THOSE FOOLS *THINK* THEY SAW ME *DIE*

I'LL KEEP UP THAT FARCE TILL THEY'VE BURIED MY "*REMAINS*" --BUT THEN I'LL HAVE MY *REVENGE!*

"AS IT HAPPENED, THAT ENTAILED GAINING ENTRANCE TO OUR *HEADQUARTERS*, AND ACTIVATING STRANGE *PURPLE LIGHTS* FROM THE CELLAR...

*THAT SHOULD HAVE DONE IT!*

4

"AND IT DID--REDUCING THE EIGHT MEMBERS PRESENT THAT DAY TO A MERE *EIGHT INCHES HIGH,* SO HE COULD IMPRISON THEM IN *SPECIAL CAGES...*

*OTHER MEN FAILED TO HALT YOU BY LEAVING YOU YOUR MIGHTY STRENGTH.*

*I DECIDED, AFTER STUDYING THE RECORDS OF YOUR ADVENTURES AND ESCAPES, TO TAKE THAT AWAY BY MAKING YOU SMALL!*

"OF COURSE, THEY SOON *RE-GAINED* THEIR STATURE, AND *CORNERED HIM*--NOT KNOWING HE'D MINED THE APPROACHES TO HIS LIGHTHOUSE HIDEOUT. BUT JOHNNY THUNDER'S *THUNDERBOLT* GOT THROUGH...

*YOU'LL NEVER GET AWAY WITH THIS, BRAIN WAVE!*

DON'T--

*FOOL! I CAN BLOW THEM UP FROM HERE-- RIGHT NOW!*

*BOOM!*

*I SUPPOSE I SHOULD'VE TOLD HIM IT WAS TOO DANGEROUS TO LEAVE MINES UNDER THE ROAD--SO I MOVED THEM UNDER HIS TOWER!*

WAIT! BACK UP, AMAZON! FIRST, I'D LIKE TO KNOW *WHY,* THOUGH THE JSA HAD SUPPOSEDLY BECOME THE *"JUSTICE BATTALION"* FOR THE DURATION OF THE WAR, IT CEASED TO BE CALLED THAT, ABOUT THIS TIME --

--AND SECOND, ABOUT THEN, A NUMBER OF SUPER-HEROES *DISAPPEARED* TOTALLY--MANY OF THEM *NEVER* TO BE SEEN *AGAIN!*

I REFER, OF COURSE, TO PEOPLE LIKE *THE RAY*-- *BLACK CONDOR*-- *UNCLE SAM*-- *PHANTOM LADY*--

--AND THEN THERE'S THE *RED BEE,* WHO DISAPPEARED IN *EARLY '42.* AND THERE WERE *OTHERS*--!

MAYBE *I'D* BETTER BACKSTOP THAT ONE, SENATOR.

PLEASE DO, HAWKMAN.

THE *BATTALION* THING'S THE EASIEST: AS THE JSA'S PERMANENT CHAIRMAN, I DISCOVERED THE AMERICAN PUBLIC HAD BECOME A BIT CONFUSED BY THE DOUBLE NAME--SO WITH THE WAR DEPT.'S PERMISSION, WE SIMPLY DROPPED IT.

THE *"VANISHED HEROES"* ARE A LITTLE HARDER TO EXPLAIN-- BUT HERE GOES...!

THE CHAMBER SITS HUSHED AS HAWKMAN TELLS OF EARTH-X... THAT ALTERNATE EARTH FOR WHICH UNCLE SAM, IN THE 1940'S, RECRUITED AN ARMY OF SUPER-HEROES TO KEEP THE AXIS POWERS FROM WINNING WORLD WAR TWO...

...BUT, IN THE LONG RUN -- ALL IN VAIN!

REACTIONS VARY, DEPENDING UPON WHETHER A SPECTATOR IS A VETERAN...

THE NAZIS WON THE BIG ONE!? NO WAY!

...OR A JSAer's WIFE LIKE INZA NELSON...

DR. FATE COULD SHOW THEM EARTH-X... IN AN INSTANT!

...OR A FRIEND, LIKE JIMMY OLSEN...

GOSH, LOIS -- THEY'RE GETTING NASTY!

...OR COUNSEL FOR THE JSA, LIKE HELENA WAYNE:

MY CLIENT TOLD YOU IT'D BE HARD TO EXPLAIN, SENATOR.

WELL, HE WASN'T WRONG! BUT WHERE ARE THESE "FREEDOM FIGHTERS" NOW?

ON THIS EARTH -- OR ON THAT "EARTH-X"?

ACTUALLY, SENATOR... NEITHER ONE.

WHAT? WHERE, THEN?

WELL... ER... UH... WOULD YOU BELIEVE--

-- ON A THIRD EARTH?

THOSE THAT ARE STILL ALIVE, ANYWAY!

IMPOSSIBLE! I, FOR ONE, DO NOT BELIEVE THAT -- YES, CONGRESSWOMAN VALDEZ?

AFTER WHAT WE SAW YESTERDAY -- WHEN THE FORMER JSAer CALLED THE SPECTRE INVADED OUR CHAMBERS AND THREATENED TO ANNIHILATE OUR WORLD, IF THE JSAers JUST GAVE HIM THE NOD--

-- I STILL CAN'T BE SURE OF THE TRUTH OF WHAT HAWKMAN'S JUST SAID -- BUT I CAN NO LONGER TRUTHFULLY SAY I THINK IT'S BEYOND POSSIBILITY!

THANK YOU FOR *THAT*, AT LEAST, CONGRESSWOMAN.

TO CONTINUE: WE ADMIT THAT MOST OF THE REST OF OUR WAR-TIME FOES WERE *NON-POLITICAL*-- LIKE THE SELF-CROWNED *KING BEE* --

--HECTOR BAUER, THE MAD MAESTRO WHO COMMITTED THE SO-CALLED *"CRIMES SET TO MUSIC"*--EVEN CAPTURING A CERTAIN *WINGED WONDER* FOR A WHILE, IN THE BARGAIN--

--OR THE VENGEFUL *MONSTER*, WHO TURNED OUT TO BE THE REPRESSED, EVIL SIDE OF A GENTLE SOUL NAMED *JASON L. ROGERS.*

NO, THEY WEREN'T *NAZIS* OR *FASCISTS* -- BUT THE WORLD'S AS WELL RID OF *THEM* AS OF ANY-BODY THIS SIDE OF HITLER!

THAT'S QUITE *ENOUGH*, HAWKMAN!

YOUR RAMBLINGS HAVE ABSOLUTELY *NOTHING* TO DO WITH THE MAIN PURPOSE OF THESE HEARINGS--

--THE *BATMAN DIARY*--

BANG!

--WHICH, IN THE *AUTHENTICATED* HANDWRITING OF THE *LATE*, GREAT CAPED CRUSADER, ACCUSES EACH OF YOU HERE BEFORE ME --EXCEPT *SUPERMAN* -- OF *TREASON!*

WE ALL *KNOW* THE CIRCUMSTANCES UNDER WHICH IT WAS GIVEN LATE IN 1979--

7

"--TO *PROF. CARTER NICHOLS*, WHO, IN THE EVENT OF THE *BATMAN'S DEATH*, WAS TO TURN THE JOURNAL OVER, *UNREAD*, TO *CLARK KENT*, MANAGING EDITOR OF THE *METROPOLIS DAILY STAR.*

"*LIKE THE SCHOLAR AND GENTLEMAN HE TRULY IS*, PROF. NICHOLS DID AS HE *VOWED* HE WOULD DO--TO THE *BATMAN* HIMSELF, THAT NIGHT IN 1979--

"--AND, AFTER A *HURRIED EXAMINATION* BY *KENT*, AND LATER BY *STAR* EDITOR *JAMES OLSEN*--THAT NEWSPAPER PRINTED THE TEXT *IN FULL!*

"IT TOLD AN *AMAZING* STORY, ADMITTEDLY--OF RAMPAGING *VALKYRIES* AND A MAGICAL *SPEAR OF DESTINY*--

"--OF THE *USA* SABOTAG-ING OF A SCIENTIFICALLY *CREATED FORCE FIELD* WHICH MIGHT HAVE KEPT AMERICA SAFE FROM *ENEMY BOMBS* DURING THE WAR--

"--AND, MOST *DAMNING* OF ALL, OF *NINE* SELF-STYLED MYSTERY-MEN, INCLUDING *BATMAN* HIMSELF, WHO IN *NOVEMBER* OF 1940, IN THE HEART OF *BERLIN*, SWORE ALLEGIANCE TO *ADOLF HITLER, FUHRER* OF THE *THIRD REICH!*

"NOW *THAT* IS SOMETHING I WOULD FIND *TRULY IMPOSSIBLE* TO BELIEVE--

8

--IF THE JSA'S ACCUSER WERE ANYONE LESS THAN THE LATE *BATMAN* HIMSELF!

HE ADMITS, IN THE DIARY, TO HAVING BEEN A *NAZI*--FROM LATE 1940 TILL HE CAME TO HIS SENSES AFTER *PEARL HARBOR.*

THE SENATOR'S WORDS STIR TWO HEARTS, PERHAPS, EVEN MORE THAN OTHERS WITHIN HEARING: THOSE OF HELENA WAYNE, WHO, UNKNOWN TO THE WORLD, WAS BATMAN'S DAUGHTER... AND ONE OTHER:

BATMAN A NAZI--THAT'S THE PART THAT *REALLY* DOESN'T MAKE ANY SENSE.!

*SNAP!*

I DON'T KNOW THE OTHERS NEARLY AS WELL--BUT BRUCE--

MAYBE HELENA'S *RIGHT.* MAYBE BRUCE *WAS* LYING WHEN HE WROTE THAT DIARY--IF IT ISN'T THE *CLEVEREST* FORGERY IN HISTORY.

IN SOME WAY, I *WANT* HER--AND *THEM*--TO CONVINCE ME AND EVERYBODY ELSE THEY'RE *INNOCENT.*

BUT IF THEY *ARE*--THEN WHAT DOES THAT MAKE *BATMAN*--

MR. CHAIRMAN--YOU'VE ASKED WHAT *RELEVANCE* THE HISTORY OF THE JSA HAS TO THE PURPOSES OF THESE HEARINGS. MAY I--ATTEMPT TO *ANSWER*--THAT QUESTION?

--AND WHERE DOES THAT LEAVE *DICK GRAYSON*--THE LAWYER WHO ONCE WAS *ROBIN, THE BOY WONDER??*

SANDMAN--*NO!* BAD ENOUGH YOU'RE HERE, AT ALL!

YOU'RE NOT *WELL* ENOUGH TO TESTIFY--YOU'RE STILL RECOVERING FROM THAT *STROKE*--!

PLEASE, STARMAN--ALL OF YOU--I'M ALL DONE WITH HAVING YOU *SHIELD* ME, OKAY?

YEAH--SURE. GO AHEAD.

MR. CHAIRMAN, WONDER WOMAN WAS *RIGHT* WHEN SHE SAID THE JSA REALLY IS ON *TRIAL* HERE.

"THE JUSTICE SOCIETY OF AMERICA"--THAT ENTITY HAS BEEN THE *LIFE'S BLOOD* OF THE THIRTEEN PEOPLE SEATED AT THIS TABLE--FOR NEARLY HALF A CENTURY--

--NOW THEIR ENTIRE CAREERS, THEIR *GOOD NAMES,* THEIR VERY *SOULS,* HAVE BEEN TINGED BY THIS ASTONISHING ACCUSATION OF *TREASON!*

I THINK THEY--WE HAVE A RIGHT TO BE *HEARD*--TO PUT OUR *WHOLE STORY* ON THE RECORD--NOT JUST THE PARTS *YOU* MIGHT WANT TO HEAR. I--

--I THINK--I'D BETTER *SIT DOWN* NOW--IF YOU DON'T MIND.

YOU WERE *GREAT*, SANDMAN-- HERE-- SOME TEA TO SOOTHE YOUR THROAT.

THE, ER, *STRAW* WILL HELP.

YOU SURE *TOLD 'EM*, SANDY!

YEAH! SO FAR THEY *AIN'T PROVED SQUAT!*

*KLAP KLAP KLAP KLAP KL*

BUT ONLY THE COMMITTEE AND *I* KNOW--WHAT'S YET TO *COME!*

WHILE, IN THE MAIN OFFICES OF THE *CAPITAL GLOBE*...

STOP BY THE DRUGSTORE AND PICK UP SOME *BANDAIDS*, WILKINS--

--FOR ALL THOSE *BLEEDING-HEARTS* OUT THERE IN *HERO-WORSHIP LAND!*

MR. O'FALLON-- WILL THERE BE ANYTHING *ELSE*, BEFORE I--?

THEY'RE GONNA NEED 'EM--AFTER OUR *SURPRISE WITNESS* BLOWS THE JSAers OUT OF THE *WATER!*

JOHN O'FALLON'S WAITED A LONG TIME TO GET THOSE COSTUMED *MURDERERS*--

--JUST LIKE THEY GOT MY *OLD MAN* YEARS AGO, AND MADE IT LOOK LIKE AN *ACCIDENT!*

BUT, BY GOD, IT'LL ALL HAVE BEEN *WORTH IT*--WHEN WE *SPRING OUR TRAP!*

YES, SIR. I'LL... BE GOING NOW.

AS, IN A HOTEL ROOM SOME-WHERE IN WASHINGTON, D.C....

--CROWD RESPONDED WITH ENTHUSIASM HERE TO SANDMAN'S *IMPASSIONED* SPEECH, AS IF ASKING THEMSELVES THE QUESTION--"IS IT *POSSIBLE* MEN SUCH AS THESE CAN BE *TRAITORS?*"

JSA ON TRIAL

YES, BY THUNDER! YES!

DON'T LET THEM OFF THE *HOOK*, YOU FOOLS! PUT THE *SCREWS* TO THEM--*NAIL* THEM TO THE *WALL!*

BECAUSE--IF YOUR *PRECIOUS* COMMITTEE *DOESN'T*--

10

**--THEN I SHALL!**

SMASSH!

--MENTION MADE OF VARIOUS JSAers *LEAVING* THE GROUP IN 1944-45--BECAUSE BY THEN, THE WAR HAD TURNED *AGAINST* HITLER, AND THERE WAS NO LONGER ANYTHING THEY COULD DO TO HELP THE AXIS CAUSE.

WOULD YOU CARE TO COMMENT ON THAT?

*I* WOULD, SENATOR--SINCE I WAS ONE OF THOSE WHO LEFT THE JSA DURING THAT PERIOD.

FOR THE RECORD: THERE WERE STILL *NINE* OF US IN THE JSA IN LATE '44 WHEN PROFESSOR *EVERSON*--OF THE "TIME TRUST" MENTIONED EARLIER--CALLED ON US FOR A VERY *SPECIAL* MISSION.

HE'D DEVELOPED HIS OWN *TIME RAY* BY THEN--AND *SENT* US BACK INTO A *DYING* MAN'S PAST--TO HELP HIM DIE WITH A *CLEAR CONSCIENCE*.

I'M PROUD TO SAY-- WE *ACCOMPLISHED* OUR TASK.

**1944**

YOU PROBABLY *WOULDN'T BELIEVE* OUR NEXT UNDER-TAKING--A LESSON IN *TOLERANCE,* INVOLVING A *LIVING INCARNATION* OF HUMAN *CONSCIENCE.*

LOVE

GREED

DESPAIR

MATTER OF FACT, *I'M* STILL NOT 100% SURE *I* BELIEVE IT MYSELF.

BUT A LOOK THROUGH OLD NEWSPAPER FILES WILL SHOW THAT WE FLUSHED THE ORIGINAL *PSYCHO-PIRATE* OUT INTO THE OPEN, ABOUT THAT TIME--

NO, WAIT--I THINK *SANDMAN* AND *DR. FATE* WERE *GONE* BY THE TIME OF THESE LAST TWO CASES--!

11

THEY WERE; I'VE CHECKED. CARE TO FILL US IN ON WHAT *YOU* WERE UP TO, SANDMAN?

SURE. I WAS IN MY PURPLE-AND-GOLD PHASE AFTER '41, OF COURSE--AND I'D PICKED UP *SANDY* AS A SIDEKICK.

'45 WASN'T MUCH OF A YEAR FOR ME, THOUGH...

IT WOULD TAKE HOURS FOR ME TO EXPLAIN TO THE COMMITTEE THE DIFFERENCE BETWEEN THE MAN I AM WHEN I WEAR THIS HELMET OF NABU--AND THE LESSER HALF-HELMET I WORE THEN.

SUFFICE IT TO SAY, I DECIDED SOMEWHAT EARLIER TO BECOME A TRUE PHYSICIAN--A HEALER OF MEN--RATHER THAN A SORCERER.

THAT LEFT ME NO TIME, EVENTUALLY, TO BE A SO-CALLED "SUPER-HERO"--

--BUT IT IS A DECISION I HAVE NEVER REGRETTED.

GOOD FOR YOU-- IF I MAY BE SO BOLD.

HAWKMAN, CAN YOU TELL US ABOUT THE SPECTRE?

CERTAINLY. HE FOUND A WAY TO JOIN THE *HUMAN BODY* TO JOIN THE *ARMED SERVICES* SO HE COULD SERVE HIS COUNTRY-- WHILE HIS ETHEREAL *GHOST-SELF* STAYED ON THE HOME FRONT TO TACKLE MOBSTERS AND SUCH.

I UNDERSTAND THAT, AT THAT TIME, THE SPECTRE LOST HIS ABILITY TO *TOUCH* HUMAN BEINGS --SO HE PROBABLY *SCARED* A FEW LOWLIFES TO DEATH.

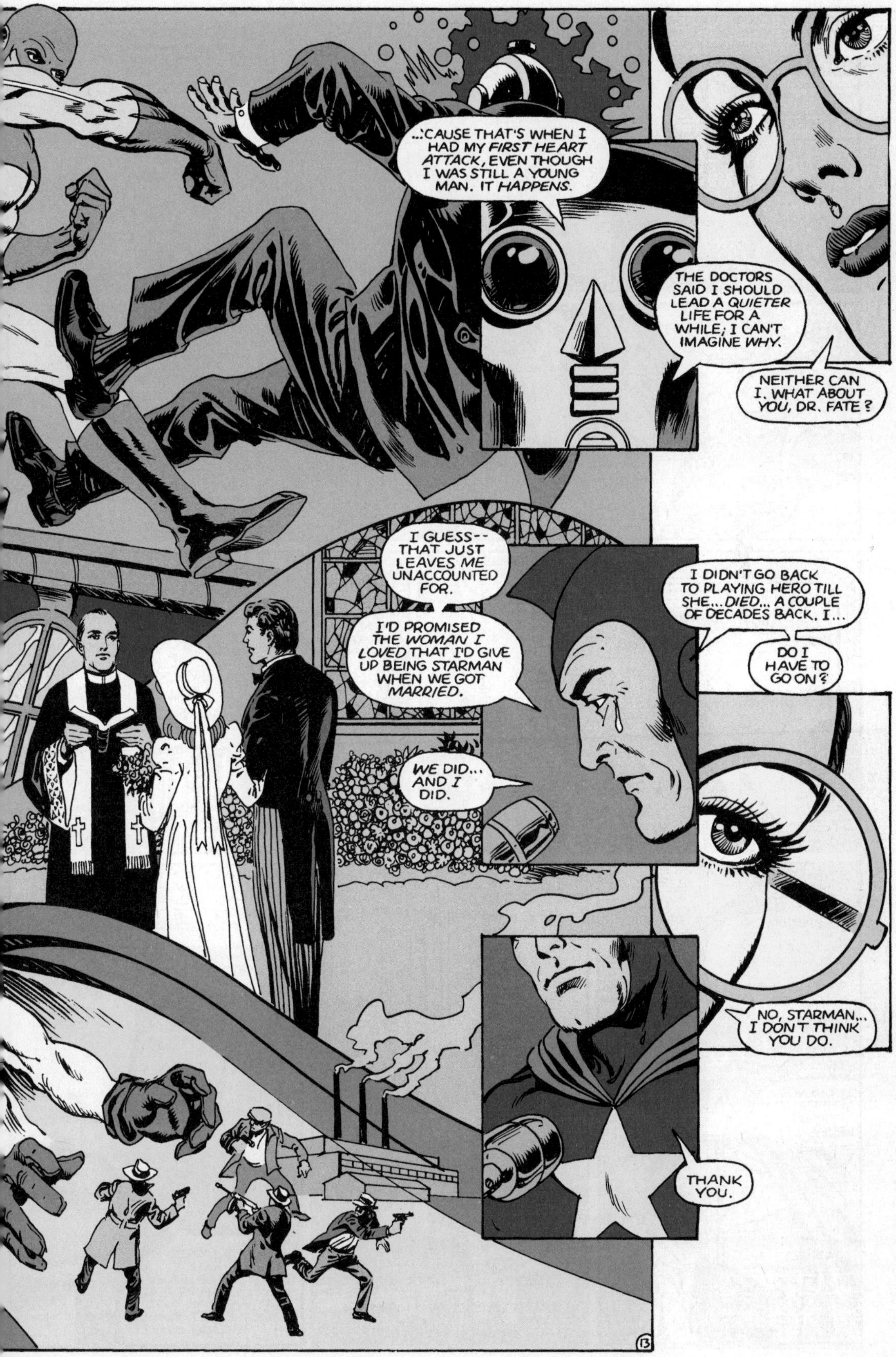
...'CAUSE THAT'S WHEN I HAD MY *FIRST HEART ATTACK*, EVEN THOUGH I WAS STILL A YOUNG MAN. IT *HAPPENS*.
THE DOCTORS SAID I SHOULD LEAD A *QUIETER* LIFE FOR A WHILE; I CAN'T IMAGINE *WHY*.
NEITHER CAN I. WHAT ABOUT *YOU*, DR. FATE?
I GUESS-- THAT JUST LEAVES *ME* UNACCOUNTED FOR.
I'D PROMISED THE *WOMAN I LOVED* THAT I'D GIVE UP BEING STARMAN WHEN WE GOT *MARRIED*.
*WE DID*... AND *I* DID.
I DIDN'T GO BACK TO PLAYING HERO TILL SHE... *DIED*... A COUPLE OF DECADES BACK. I...
DO I HAVE TO GO ON?
NO, STARMAN... I DON'T THINK YOU DO.
THANK YOU.
13

I...THINK I SPEAK FOR THE COMMITTEE IN SAYING WE WERE QUITE *MOVED* BY THE PRECEDING TESTIMONY...THOUGH OF COURSE THERE'S NO WAY ITS *TRUTH* OR *FALSEHOOD* CAN BE READILY CHECKED.

MR. CHAIRMAN, MAY I SUGGEST A RECESS?

I'LL *SECOND* THAT.

THAT *WOULD* SEEM TO BE IN ORDER. ER--IF YOU *JSAers* WILL WAIT UNTIL AN ESCORT CAN BE SUMMONED...

OUR JAILERS, HE MEANS!

THERE IS NO NEED TO BOTHER YOURSELF OR THEM, SUCH PRIVACY AS THE *JUSTICE SOCIETY* REQUIRES--

DR. FATE CAN WELL PROVIDE!

NO MAN PRESENT UNDERSTANDS THE WORDS THE MASTER MAGE SPEAKS NEXT. THEY SEEM, TO SOME, LIKE STRANGE *NONSENSE WORDS*--AS FULL OF JUMBLED CONSONANTS AND DIPTHONGS AS THEY ARE DEVOID OF MEANING.

YET, WHEN THE SUDDEN BURST OF LIGHT AND TORRENT OF SYLLABLES FADE, MOMENTS LATER--

UH-- I GUESS HE CAN, AT THAT!

SOON, IN A SMALLER CHAMBER OF A BUILDING IN THE SHADOW OF THE CAPITOL...

I REALLY APPRECIATE YOUR MEETING ME HERE, DICK...

...ESPECIALLY SINCE I KNOW YOU'VE *BRISTLED* AT SOME OF THE THINGS I'VE SAID AS THE JSA'S *COUNSEL.*

YOU KNOW WHERE I STAND, HELENA.

DO I? I ALWAYS THOUGHT IT WAS FOR... THE *TRUTH.*

SO WHO'S GOT A MONOPOLY ON THAT? *YOU?* THE *JSA?*

YOU'VE AS MUCH AS *ACCUSED* BATMAN--THE MAN WHO BROUGHT ME UP--YOUR OWN *FATHER,* FOR GOD'S SAKE--OF CREATING THAT "DIARY" AS A MONSTROUS *LIE!*

WHAT'S MORE, YOU'VE TOLD ME THAT, IF NECESSARY, YOU'LL EVEN REVEAL THAT BATMAN WAS REALLY *BRUCE WAYNE.* WHY, HELENA? *WHY??*

14

BECAUSE I WON'T SEE THE JSA WRONGLY CONVICTED OF *TREASON*-- BY THE WORDS OF A MAN WHO'D CONCEIVED AN *IRRATIONAL DISTRUST* OF THE GROUP DURING HIS FINAL YEARS.

YOU KNEW HIM, DICK. YOU *KNOW* THAT'S HOW HE WAS.

THE COMMITTEE AND THE PUBLIC COULD LOOK AT *BRUCE WAYNE'S RECORD*-- AND MAKE UP THEIR OWN *MIND*. IF THEY KNEW HE HAD BEEN THE *BATMAN* IN EARLIER YEARS--

--IT MIGHT *DESTROY* HIS CREDIBILITY, EVEN FROM THE *GRAVE!* I KNOW THAT.

THE MAN'S *DEAD*, HELENA! CAN'T YOU LET HIM--AND THE *GOOD* HE DID-- REST IN *PEACE?*

NOBODY DOES *ALL GOOD,* DICK--NOT EVEN *DAD!* YOU KNOW I WOULDN'T BE DEFENDING THE JSA IF I THOUGHT THEY WERE GUILTY.

OR MAYBE IT'S JUST THAT, AS THE *HUNTRESS,* YOU'RE A JSAer *YOURSELF.*

MAYBE YOU'VE GOT AN *AXE* TO GRIND-- SOME SECRET *GRUDGE* YOU NURTURED AGAINST BRUCE ALL THESE YEARS.

WHAT I REALLY THINK IS THAT DAD HAD A *REASON* FOR WRITING THOSE LIES-- OR ELSE--

OR ELSE HE'D GONE TOTALLY *BONKERS* BY THE END, RIGHT?

WELL, YOU BELIEVE WHAT YOU *WANT,* LADY--

I'M STICKING UP FOR THE *BATMAN*--TILL THE *END!*

SLAM

AND ELSEWHERE...

DON'T SEE HOW YOU GUYS CAN *PLAY CARDS* AT A TIME LIKE THIS. *JOAN'S* SO UPSET, IT TORE ME UP JUST TO *TALK* TO HER FOR A MINUTE.

THEY GOTTA TAKE THEIR MINDS OFF THIS CRAZY THING *SOMEHOW,* DON'T THEY, FLASH? *ME,* I JUST WISH I HAD A *PUNCHIN'* BAG HANDY.

ACTUALLY, WILDCAT, JAY'S *RIGHT.* I CAN BARELY KEEP MY MIND ON *WHICH* GAME WE'RE PLAYING.

IT'S THE GAME IN THE *COURTROOM* THAT CONCERNS *ME.* RIGHT NOW WE SEEM TO BE HOLDING OUR OWN, BUT...

HEY, SANDMAN-- YOU *OKAY?*

HUH? OH, SURE, TED... *FINE.*

HEY, IF I'D KNOWN YOU WERE ALL GONNA *PATRONIZE* ME, WES DODD WOULD'VE STAYED IN THAT *HOSPITAL.*

YOU THINK IT'S FUN AND GAMES SITTING THROUGH THESE HEARINGS IN A *GASMASK?*

NOW *THAT'S* THE SANDMAN WE ALL KNOW AND LOVE!

THIS IS ALL *MY* FAULT! I SHOULD'VE *HEAT-VISIONED* THAT DIARY, THE MOMENT I--

YOU'RE A *REPORTER* AS WELL AS A *JSAer,* CLARK.

RIGHT. LET'S LET THE *AMERICAN PEOPLE* DECIDE WHAT THE *TRUTH* IS, SHALL WE?

NO MORE COFFEE, DIANA. I'M WOUND UP TIGHT AS A DRUM AS IT IS.

AH... *SENATOR HOPKINS* SAID I MIGHT FIND YOU HERE. THE HEARING'S ABOUT TO RECONVENE.

I *KNEW* THAT-- SOON AS I DREW MY *THIRD* ACE.

WELL, FELLAS, LET'S GET CRACKING.

YOU *ARE* ALL RIGHT THEN, SANDMAN?

NEVER FELT BETTER.

IF I LET ON HOW MY HEART WAS *REALLY* POUNDING--DR. MID-NITE'D HAVE ME BACK IN THE *WARD* IN A SECOND!

AS IT'S A BIT *WARM* IN THE HALL THIS AFTERNOON--

--I HOPE THAT ANYONE WHO *WISHES* TO, WILL FEEL FREE TO REMOVE HIS *COAT*-- OR *CAPE*, OR WHATEVER.

MINE *STAYS*, THANK YOU, MR. CHAIRMAN--BUT I AM LOOKING FORWARD TO HEARING THE REMAINDER OF THE *JSA'S* COLORFUL *HISTORY.*

CERTAINLY--AS LONG AS MY FELLOW COMMITTEE MEMBERS FEEL IT *RELEVANT.*

WE HAD GOTTEN, I BELIEVE, AS FAR AS *1945*-- WHEN SEVERAL LONGTIME MEMBERS LEFT FOR VARIOUS PERSONAL REASONS.

*HAWKMAN,* WOULD YOU *CARE* TO CONTINUE?

ACTUALLY, SENATOR, I THINK IT'S TIME WE HEARD FROM ONE WHO HAD *NOT* BEEN A *JSA*er BEFORE '45-- *WILDCAT.*--

THANKS, HAWK. GUESS THE *ONLY* THING YOU LAWMAKERS ARE AFTER *ME* ABOUT IS THAT I *MIGHT'VE* HELPED WITH THE SO-CALLED *"COVER-UP"* AFTER THE WAR, SO--

NOW, WILDCAT... IF YOU'LL *PROCEED?*

SURE, SURE. THE WAR WAS *WINDIN'* DOWN WHEN *MR. TERRIFIC* AN' ME WERE CALLED IN FOR A VERY *SPECIAL* CASE-- ONE WHICH CAUSED A *C.O.** NAMED *DICK AMBER* TO DECIDE HE HAD A STAKE IN THE WAR, AFTER ALL. HE WENT ON TO DO AMERICA PROUD.

DAILY BUGLE

**SGT. DICK AMBER GIVEN CONGRESSIONAL MEDAL OF HONOR!**
ENTIRE NATION HONORS HERO

PLEASE--*MUST* WE KEEP REMINDING YOU ALL THAT NO ONE IS ON *TRIAL* HERE? WE'RE ONLY AFTER THE *TRUTH.*

IF YOU KNEW *NOTHING* OF SUPPOSEDLY TREASON-OUS ACTIVITIES ON THE PART OF THE *JSA*--WE WANT TO KNOW *THAT,* TOO.

"THAT'S ABOUT THE TIME *THE FLASH* AND *GREEN LANTERN* CAME BACK ON BOARD, TOO-- OR ELSE I FIGURE WE BOTH WOULD'VE BEEN MADE REGULARS."

*CONSCIENTIOUS OBJECTOR. --Roy.

107

THE *TRUTH* IS, WILDCAT-- I'VE *CHECKED* OUT THIS "DICK AMBER," AND HE WASN'T REALLY A BONA FIDE CONSCIENTIOUS OBJECTOR AT ALL.

HE WAS MERELY AN *ULTRA-ISOLATIONIST*--A YOUNG MAN WHO DIDN'T THINK THE WAR WAS ANY OF *OUR* BUSINESS.

OKAY, SO I'M A LITTLE *SLOPPY* WITH *WORDS*... SO *SUE* ME! I'M A CRIME-BUSTER, NOT A POLITICIAN.

ANYWAY, SORRY YOU CAN'T ASK MR. T. ABOUT ANY OF THIS--BUT I GUESS YOU ALREADY KNOW HE WAS *MURDERED* A COUPLE OF YEARS BACK, BY AN OLD ENEMY OF HIS CALLED THE *SPIRIT KING*.

THE JSA NEVER *DID* QUITE CATCH UP WITH THAT SUCKER. THAT'S SOMETHIN' WE'RE GONNA HAVE TO *TAKE CARE* OF, ONE'A THESE DAYS.

"ALONG THE WAY, *PRESIDENT ROOSEVELT* DIED, GOD REST HIS SOUL-- THE GUY WHO, IN A WAY, *FOUNDED* THE JUSTICE SOCIETY.

"--AND EVEN BATTLED SOME METAL-EATIN' LIVING ROBOTS FROM OUTER SPACE, NO LESS.

"MEANTIME, THE JSA GOT INVOLVED IN CASES LIKE THE ONE THEY CALLED 'THE FORGOTTEN CRIME'--

"I SWEAR, HE'D ROLL OVER IN HIS *GRAVE* IF HE KNEW THEY WAS BEIN' ACCUSED OF *TREASON* TODAY!

"I *DID* COME BACK TO HELP THE USA OUT ONE MORE TIME--IN EARLY '46-- A SPECIAL ASSIGNMENT DEALIN' WITH *HANDICAPPED* PEOPLE-- ESPECIALLY *RETURNIN'* SOLDIERS WHO'D LOST A LIMB IN THE WAR.

"LOOK IT UP. *THAT* ONE'S EVEN MENTIONED IN THE *WORLD BOOK ENCYCLOPEDIA* A FEW YEARS LATER-- NO LIE!

18

NEXT, JOHNNY THUNDER HAS HIS SAY:

I--I'M NOT TOO GREAT AT TALKING IN PUBLIC--NOT AT MAKING SENSE, ANYWAY-- BUT I'LL DO MY BEST.

LET'S SEE NOW--WE HAD SOME REALLY BIZARRO CASES RIGHT AFTER THAT. LIKE THERE WAS THIS WEIRD PAINT FROM ANCIENT ATLANTIS--IT MADE ANYTHING THAT WAS PAINTED WITH IT COME ALIVE WHEN THE MOON CAME OUT. PRETTY WEIRD, HUH?

EVEN THE FLASH HAD TO DO SOME HUSTLING, I REMEMBER, TO KEEP AN ARTIST NAMED NELS FARROW FROM GETTING REVENGE ON SOME OLD RIVALS--BY FIXING THINGS SO THEIR OWN PAINTINGS WOULD COME TO LIFE AND TRY TO KILL THEM.

"THE PAINTINGS THAT WALKED THE EARTH"-- THAT'S WHAT WE CALLED 'EM. PRETTY CLASSY, HUH?

THEN THERE WAS THIS GUY LANDOR. HE WAS FROM THE FUTURE, SEE-- A THROWBACK WHO WANTED MORE EXCITEMENT THAN HE COULD SCRAPE UP IN THE 25TH CENTURY, I RECKON.

HE FOUND PLENTY-- BEFORE THE USA TOSSED 'IM BACK TO WHERE HE CAME FROM!

POW

"HEY, THAT'S WHEN THE BRAIN WAVE POPPED UP AGAIN, TOO-- DISGUISED AS AN OLD MAN--

"--TRYING TO GET HIS REVENGE BY PUTTING 'DREAMS OF MADNESS' INSIDE OUR HEADS.

"IT WORKED WITH THE OTHERS, BUT SOMEHOW--I DUNNO HOW-- IT JUST KIND'A MADE ME SMARTER, FOR A WHILE, ANYWAY.

19

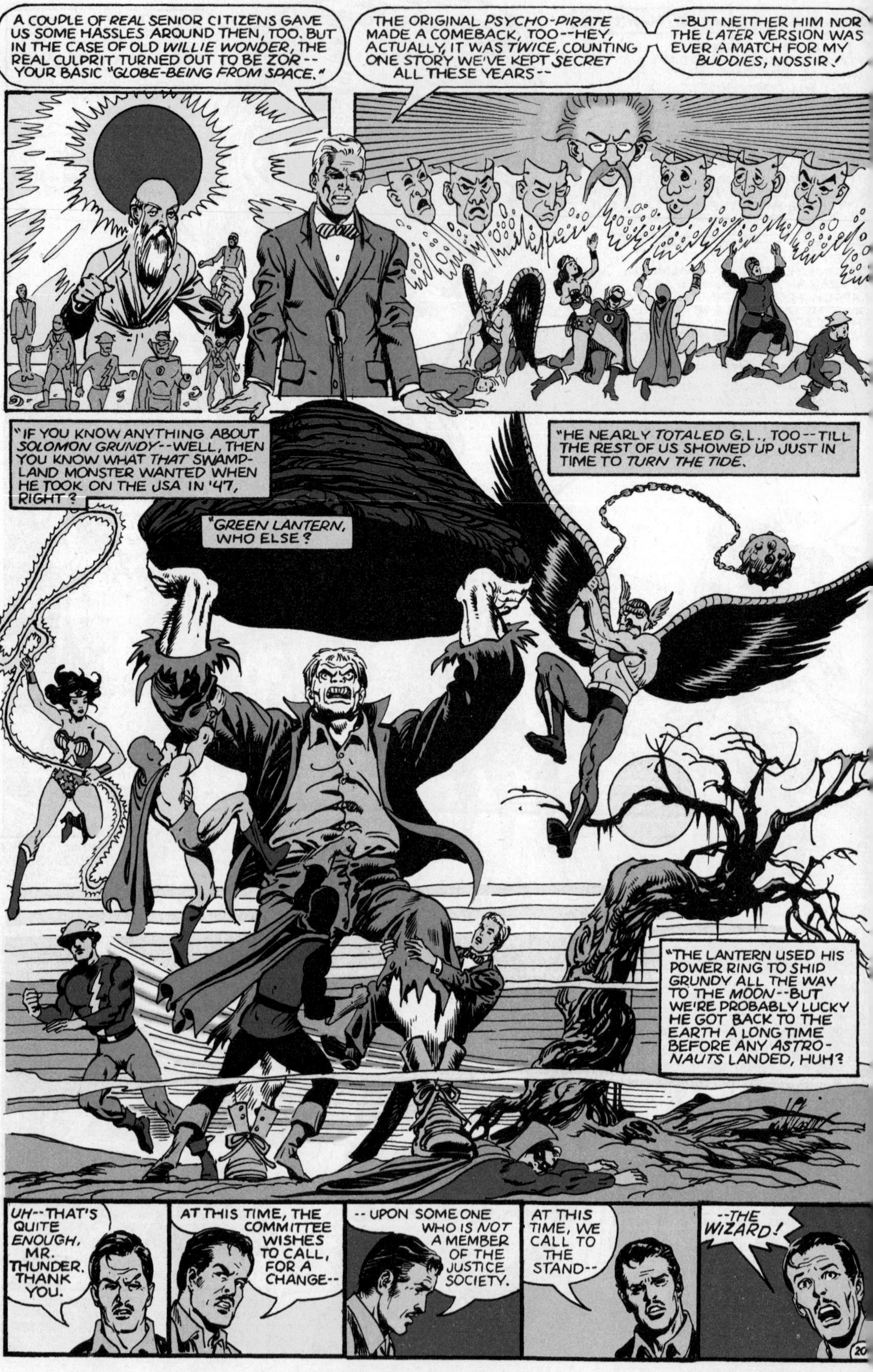

A COUPLE OF REAL SENIOR CITIZENS GAVE US SOME HASSLES AROUND THEN, TOO. BUT IN THE CASE OF OLD WILLIE WONDER, THE REAL CULPRIT TURNED OUT TO BE ZOR-- YOUR BASIC "GLOBE-BEING FROM SPACE."
THE ORIGINAL PSYCHO-PIRATE MADE A COMEBACK, TOO--HEY, ACTUALLY, IT WAS TWICE, COUNTING ONE STORY WE'VE KEPT SECRET ALL THESE YEARS--
--BUT NEITHER HIM NOR THE LATER VERSION WAS EVER A MATCH FOR MY BUDDIES, NOSSIR!
"IF YOU KNOW ANYTHING ABOUT SOLOMON GRUNDY--WELL, THEN YOU KNOW WHAT THAT SWAMP-LAND MONSTER WANTED WHEN HE TOOK ON THE JSA IN '47, RIGHT?
"GREEN LANTERN, WHO ELSE?
"HE NEARLY TOTALED G.L., TOO--TILL THE REST OF US SHOWED UP JUST IN TIME TO TURN THE TIDE.
"THE LANTERN USED HIS POWER RING TO SHIP GRUNDY ALL THE WAY TO THE MOON--BUT WE'RE PROBABLY LUCKY HE GOT BACK TO THE EARTH A LONG TIME BEFORE ANY ASTRO-NAUTS LANDED, HUH?
UH--THAT'S QUITE ENOUGH, MR. THUNDER. THANK YOU.
AT THIS TIME, THE COMMITTEE WISHES TO CALL, FOR A CHANGE--
--UPON SOME ONE WHO IS NOT A MEMBER OF THE JUSTICE SOCIETY.
AT THIS TIME, WE CALL TO THE STAND--
--THE WIZARD!
20

KRA-KOOM

AT YOUR SERVICE, MR. CHAIRMAN!

YEAH? YOU'LL GET PLENTY OF ATTENTION FROM THIS FIST, IF--

MY APOLOGIES, SENATOR HOPKINS. BUT I'VE ALWAYS FOUND THAT A FLAMBOYANT APPROACH GAINS ME A CERTAIN AMOUNT OF ATTENTION.

HOLD IT, JSAers! IF HE'S HERE--IT'S BECAUSE THE COMMITTEE WANTS HIM HERE, REMEMBER!

WELL PUT, "WINGED WONDER"-- OR ARE THEY CALLING YOU "FEATHERED FURY" THESE DAYS?

MR. CHAIRMAN, WE WERE EXPECTING A SURPRISE WITNESS--BUT I CAN'T BELIEVE YOU'RE REALLY INTERESTED IN THE TESTIMONY OF THIS AVOWED CRIMINAL!

WONDER WHAT HE'S UP TO?! LAST WE KNEW, EARTH ONE'S JUSTICE LEAGUE HAD HELPED US PUT HIS LATEST INJUSTICE CREW OUT OF COMMISSION!

EVEN IF HE'S HERE LEGALLY, I'M BETTING HE'LL NEVER RELENT TO GOING BACK TO A PRISON CELL..

WELL, MY RING'S ALL CHARGED UP-- SO JUST LET HIM MAKE A BREAK FOR IT!

NOW, NOW, MS. WAYNE. I'M ONLY HERE AS A PATRIOTIC CITIZEN, TO GIVE EVIDENCE AGAINST A NEST OF TRAITORS-- THE JUSTICE SOCIETY OF AMERICA!

ULP! -DID YOU HAVE TO APPEAR SO-- SO MELODRAMAT- ICALLY, WIZARD?

MAY I GO NOW, MR. O'FALLON?

I DON'T SEE HOW YOU CAN LEAVE AT A TIME LIKE THIS, WILKINS.

IT TOOK ALL THE INFLUENCE I COULD WIELD TO GET HOPKINS TO SPRING THE WIZARD FOR THE HEARING--

--BUT IF I'M LUCKY, NOT ONLY WILL HIS TESTIMONY CONDEMN THE JSA-- BUT I MAY EVEN LEARN THE TRUTH ABOUT HOW THEY KILLED MY FATHER WHEN HE WAS A SENATOR!

I... HOPE YOU DO, SIR... IF IT'S TRUE.

21

NOW, *ER*--*WIZARD*--IF YOU'D TELL US WHAT YOU KNOW THAT MIGHT HAVE A *BEARING* UPON THESE *DELIBERATIONS?*

MOST *READILY*, MR. CHAIRMAN. BUT *FIRST*, I SHOULD STATE THAT EVERY-THING MS. WAYNE HAS SAID IS *TRUE.*

I AM INDEED AN *"AVOWED CRIMINAL"*-- NOR AT ANY TIME IN MY LONG CAREER HAVE I EVER CLAIMED TO BE ANYTHING *ELSE.*

THAT BIT OF *HONESTY* ALONE WOULD PUT ME ON QUITE A DIFFERENT *PLANE* FROM THOSE *HOODED HOODLUMS* YONDER IN THE *DOCK!*

PERHAPS, NONETHELESS, A BIT OF *BACKGROUND* CONCERNING MYSELF IS IN ORDER.

MY FULL NAME IS *WILLIAM ASMODEUS ZARD*--A HAPPY *ACCIDENT* WHICH LED TO MY INITIALS BEING *"W. I. ZARD,"* AND WHICH PERHAPS INFLUENCED MY CHOICE OF A *VOCATION.*

AS I ONCE TOLD THE *JSA:* IN MY YOUTH, I WAS JUST A STUPID, TRIGGER-HAPPY *GUNMAN.*

IN DUE TIME, I WAS *CAUGHT* AND *IMPRISONED*... AND DURING MY *INCARCERATION* I HAD AMPLE OPPORTUNIT' TO REFLECT ON WHAT A *FOOL* I'D BEEN.

"CRIME, I SAW, IS *BIG BUSINESS*--WITH ALL THE *PITFALLS* AND *COMPETITION* OF ANY *OTHER* BUSINESS."

"TO BE *SUCCESSFUL*, ONE MUST *STUDY HARD*...LEARN THE LATEST *METHODS*...DIFFERENT *ANGLES.*"

"WHEN I WAS EVENTUALLY *RELEASED*, I WENT AWAY-- TO *STUDY* IN AN OBSCURE *LAMASERY* IN MYSTIC *TIBET.*"

"I *PAID* WELL TO LEARN THE *MAGIC ARTS.*"

I WAS *TAUGHT* THE *COMPLETE* ART OF *HYPNOTISM*... *ASTRAL PROJECTION*...

22

IN TIME, I LEARNED ENOUGH TO FINALLY TEACH MYSELF-- *BLACK MAGIC!*

MR. CHAIRMAN! DO WE HAVE TO *SIT* HERE AND *LISTEN* TO THIS--??

PLEASE, ATOM-- I WAS ABOUT TO ADMIT HOW I *REPAID* MY LAMA-MASTER FOR HIS HELP-- BY MAGICALLY SLAYING HIM!

MR. CHAIRMAN, MY CLIENT'S OUTBURST IS TOTALLY *UNDER-STANDABLE*--WHEN YOU REALIZE WHAT A *MONSTER* YOU HAVE BROUGHT HERE TO TESTIFY!

YOU *SEE*, LITTLE FRIEND? YOU WOULDN'T HAVE WANTED TO INTERRUPT MY FIRST *PUBLIC* CONFESSION OF MY *HEINOUS* CRIMES, WOULD YOU?

*"MONSTER"* MS. WAYNE? MY PARDON, BUT YOU DO NOT KNOW THE *MEANING* OF THE WORD.

TAKE IT FROM ONE WHO *KNEW WELL* THE MAN WHO WAS THE FOREMOST MONSTER, DOUBTLESS, OF THIS *TWENTIETH CENTURY*-- NONE OTHER THAN *ADOLF HITLER.*

" I WAS PRESENT, FOR INSTANCE, AT SOME OF THE GIGANTIC *NUREMBERG RALLIES* HE STAGED, FOR BENEFIT OF CITIZENRY AND CAMERAS...

"AND WHEN HE *SPOKE*, I SENSED AT ONCE THAT THIS WAS NOT ANOTHER MERE *POLITICIAN*--NO, NOT EVEN A RUN-OF-THE-MILL *DICTATOR*--

"--BUT A MAN WHO REALIZED THAT *MYSTIC FORCES*, BEHIND THE SCENES, ARE THE *REAL RULERS* OF MANKIND!

"THAT IS WHY I OFFERED MY *SERVICES* TO HIM AT ONCE--

"--OBTAINING FOR HIM THE *SPEAR OF DESTINY*, WITHOUT WHICH HE WOULD NEVER HAVE *DARED* BEGIN HIS MARCH TOWARD CONQUEST.

I *BLUSH*, EVEN NOW, TO RECALL HOW, UPON RETURNING FROM TIBET IN 1934, I BECAME *FASCINATED* WITH HITLER AND HIS *THIRD REICH.*

"I WAS NEVER A *NAZI*, MIND YOU-- AND AT THAT STAGE, NO ONE WAS EVEN AT *WAR* WITH HITLER'S REICH.

"NOR WAS *AMERICA* YET AT WAR WITH GERMANY WHEN, IN NOVEMBER 1940, I BEHELD NINE SELF-STYLED 'MYSTERY-MEN' SWEAR ALLEGIANCE TO DER FÜHRER.

23

THEY WERE THE *SAME NINE,* OF COURSE, WHO--WITH *SUPERMAN* PIPING HIMSELF ABOARD LATER-- BECAME THE *CHARTER MEMBERS* OF THE JSA!

*LIAR!*

FLASH-- *PLEASE!* YOU'LL GET YOUR *CHANCE*--!

FORGET IT, HELENA! *NO WAY* I'M GOING TO LET THAT PASS-- WITHOUT CALLING THE CAPED *CHARLATAN* EXACTLY WHAT HE OBVIOUSLY *IS*--

--NAMELY, A WILLING *ACCOMPLICE* IN SOME *CONSPIRACY* TO CONVICT US OF *TREASON!*

ANOTHER *CONSPIRACY THEORY,* EH? STILL, WHATEVER ELSE I MAY HAVE BEEN, MR. GARRICK, I WAS DEFINITELY *NOT* A *CHARLATAN.*

"AT ANY RATE: ONCE HITLER DECLARED WAR ON MY NATIVE LAND, I ELECTED TO *SIT OUT* THE REMAIN- DER OF THE WAR IN A SECLUDED EUROPEAN CASTLE-- STUDYING ADDITION- AL MAGIC.

"BY 1947, I HAD DECIDED TO BEGIN A *SECOND* CRIMINAL CAREER-- AND SINCE THE JSA WERE STILL PASSING THEMSELVES OFF AS *HEROES,* I TRIED TO *JOIN* THEM. BUT THEY DIDN'T APPRECIATE THE *COMPETITION,* AND *ATTACKED* ME, INSTEAD.

"THEY MANAGED TO OVERCOME THE EARLY, CRUDE *ILLUSIONS* I HURLED AT THEM--

"--LEAVING ME NO RECOURSE BUT TO COMMIT *SUICIDE,* BY LEAPING INTO A CONVENIENT VAT OF *ACID.*

GENTLEMEN-- I *CONCEDE* DEFEAT. I AM *BEATEN!*

MERELY AN ADDITION- AL *ILLUSION,* OF COURSE. THE JSA WERE BETTER AT BEING *AXIS AGENTS* THAN THEY WERE AT OUTSMARTING THE *WIZARD.*

AND THAT, LADIES AND GENTLEMEN OF THE COMMITTEE, CONCLUDES MY *TESTIMONY.*

THE *FLASH* WAS *RIGHT!* IT IS JUST A *PACK OF LIES.*

MUST I REMIND YOU, MS. WAYNE, THAT WE ARE NOT *UNEQUIVOCALLY* TAKING THE WIZARD'S *WORD* FOR ANYTHING; IT IS MERELY ONE MORE THING, PLACED INTO THE *BALANCE.*

24

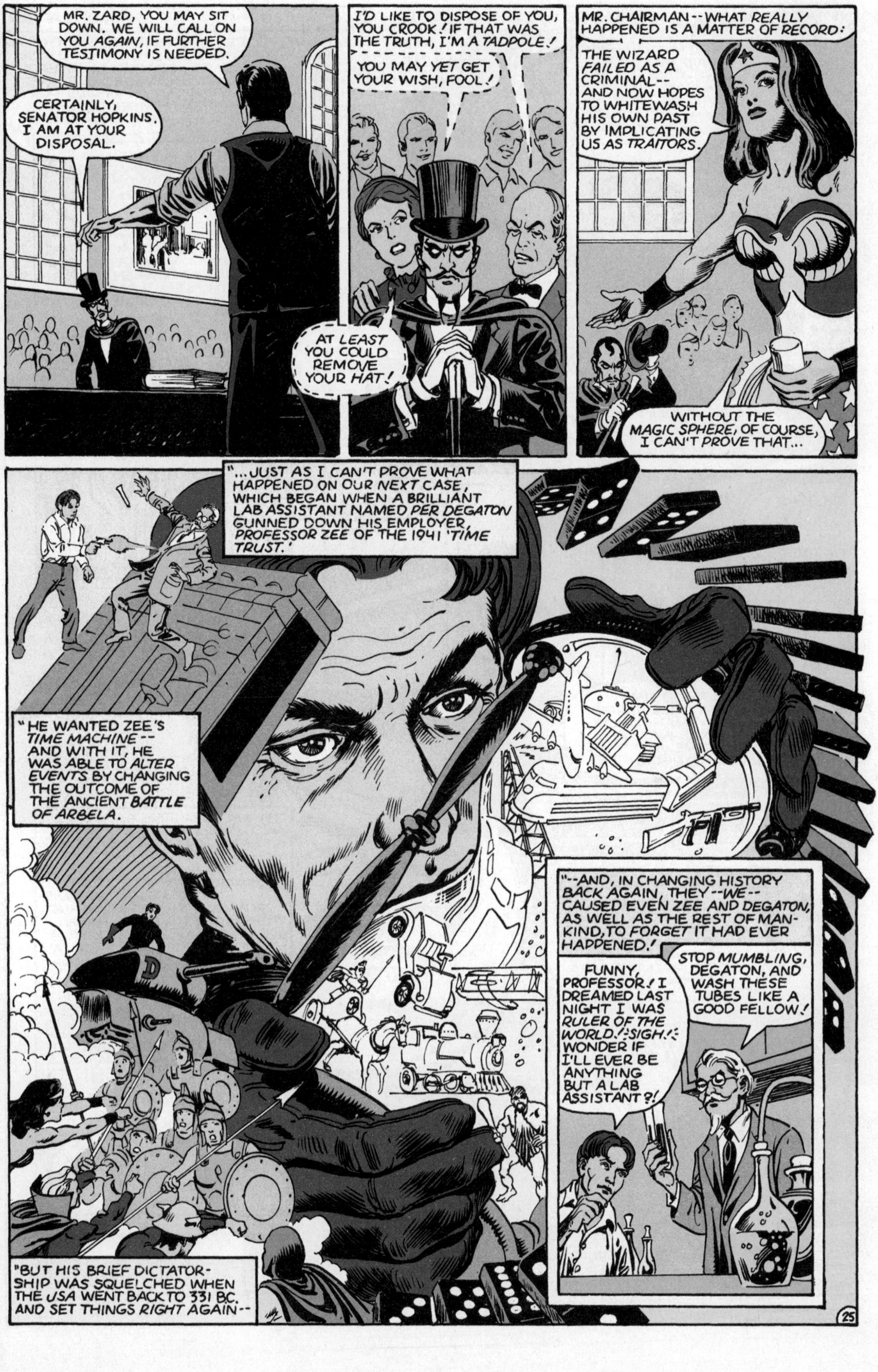
MR. ZARD, YOU MAY SIT DOWN. WE WILL CALL ON YOU AGAIN, IF FURTHER TESTIMONY IS NEEDED.
CERTAINLY, SENATOR HOPKINS. I AM AT YOUR DISPOSAL.
I'D LIKE TO DISPOSE OF YOU, YOU CROOK! IF THAT WAS THE TRUTH, I'M A TADPOLE!
YOU MAY YET GET YOUR WISH, FOOL!
AT LEAST YOU COULD REMOVE YOUR HAT!
MR. CHAIRMAN--WHAT REALLY HAPPENED IS A MATTER OF RECORD:
THE WIZARD FAILED AS A CRIMINAL--AND NOW HOPES TO WHITEWASH HIS OWN PAST BY IMPLICATING US AS TRAITORS.
WITHOUT THE MAGIC SPHERE, OF COURSE, I CAN'T PROVE THAT...
"...JUST AS I CAN'T PROVE WHAT HAPPENED ON OUR NEXT CASE, WHICH BEGAN WHEN A BRILLIANT LAB ASSISTANT NAMED PER DEGATON GUNNED DOWN HIS EMPLOYER, PROFESSOR ZEE OF THE 1941 'TIME TRUST.'
"HE WANTED ZEE'S TIME MACHINE--AND WITH IT, HE WAS ABLE TO ALTER EVENTS BY CHANGING THE OUTCOME OF THE ANCIENT BATTLE OF ARBELA.
"BUT HIS BRIEF DICTATORSHIP WAS SQUELCHED WHEN THE USA WENT BACK TO 331 BC. AND SET THINGS RIGHT AGAIN--
"--AND, IN CHANGING HISTORY BACK AGAIN, THEY--WE--CAUSED EVEN ZEE AND DEGATON, AS WELL AS THE REST OF MANKIND, TO FORGET IT HAD EVER HAPPENED!
FUNNY, PROFESSOR! I DREAMED LAST NIGHT I WAS RULER OF THE WORLD! SIGH! WONDER IF I'LL EVER BE ANYTHING BUT A LAB ASSISTANT?!
STOP MUMBLING, DEGATON, AND WASH THESE TUBES LIKE A GOOD FELLOW!
25

IS THAT THE ALLEGED PLOT WHICH *YOU*, THE *SHINING KNIGHT*, AND *DR. CHARLES GRAYSON* TOLD US ABOUT, EARLIER IN THESE HEARINGS?

ER, I'M AFRAID NOT, CONGRESS-WOMAN VALDEZ.

YOU SEE, EVIDENTLY, *LATER* IN 1947, DEGATON SOMEHOW REMEMBERED THOSE EVENTS WHICH BOTH *HAD* AND HAD *NOT* HAPPENED.

*THAT* TIME, WITH THE AID OF SOME *SUPER-CRIMINALS*, HE NEARLY MANAGED TO CARVE OUT AN *EMPIRE* FOR HIMSELF DURING WORLD WAR TWO--

--BEFORE THE FLEDGLING *ALL-STAR SQUADRON* CAME TO THE RESCUE, AND EVENTS *AGAIN* RETURNED TO NORMAL IN 1947.

FUNNY, PROFESSOR! I DREAMED LAST NIGHT I WAS *RULER OF THE WORLD*! ⸰SIGH!⸰ WONDER IF I'LL EVER BE ANYTHING BUT A LAB ASSISTANT?!

STOP MUMBLING, DEGATON, AND WASH THESE TUBES LIKE A GOOD FELLOW!

AND *THAT* WAS THE END OF PER DEGATON, WAS IT?

NO, SIR. A *THIRD* TIME IN '47, DEGATON REGAINED HIS *MEMORY* AND--MAKING SURE PROF. ZEE WAS REALLY *DEAD* THIS TIME, AND THUS UNABLE TO HELP *FOIL HIM*--

--HE STOLE SOME RUSSIAN *ATOMIC* MISSILES FROM CUBA IN 1962, AND USED THEM TO TRY TO *BLACKMAIL* THE U.S. INTO SURRENDERING TO HIM IN 1942.

"THANK HERA, THE *ALL-STARS* AND *USAers* TOGETHER--WITH A BIT OF HELP FROM SOME *FRIENDS*--MANAGED TO BEAT HIM *THAT* TIME, TOO, AND --

FUNNY, PROFESSOR! I DREAMED LAST NIGHT I WAS *RULER OF THE WORLD*! ⸰SIGH!⸰ WONDER IF I'LL EVER BE ANYTHING BUT A LAB ASSISTANT?!

STOP MUMBLING, DEGATON, AND WASH THESE TUBES LIKE A GOOD FELLOW!

26

ANDREW VINSON HERE-- SPEAKING FROM JUST OUTSIDE THE CHAMBER.

ONE CAN HARDLY **BLAME** SENATOR HOPKINS OR HIS FELLOW COMMITTEE MEMBERS FOR BEING TOTALLY CONFUSED BY WONDER WOMAN'S TESTIMONY CONCERNING *PER DEGATON,* TIME TRAVEL, AND THE LIKE.

LIVE

FORTUNATELY, IT SEEMS HIGHLY UNLIKELY THAT ANY OF THOSE PERMUTATIONS--EVEN IF *TRUE*-- WILL HAVE ANY BEARING WHATEVER ON THE OUTCOME OF THESE HEARINGS...

...OR ELSE WE'D ALL HAVE TO HANG ONTO OUR SANITY.

LIVE

Andrew Vinson UBS NEWS

ANDREW VINSON HERE, FOR *UBS* NEWS. MORE NEWS--MORE OFTEN!

LIVE

NOW, IF YOU'LL EXCUSE ME, I'VE GOT TO SNEAK BACK IN.

UBS

IF YOU'LL ALLOW ME TO SPEAK ON SOMETHING DOUBTLESS MORE *RELEVANT* TO THESE PROCEEDINGS, MR. CHAIRMAN--

PLEASE!

IN HIS SUPPOSED DIARY, BATMAN CLAIMS HE *DISASSOCIATED* HIMSELF FROM THE JUSTICE SOCIETY AFTER PEARL HARBOR, WHEN HE *RENOUNCED* HIS EARLIER ALLEGIANCE TO HITLER.

"IF THAT WERE *TRUE,* HOWEVER --

JUSTICE SOCIETY OF AMERICA

"--WOULD HE REALLY HAVE BEEN LIKELY TO STAND IN FOR *THE ATOM* IN ONE CASE, LATER IN '47--

"--JUST AS *SUPERMAN* FILLED IN FOR *JOHNNY THUNDER?*

"YES, THAT WAS THE FAMOUS 'STREAM OF RUTHLESSNESS' EPISODE--WELL DOCUMENT- ED, ESPECIALLY AFTER THOSE SAME WATERS WERE USED ON SEVERAL OF US JSAers RECENTLY BY THE ULTRA-HUMANITE.

"AS FOR *THE WIZARD*--I THINK HIS INCORRIGIBLE CRIMINAL NATURE IS CLEARLY SHOWN BY THE FACT THAT HE WAS SOON LEADING HIS OWN 'INJUSTICE SOCIETY OF THE WORLD,' AS HE CALLED IT, TRYING TO TAKE OVER THE COUNTRY.

"THAT CONSTITUTES *PROVEN* TREASON-- EVEN IF HE ESCAPED ALL BUT CRIMINAL CHARGES ON TECHNICALITIES.

"IF NOT FOR THE JUSTICE SOCIETY--HIS SCHEME MIGHT HAVE SUCCEEDED."

21

IN KEEPING WITH OUR *INFORMAL RULES*, MR. ZARD-- HAVE YOU ANYTHING TO SAY TO THAT ?

ONLY THAT, THOUGH A CONFESSED *CRIMINAL*, I'VE NEVER GIVEN AID OR COMFORT TO ANY NATION WITH WHOM THE UNITED STATES WAS AT *WAR*--

--UNLIKE *SOME* PUBLIC FIGURES I MIGHT NAME, MR. CHAIRMAN.

THANK YOU, *WONDER WOMAN* ?

IN EARLY 1948, ONE OF THE *JSA'S* MOST *BIZARRE* ADVENTURES OCCURRED.

BUT THAT WAS NO STRANGER THAN OUR ENCOUNTER WITH DWELLERS IN AN OTHER-DIMENSIONAL *FAIRYLAND*, RULED OVER BY THE EVIL *LORELEI.*

IT SEEMS AN OBSCURE *GUARD* IN A WAX MUSEUM WENT MAD--AND TOOK ON THE PERSONALITIES, EVEN THE *FEROCITY* OF SOME OF HISTORY'S GREATEST *ARCH-VILLAINS*...

...*GENGHIS KHAN*... *GOLIATH*... *ATTILA THE HUN*... *CAPTAIN KIDD*... *NERO*... AND *CESARE BORGIA.*

BEFORE WE DEFEATED HER WEIRD ARMY OF GIANTS AND TROLLS, THEY HAD EVEN BRIEFLY INVADED *GOTHAM CITY*--

--THOUGH ALL MEMORY OF THAT NIGHT SEEMS TO HAVE *FLED* MAGICALLY, ONCE THE DIMENSIONAL DOORWAY WAS *SEALED* FOR ANOTHER HUNDRED YEARS.

WE *DEFEATED* HIM, OF COURSE-- BUT ONLY AFTER OUR AMAZON *PURPLE HEALING RAY* BROUGHT SIX JSA MEMBERS BACK FROM WHAT SEEMED TO BE A STATE OF *DEATH* ITSELF!

OH, AND THAT WAS THE CASE IN WHICH THE *BLACK CANARY* FIRST TEAMED UP WITH US-- AFTER FINDING HER FRIEND *JOHNNY THUNDER* LEFT FOR DEAD BY "*ATTILA*."

EVIDENTLY-- SINCE I'VE NEVER HEARD OF IT, CERTAINLY!

MORE SO THAN AN AMAZON PRINCESS-- A SURVIVOR OF KRYPTON-- A MAGICAL POWER RING?

GOOD POINT, WONDER WOMAN. SURELY EVEN FAIRYLAND IS SCARCELY MORE UNBELIEVABLE THAN VALKYRIES--

CORRECT! AFTER ALL, IF WE DENY THE PLAUSIBILITY OF THE ONE, IS THE OTHER, THEN, PLAUSIBLE?

PLEASE PROCEED.

THANK YOU. ER--PERHAPS I SHOULD ADD THAT, AFTER THE FAIRYLAND EPISODE, JOHNNY THUNDER LEFT THE SOCIETY.

REALLY, MS. TREVOR-- AREN'T YOU REACHING? SOME OF THESE JSA "MISSIONS" SOUND IMPOSSIBLY FAR-FETCHED.

OR MAYBE YOU'LL ONLY BELIEVE SUCH CASES AS THE ONE WHERE WE SAVED SOME JUVENILE DELINQUENTS FROM A LIFE OF ADULT CRIME?

--AND THOSE ARE VOUCHED FOR EVEN BY THE BATMAN DIARY WHICH CHARGES YOU WITH TREASON.

HE HAD LOST MUCH OF HIS POWER OVER HIS BAHDNISIAN THUNDERBOLT BY THEN--AND DECIDED TO DEVOTE HIMSELF TO HIS PRIVATE LIFE.

119

THEN, THE *WIZARD* STRUCK AGAIN, WITH HIS *SECOND* INJUSTICE GANG.

DO YOU EXPECT ME TO *DENY* IT, DEAR LADY?

THE *FIDDLER*-- *SPORTSMASTER*-- THE *ICICLE*-- AND THE *ORIGINAL HUNTRESS* WERE ALL MEMBERS...

"...AND, BY MEANS OF THE *WIZARD'S MIND-INDUCER RAY*, THEY EVEN SUCCEEDED FOR A TIME IN TURNING ALL *SIX* THEN-JSAers INTO *SOULLESS SLAVES.*

"THE *HARLEQUIN'* HAD BEEN *BRIEFLY* A MEMBER, TOO--

"--BUT SHE *BETRAYED* THE WIZARD, AND *FOUGHT* THEM, ALONGSIDE THE *BLACK CANARY.*

"WHEN WE FINALLY *TRIUMPHED* WITH THEIR HELP, THE HARLEQUIN *SNEAKED AWAY--*

"--FOR, THOUGH SHE *WAS* A *CROOK*, ALL RIGHT, HER MAIN AIM WAS ALWAYS TO ATTRACT THE *ATTENTIONS* OF *GREEN LANTERN.*"

THE *HARLEQUIN!* AFTER ALL THESE YEARS-- SO MANY ENCOUNTERS-- I *STILL* DON'T KNOW WHO SHE *REALLY* WAS. AND SHE'S *BACK*, OR AT LEAST SOMEBODY CLAIMING TO BE HER SURE DISRUPTED THAT *PRESS CONFERENCE* HELD BY *INFINITY, INC.* OUT IN HOLLYWOOD, A LITTLE WHILE BACK.

IT'S HIGH TIME I *SOLVED* THE MYSTERY OF THE *HARLEQUIN*-- FOR *ONCE AND FOR ALL!*

"OH YES-- AND AT THE CON-CLUSION OF THIS '*CASE OF THE PATRIOTIC CRIMES*,' *BLACK CANARY* WAS FINALLY MADE AN OFFICIAL JSAer, REPLACING *JOHNNY.*

ABOUT *TIME!*

AND WHERE *IS* BLACK CANARY, MRS. TREVOR? SHE'S NOT BEEN HEARD FROM FOR SEVERAL *YEARS* NOW.

I'M... AFRAID SHE'S *DECEASED,* MR. CHAIRMAN.

AND HER *DAUGHTER'S* OVER ON *EARTH-ONE*... BUT NO USE GETTING INTO *THAT!*

MMM, WELL, THIS SEEMS AS GOOD A MOMENT AS ANY FOR *ADJOURNING.*

GUARDS, IF YOU'LL KINDLY *RETURN* THE *WIZARD* TO HIS *CELL*...

OKAY, TOP-HAT. IT'S BACK TO THE BIRDCAGE FOR YOU.

SURELY YOU *JEST.* I HAVE *OTHER* ENGAGEMENTS.

UH-OH! *WATCH* HIM, YOU GUYS!

30

WE MIGHT'VE KNOWN HE'D TRY SOMETHING LIKE THIS!

GET HIM!

TOO LATE!

H-HE VANISHED-- JUST LIKE THAT!

POOF!

BUT WHAT HAS VANISHED, MY FRIENDS--

--MAY JUST AS EASILY APPEAR ANEW!

SO IT SEEMS!

THIS IS-- UNHEARD-- OF!

POP!

ALL MY MAGIC ARTS--MY MATCHLESS ILLUSIONS-- OVERCOME BY THE MEREST GESTURE OF SOME POPINJAY IN A GOLDEN HELMET!

GUESS YOU'RE JUST A FEATHERWEIGHT, WIZ, WHEN YOU STEP IN THE RING WITH DR. FATE!

SENATOR HOPKINS--UNDER THE CIRCUMSTANCES, I WONDER IF WE OUGHT TO SERIOUSLY CONSIDER ZARD'S TESTIMONY--OR EVEN CONTINUE THESE HEARINGS.

I CONCUR. THE ONE PERSON WHO HAS STEPPED FORWARD TO CORROBORATE ANYTHING IN THE ALLEGED "BATMAN DIARY" HAS NOW ADDED TO HIS PREVIOUS INFAMY-- BY TRYING TO USE US AS AN OPPORTUNITY FOR A JAILBREAK!

NO! I WILL ACCEPT THE RESIGNATIONS OF MY FELLOW COMMITTEE-MEMBERS, IF I MUST--BUT THESE HEARINGS WILL CONTINUE--

--UNTIL AND UNLESS SOMEONE GIVES CONCLUSIVE EVIDENCE THAT BATMAN DID NOT WRITE THE WORDS ATTRIBUTED TO HIM!

MR. CHAIRMAN, I BEG YOU TO RECONSIDER. EVEN DURING HIS TESTIMONY, THE WIZARD OFFERED NO SHRED OF PROOF THAT HE WAS ACTUALLY IN NAZI GERMANY DURING WORLD WAR TWO--LET ALONE THAT HE SAW THE JUSTICE SOCIETY THERE! WHAT IS MORE--

THAT IS ENOUGH FOR TODAY, MS. WAYNE.

WE STAND ADJOURNED-- UNTIL TOMORROW!

KRAK!

LIVE

IT REMAINS TO BE SEEN WHETHER THESE HEARINGS CAN SURVIVE THE TREACHEROUS BEHAVIOR ON THE PART OF THE WIZARD. NOW, BACK TO--

--AND THAT'S THE WAY IT WENT TODAY... WITH THIS ROUND DEFINITELY GOING TO THE JSA.

UBS

31

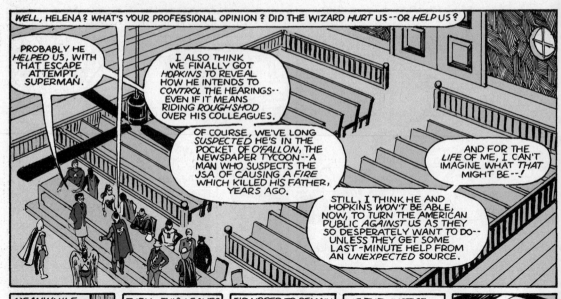

WELL, HELENA? WHAT'S YOUR PROFESSIONAL OPINION? DID THE WIZARD *HURT* US--OR *HELP* US?

PROBABLY HE *HELPED* US, WITH THAT ESCAPE ATTEMPT, SUPERMAN.

I ALSO THINK WE FINALLY GOT *HOPKINS* TO REVEAL HOW HE INTENDS TO *CONTROL* THE HEARINGS-- EVEN IF IT MEANS RIDING *ROUGHSHOD* OVER HIS COLLEAGUES.

OF COURSE, WE'VE LONG *SUSPECTED* HE'S IN THE POCKET OF *O'FALLON*, THE NEWSPAPER TYCOON--A MAN WHO SUSPECTS THE *JSA* OF CAUSING A *FIRE* WHICH KILLED HIS FATHER, YEARS AGO.

AND FOR THE *LIFE* OF ME, I CAN'T IMAGINE WHAT *THAT* MIGHT BE--!

STILL, I THINK HE AND HOPKINS *WON'T* BE ABLE, NOW, TO TURN THE AMERICAN PUBLIC *AGAINST* US AS THEY SO DESPERATELY WANT TO DO-- UNLESS THEY GET SOME LAST-MINUTE HELP FROM AN *UNEXPECTED* SOURCE.

*MEANWHILE...*

THAT EGOCENTRIC, MISGUIDED FOOL! I MIGHT HAVE *KNOWN* HE'D BLOW HIS CREDIBILITY BY TRYING TO *ESCAPE!*

THEN--THIS LEAVES ME *NO CHOICE!*

I'D HOPED TO REMAIN *OUT OF SIGHT* UNTIL MY OWN PERSONAL *"H-HOUR"* TOMORROW--

--BUT I SEE THAT IS NO LONGER *POSSIBLE*.

IF THE JUSTICE SOCIETY IS TO BE DISGRACED--DEFEATED--EVEN DESTROYED--

--IT MUST BE BY THE MAN WHO WAS *TRULY* THEIR GREATEST, THEIR MOST *IMPLACABLE* AND *UNRELENTING* FOE--

--PER DEGATON!

BY THIS TIME TOMORROW, THE *JSA* WILL BE NO *MORE*--

--AND THE *ENTIRE PLANET* WILL COME FALLING INTO MY HAND, LIKE THE *LAST LEAF OF AUTUMN!*

32

*NEXT ISSUE:* THE DYNAMIC *CONCLUSION* OF THIS OFFBEAT, EPOCH-SPANNING SAGA!

# VERDICT AND VENGEANCE!

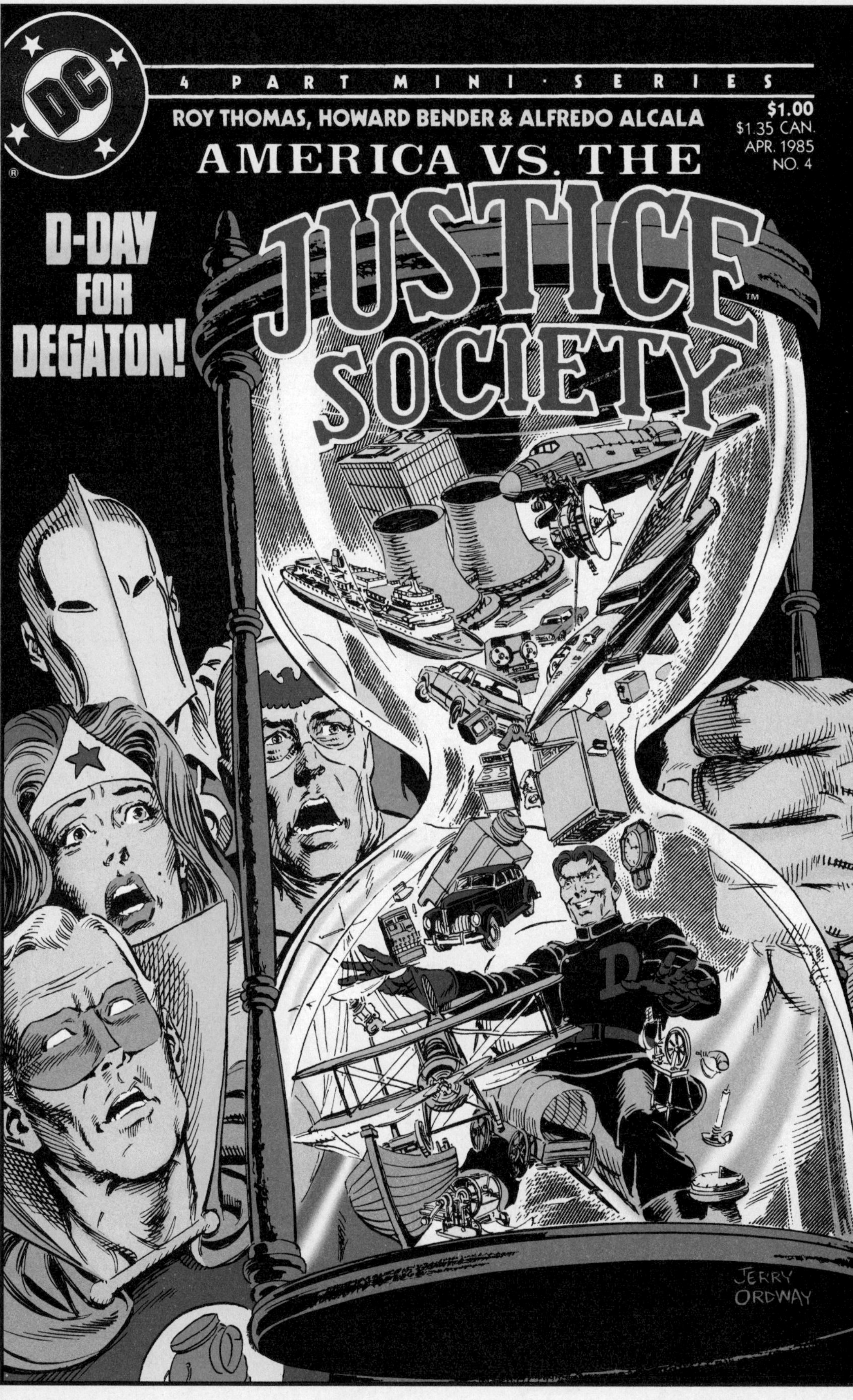

4 PART MINI·SERIES
ROY THOMAS, HOWARD BENDER & ALFREDO ALCALA
$1.00
$1.35 CAN.
APR. 1985
NO. 4
AMERICA VS. THE
JUSTICE SOCIETY
D-DAY FOR DEGATON!
JERRY ORDWAY

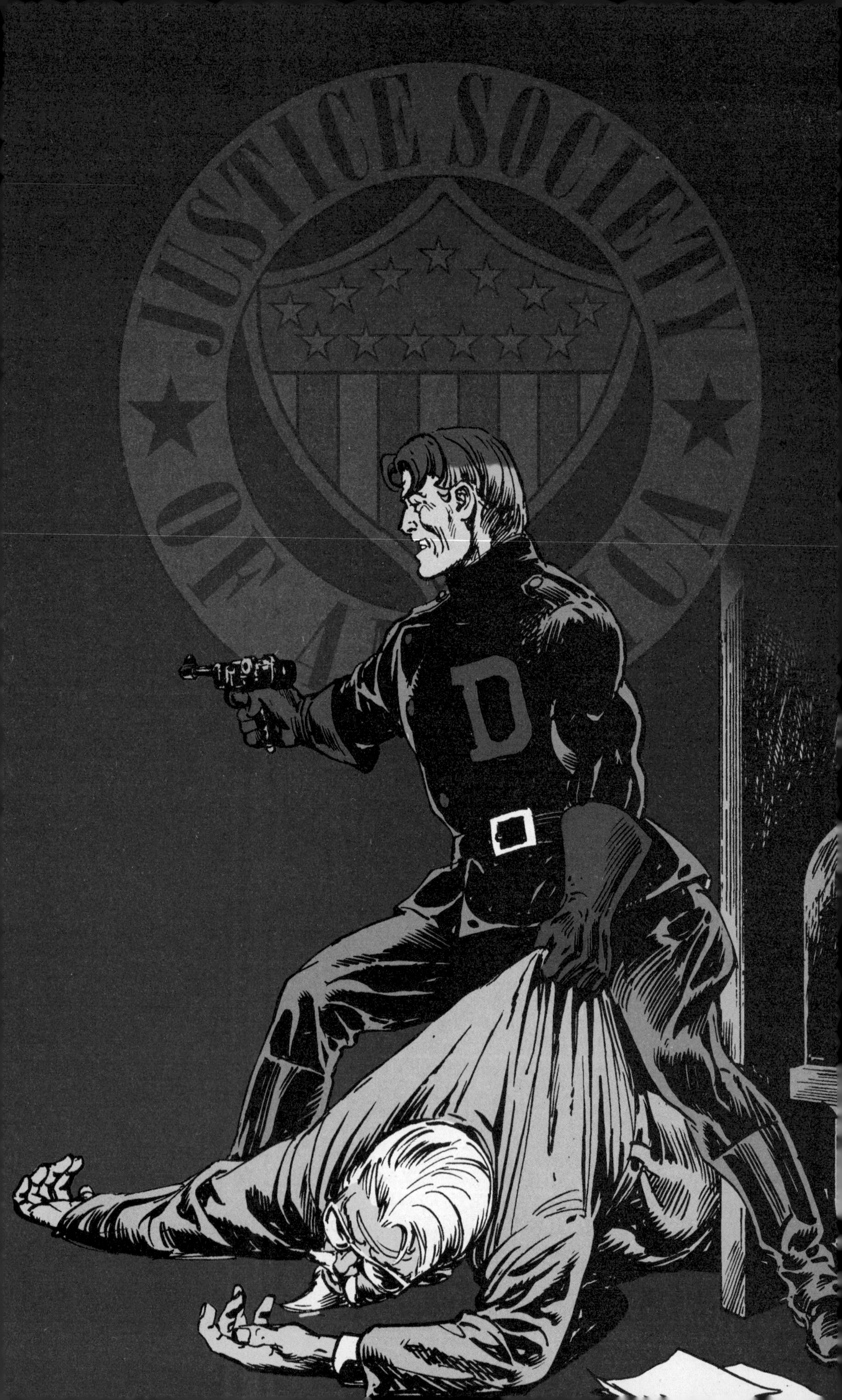
JUSTICE SOCIETY

INSTANT RECAP DEPT.: THINGS HAVEN'T BEEN GOING SO WELL FOR THE "PROSECUTION" IN THE CONGRESSIONAL HEARINGS THE WORLD IS CALLING THE CASE OF AMERICA VS. THE JUSTICE SOCIETY

THUS, IN A HIDDEN ROOM ELSEWHERE IN THE NATION'S CAPITAL, THE DISCREDITING OF THE TESTIMONY OF THE WIZARD* IS MET BY AN ANGRY, OUTRAGED BELLOWING:

I'D HOPED TO REMAIN *OUT OF SIGHT* UNTIL MY OWN PERSONAL *"H-HOUR"* TONIGHT--BUT I SEE THAT IS NO LONGER *POSSIBLE.*

IF THE JUSTICE SOCIETY IS TO BE *DISGRACED--DEFEATED--* EVEN *DESTROYED*--IT MUST BE BY THE MAN WHO WAS TRULY THEIR GREATEST, THEIR MOST *IMPLACABLE* AND *UNRELENTING* FOR--*PER DEGATON!*

BY THIS TIME TOMORROW, THE *USA* WILL BE NO MORE--

--AND THE *ENTIRE PLANET* WILL COME FALLING INTO MY HAND-- LIKE THE *LAST LEAF* OF AUTUMN!

# D-DAY FOR DEGATON!

"The time has come, the Walrus said..." --Lewis Carroll.

ROY THOMAS — WRITER/EDITOR
HOWARD BENDER — PENCILLER
ALFREDO ALCALA — EMBELLISHER

DANN THOMAS, CO-PLOTTER
CODY, LETTERER
CARL GAFFORD, COLORIST

MEANWHILE, BACK AT THE RESUMED CONGRESSIONAL HEARINGS, DR. MID-NITE CONTINUES THE RECOUNTING OF THE HONORED HISTORY OF THE JSA—A LEGENDARY GROUPING NOW CHARGED WITH TREASON BY A DIARY IN THE HANDWRITING OF THE LATE, LAMENTED BATMAN:

HAHAHAHA SO THIS IS THE IRONIC END OF THE JUSTICE SOCIETY—

"WITH THE WIZARD'S SECOND INJUSTICE GANG OUT OF BUSINESS, WE TURNED OUR ATTENTION TO ONE PROFESSOR ZODIAK, A.K.A. THE ALCHEMIST...

"...BUT WE SURE LOST THE FIRST ROUND ON THAT ONE.

—DOOMED TO TRAVEL AROUND AND AROUND BY A PERPETUAL MOTION MACHINE WHICH NEEDS NO POWER— AND WILL NEVER STOP TURNING!

"WE MANAGED, THOUGH, TO USE ZODIAK'S OWN ELIXIR OF YOUTH TO TURN OURSELVES BACK INTO KIDS—

"—ENABLING US TO SLIP OUT OF HIS INFERNAL DEVICE, AND TURN THE TABLES ON HIM.

"AND, DESPITE THE FACT THAT NONE OF US HAS GOTTEN ANY YOUNGER SINCE THAT DAY IN 1948—

"—I THINK WE'RE ALL GLAD THE REVERSION WAS ONLY TEMPORARY.

AS YOU SAID, DR. MID-NITE, THAT CASE IS WELL-DOCUMENTED.

STILL, NONE OF THIS DISPROVES THE DECEASED BATMAN'S ALLEGATION THAT YOU JSAers WERE AGENTS OF ADOLF HITLER DURING THE SECOND WORLD WAR.

PERHAPS NOT, SENATOR HOPKINS— BUT SOMEHOW, THE MORE I HEAR THAT PHRASE BANDIED ABOUT, THE MORE LUDICROUS IT SOUNDS TO ME.

NOT TO US, CONGRESSWOMAN VALDEZ.

②

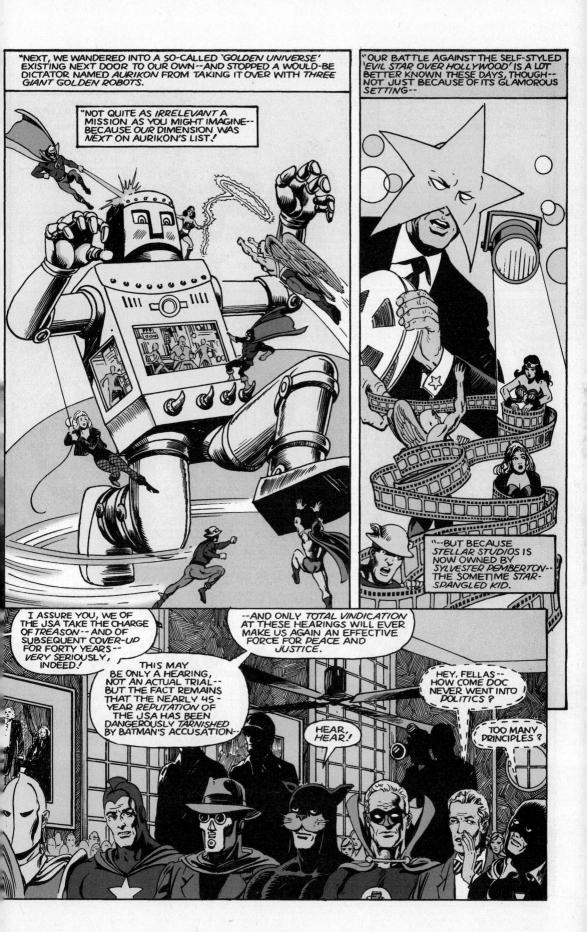

"NEXT, WE WANDERED INTO A SO-CALLED 'GOLDEN UNIVERSE' EXISTING NEXT DOOR TO OUR OWN--AND STOPPED A WOULD-BE DICTATOR NAMED *AURIKON* FROM TAKING IT OVER WITH *THREE GIANT GOLDEN ROBOTS.*

"NOT QUITE AS *IRRELEVANT* A MISSION AS YOU MIGHT IMAGINE-- BECAUSE *OUR* DIMENSION WAS *NEXT* ON AURIKON'S LIST!"

"OUR BATTLE AGAINST THE SELF-STYLED 'EVIL STAR OVER HOLLYWOOD' IS A LOT BETTER KNOWN THESE DAYS, THOUGH-- NOT JUST BECAUSE OF ITS GLAMOROUS SETTING--

"--BUT BECAUSE *STELLAR STUDIOS* IS NOW OWNED BY *SYLVESTER PEMBERTON*-- THE SOMETIME *STAR-SPANGLED KID.*

I ASSURE YOU, WE OF THE JSA TAKE THE CHARGE OF *TREASON*-- AND OF SUBSEQUENT *COVER-UP* FOR FORTY YEARS-- *VERY SERIOUSLY,* INDEED!

THIS MAY BE ONLY A HEARING, NOT AN ACTUAL TRIAL-- BUT THE FACT REMAINS THAT THE NEARLY 45- YEAR *REPUTATION* OF THE JSA HAS BEEN DANGEROUSLY *TARNISHED* BY BATMAN'S ACCUSATION--

--AND ONLY *TOTAL VINDICATION* AT THESE HEARINGS WILL EVER MAKE US AGAIN AN EFFECTIVE FORCE FOR *PEACE* AND *JUSTICE.*

HEAR, HEAR!

HEY, FELLAS-- HOW COME DOC NEVER WENT INTO *POLITICS* ?

TOO MANY *PRINCIPLES* ?

A SIDETRIP: THE JSAers YOU ALREADY KNOW--BUT PERHAPS WE WOULDN'T BE REMISS AT THIS POINT TO INTRODUCE, IN ADDITION TO SENATOR HOPKINS AND HIS TWO JOINT-COMMITTEE COLLEAGUES, THE STRANGELY-MATCHED LEGAL COUNSEL FOR THE TWO SIDES:

FOR THE COMMITTEE: A VERY TROUBLED RICHARD GRAYSON-- HE WHO WAS ONCE BATMAN'S WARD, WHEN HE WAS KNOWN AS ROBIN, THE BOY WONDER...

...AND, FOR THE ACCUSED: HELENA WAYNE, ALIAS JSA MEMBER THE HUNTRESS-- THE NATURAL DAUGHTER OF BRUCE WAYNE, ALIAS BATMAN.

YES, MS. WAYNE?

ONCE AGAIN I ASK THAT, IN THE NAME OF DECENCY, THESE HEARINGS BE TERMINATED, AND THE JSA DECLARED BLAMELESS OF ALL CHARGES.

WE WILL PROBABLY NEVER KNOW BATMAN'S TRUE MOTIVES IN WRITING HIS ODD, ACCUSATORY JOURNAL IN 1979--

"--BUT NEED WE BRING ADDITIONAL HEARTBREAK TO THE LOVED ONES OF THE JSA--THEIR WIVES, THEIR CHILDREN, THEIR FRIENDS-- SOME OF WHOM ARE DOUBTLESS IN THIS CHAMBER AT THIS VERY MOMENT?

AS HELENA SPEAKS, WHAT THOUGHTS MUST PASS THROUGH THE MIND OF SUCH AS SHIERA HALL, NOW KNOWN TO HAVE BEEN HAWKMAN'S PARTNER HAWKGIRL IN THE 1940'S--

--OF INZA NELSON, WIFE OF DR. FATE'S HUMAN ALTER EGO--

-- OF LOIS LANE KENT, ALREADY MADE DISTRAUGHT BY HER HUSBAND'S INCREASED MELAN-CHOLY OVER THE TRAGIC DESTINY OF HIS BELOVED KRYPTON?

BUT PERHAPS WE DO KNOW BATMAN'S MOTIVES, MS. WAYNE, PERHAPS THEY WERE-- TRUTH!

EVEN THE WIZARD, FOR ALL HIS PERFIDY, MAY HAVE BEEN SPEAKING THE TRUTH WHEN HE SWEARS HE SAW THE JSA CHARTER MEMBERS SWEARING AN OATH OF ALLEGIANCE TO HITLER IN 1940...

AND MAYBE GOATS CAN FLY, TOO-- IF THEY EAT ENOUGH OF HAWKMAN'S NINTH METAL.

HAHAHAHA

PLEASE, MS. WAYNE. I ASSURE YOU, IF THE JUSTICE SOCIETY ARE TRULY INNOCENT, NO ONE WANTS TO SEE THEM VINDICATED ANY MORE THAN WE DO.

NOW, IF ONE OF THE JSA WILL CONTINUE...?

I'LL DO THE HONORS, MR. CHAIRMAN.

1949 DIDN'T EXACTLY START OUT AS ONE OF OUR MOST EVENTFUL YEARS...

4

"...STARTING AS IT DID WITH THE LACKLUSTER *DR. EGRI* TRYING TO KILL US ALL WITH A BUNCH OF OBJECTS WHICH HAD SOMEHOW BEEN DOUSED WITH *COSMIC POWER*--

"--NOT TO MENTION THE EQUALLY FORGET-TABLE *'ADVENTURE OF THE INVISIBLE BAND,'* IN WHICH OUR UNSUSPECTING *CLEANING-WOMAN* FOUND SOME SKETCHES WE LEFT IN OUR SECRET HQ--

"--WHICH LED, BY A WEIRD CHAIN OF EVENTS, TO HER WOULD-BE DETECTIVE NEPHEW *ELMER DOOLITTLE* HELPING US CAPTURE A WHOLE GANG OF CRIMINALS.

"NOT MUCH MORE MEMORABLE WAS OUR ENCOUNTER WITH A *RODEO STAR* WHO PASSED HIMSELF OFF AS THE REINCARNATION OF *BILLY THE KID.*

I KNOW, MR. CHAIRMAN, THAT EVIDENCE SEEN ONLY ON MY *MAGIC SPHERE* HAS BEEN DEEMED INADMISSIBLE.

STILL, OUR *NEXT* TASK -- WHICH UTILIZED THE SPHERE--STARTED OUT AS MOSTLY A *HUMANE* UNDERTAKING.

BLAM
BLAM
BLAM

"IT WOULD'VE BEEN A BIT MORE MEMORABLE, I SUPPOSE, IF THE *STAGECOACH* HE TIED US TO HAD CRASHED AS HE INTENDED--

"BUT IT *DIDN'T*, OF COURSE--AND WE DIDN'T NEED *PAT GARRETT* TO TAKE CARE OF *THAT* PARTICULAR BUSHWHACKER.

IT CONCERNED A BOY NAMED *EDMUND BLAKE*, WHO WAS DYING IN A HOSPITAL IN *CIVIC CITY*...

THEN WHY DON'T YOU LET *ME* TELL THEM ABOUT THAT ONE, WONDER WOMAN?

WHO--?

EDMUND!? AND JOAN!

SORRY WE COULDN'T MAKE IT BACK ANY FASTER, JAY.

WE WERE ON THIS DIG IN THE AUSTRALIAN OUTBACK, AND IT TOOK A WHILE FOR MS. WAYNE'S WIRE TO CATCH UP WITH--

WILL SOMEONE PLEASE TELL THIS COMMITTEE JUST WHAT IN BLAZES IS GOING ON AROUND HERE?

MR. CHAIRMAN, MAY I PRESENT THE AFOREMENTIONED EDMUND BLAKE... AND HIS WIFE, JOAN NEVINS BLAKE.

I'M SURE WE'VE ALL HEARD OF ONE OF AMERICA'S FOREMOST NATURALISTS, WONDER WOMAN.

THEN MAYBE YOU'LL BELIEVE ME WHEN I TELL YOU THE JUSTICE SOCIETY GAVE ME THE WILL TO LIVE THAT DAY IN 1949, SIR...

"IF THEY HADN'T, I'D NOT HAVE BEEN AROUND TO SAVE JOAN'S LIFE FROM A JEALOUS SUITOR MORE THAN A DECADE LATER.

CRAK!

AIIEEE

"I OWE THEM MY LIFE--AND MORE!"

WHAT EDMUND ISN'T TELLING, SENATOR, IS HOW WE ACTUALLY THOUGHT WE'D FAILED, THAT DAY.

YOU SEE, WE'D TRIED TO HELP HIM BY SHOWING HIM VISIONS OF HIS FUTURE... BUT THEY WEREN'T ENOUGH...

"LATER, AFTER WE'D LEFT HIS BEDSIDE, THE MAGIC SPHERE SHOWED HIM A POWERFUL IMAGE OF THE SEVEN OF US IN DEADLY PERIL--ONLY A WEEK IN THE FUTURE:"

THOSE CROOKS--THEY'RE LOWERING THAT STEAM-SHOVEL CLAW ON THE JUSTICE SOCIETY! IT'LL KILL THEM!

WHAT THE FLASH IS SAYING, DR. BLAKE, IS THAT SEEING THAT IMAGE GAVE YOU THE WILL TO GO ON LIVING?

YES, SIR, A WEEK AFTER MY OPERATION, I AWOKE-- BUT I COULDN'T GET THE DOCTORS TO BELIEVE WHAT I'D SEEN.

SO HE GOT UP FROM HIS BED AND ARRIVED ON THE SCENE JUST IN TIME TO STOP THE JSA FROM BECOMING STATISTICS.

I OWED THEM--I STILL DO! IF THE JUSTICE SOCIETY ARE TRAITORS--THEN MY WHOLE LIFE IS A LIE!

SCORE ONE FOR OUR SIDE, PEOPLE.

A PENTHOUSE IN WASHINGTON, D.C.:

DAMN THAT HOPKINS! WHAT DO I MAKE MY CAMPAIGN CONTRIBUTIONS FOR EVERY SIX YEARS, ANYWAY?

THAT'S NOT GOING TO GET ME MY REVENGE!

SO HE CAN LET THE WIZARD SCREW THINGS UP--AND LET CHARACTER WITNESSES LIKE BLAKE CRAWL OUT OF THE WOODWORK?

DON'T WORRY, MR. O'FALLON. I'LL GET THAT FOR YOU-- TODAY!

WH--? YOU!?

DID YOU THINK YOU'D NEVER HEAR FROM PER DEGATON AGAIN, YOU SIMPERING EXCUSE FOR A MEDIA TYCOON?

AFTER ALL, YOU'VE BEEN FINANCING MY LAB SINCE I WAS PAROLED LAST YEAR, HAVEN'T YOU-- WITH YOUR PRECIOUS VENGEANCE IN MIND?

WELL, ER--YES, BUT--

YOU DIDN'T THINK FOR ONE MOMENT THAT I'D COME THROUGH, DID YOU?

YOU WERE JUST HEDGING YOUR BETS-- JUST IN CASE POOR, CRAZY OLD DEGATON WASN'T QUITE AS INSANE AS HE SEEMED, WEREN'T YOU?

UNLESS YOU'RE READY TO DELIVER-- GET OUT!

THOSE MASKED FASCISTS KILLED MY FATHER YEARS AGO--AND I MEAN TO BE WATCHING WHEN THEY GET THEIRS, ON NATIONWIDE TELEVISION!

YOU'RE A FOOL, O'FALLON. WITH YOUR MONEY, I'VE SPENT THE PAST YEAR CHECKING OUT YOUR VERSION OF THINGS--

--AND EVERYBODY BUT YOU KNOWS THE FIRE THAT KILLED YOUR OLD MAN IN '58 WAS AN ACCIDENT.

TAL ⊕ GLOBE
IETY DISBANDS FOR GOOD

SURE, AS A SENATOR, HE SPEARHEADED THE COMMITTEE THAT PUSHED THE JUSTICE SOCIETY INTO RETIRING BACK IN '51-- BUT THEY DIDN'T WASTE HIM FOR IT.

HIS DEATH WARPED YOUR LIFE, MAN--

-- BUT THE MONEY YOU FUNNELED TO ME WAS WELL SPENT, JUST THE SAME!

YOU DO HAVE SOMETHING UP YOUR SLEEVE! WHAT?

YOU'LL SOON SEE! I'VE WAITED YEARS FOR MY OWN REVENGE--AND ANOTHER CRACK AT WORLD CONQUEST--

VANISHE

--AND THIS IS D-DAY!

I JUST THOUGHT THAT--AS THE MAN WHO PAID FOR IT-- YOU SHOULD BE THE FIRST TO KNOW!

7

GREEN LANTERN TAKES OVER:

SOON AFTERWARD, THE WORLD SUFFERED A SPATE OF *ALIEN INVASIONS*-- FIRST, *FIRE PEOPLE* FROM THE "*YELLOW COMET*"--

--THEN *DIAMOND MEN* FROM BENEATH EARTH'S SURFACE--

"--AND FINALLY, THE MENACE OF THE LEGEND-ARY '*FOUR KINGS*' OF PREHISTORIC TIMES, WHO PUT US TO *SLEEP* FOR AN ENTIRE YEAR--

--AND TRIED TO CARRY OUT WHAT'S BEEN CALLED "*THE SECRET CONQUEST OF THE EARTH*." WE--

HE'S TELLING THE *TRUTH!* I WAS IN THE NATIONAL GUARD AGAINST SOME OF THOSE *OUTER-SPACERS!*

IF IT WASN'T FOR THE JSAers, WE'D HAVE WOUND UP LIKE THE PEOPLE ON THAT "*V*" SHOW ON TV!

YOU *TELL 'EM*, POPS!

UH-- IF I MAY CONTINUE: GREEN LANTERN FORGOT TO MENTION AN INTERIM CASE WHERE AN OLD *COLLEGE CHUM* OF MINE TURNED OUT TO BE A BAD GUY CALLED *MR. ALPHA*.

FRED KINCAID WENT *STRAIGHT*, THOUGH-- AFTER HE'D SERVED HIS TIME.

*TIME*, MR. CHAIRMAN, IS JUST WHAT *WE* SERVED LATER IN 1950-- WHEN OUR OLD FRIEND *DR. SWANLEY* OF THE "*TIME TRUST*" WAS *KILLED*, AND THE MURDER WEAPON BECAME "*THE GUN THAT DROPPED THROUGH TIME*."

HIS "*TIME CHUTE*" HAS BEEN SAFE IN OUR KEEPING FOR YEARS--

"--SINCE WE *RETRIEVED* THE PISTOL, BY CHASING IT ACROSS THE *CENTURIES*.

AFTER THAT, IT SEEMED AS IF THINGS WERE GOING TO *EASE UP* FOR A WHILE.

SURE, WE HAD SOME PRETTY *HARROWING* MOMENTS WHEN WE TOOK ON *"THE CIRCUS OF A THOUSAND THRILLS."*

THAT TURNED OUT TO BE A *CRIME CARNIVAL* SECRETLY MADE UP OF *IDENTICAL TWINS*--ONE TWIN OUT COMMITTING CRIMES, WHILE THE OTHER WAS HIS *ALIBI.*

STILL, THAT CASE WAS A *SNAP,* COMPARED TO--

--*"THE MAN WHO CONQUERED THE SOLAR SYSTEM,"* RIGHT, HAWK?

ACTUALLY, IT WASN'T REALLY OUR SOLAR SYSTEM, AS WE LATER FOUND OUT-- BUT ONE IN *ANOTHER DIMENSION,* WHERE ALL THE PLANETS WERE *HABITABLE.*

*" OUR BIGGEST SHOCK, THOUGH, CAME WHEN THE HELMETED MAN WE WERE FIGHTING-- THE CONQUEROR-- TURNED OUT NOT TO BE A BADDIE, AT ALL --*

*"--BUT ONLY OUR OLD FRIEND PROF. ELWOOD NAPIER, THE EMINENT SCIENTIST--UNDER THE SPELL OF SOME WEIRD ALIEN HEADGEAR!"*

9

YEP, THAT'S RIGHT-- THE *SAME* PROF. NAPIER WHO'D DESIGNED THE INFAMOUS "FLYING EYE" THAT TERRORIZED WASHINGTON BACK IN '42.

BUT THE *TERROR* PART HAD BEEN A *SUPER-VILLAIN'S* DOING-- NOT NAPIER'S!

NOBODY IN THIS ROOM BUT *US* COULD POSSIBLY KNOW THAT OUR NEXT MISSION TOOK US TO THE 31st CENTURY-- WHERE MANKIND WAS BEING MENACED BY UGLY LITTLE CRITTERS CALLED *CHAMELEONS*.

WE FORGOT IT, TOO, WHEN WE RETURNED-- TILL WONDER WOMAN'S *MAGIC SPHERE* FILLED US IN.

To the Seven Greatest Detectives in the World--

"AND THEN CAME *THE KEY*-- A MASTER CRIMINAL WHO KIDNAPPED FOUR OF THE WORLD'S MOST FAMOUS *DETECTIVES* AND DARED US TO RESCUE THEM.

"WE *DID*-- AND THE KEY JUMPED TO HIS DEATH, SO *UNEXPECTEDLY* THAT WE DIDN'T HAVE A CHANCE TO *SAVE* HIM.

"*ARTISTS* USUALLY RENDER HIM AS A GUY WITH A *KEY-SHAPED MASK*. BUT ACTUALLY HE WAS JUST A MAN WITH THE MOST *PURELY EVIL* FACE I'VE EVER SEEN!"

GOOD LORD! JUST *HEARING* ALL THIS--!

BATMAN AND I SOLVED SCORES OF CASES, TOO-- BUT I NEVER REALIZED BEFORE JUST *HOW MUCH* THE JSA HAD ACCOMPLISHED IN THOSE TEN YEARS!

IF ONLY I COULD *BELIEVE* THEY'RE INNOCENT OF TREASON--

--WITHOUT THAT MAKING *BRUCE WAYNE* GUILTY-- OF TRYING TO *FRAME* THEM FROM HIS *GRAVE*!

MR. CHAIRMAN-- THE JUSTICE SOCIETY'S *FINAL* 1950's EXPLOIT WAS THE SUBJECT OF THE JOINT CONGRESSIONAL HEARING IN 1951.

I PRESUME YOU WON'T OBJECT TO THEIR ELABORATING ON *IT*, AS WELL?

ON THE CONTRARY, MS. WAYNE! AFTER ALL, DUE TO-- *ER*-- CIRCUMSTANCES, THE JSAers *NEVER DID* REVEAL MUCH INFORMATION ABOUT THAT BUSINESS.

ATOM? WOULD YOU CARE TO PROCEED?

"CHECK! IN EARLY '51, THE HEAD OF A CRIME-SERVICES GROUP CALLED *ELIMINATIONS, INC.* LURED US TO AN EARLY *SPACE SATELLITE...*

Eliminations, Inc.

"...WITH PROMISES THAT IT WOULD BE OUR *NEW* HEADQUARTERS, PROVIDED BY A *GRATEFUL* GROUP OF *PRIVATE* CITIZENS.

"ONCE THERE, WE FOUND OURSELVES *ATTACKED* INSTEAD BY DEADLY ROBOTS...

"OH, SURE, WE *MUDDLED THROUGH,* ALL RIGHT--EVEN CAPTURED OUR *HOST*--

"--THOUGH WE NEVER *DID* SOLVE THE MYSTERY OF HIS ADVANCED *TECHNOLOGY,* OR--"

"*I'LL* TAKE IT, ATOM. BACK ON EARTH, OUR WELCOME WAS A *SUBPOENA...*

Subpoena

"...AN 'INVITATION' TO APPEAR BEFORE THE *JOINT CONGRESSIONAL UN-AMERICAN ACTIVITIES COMMITTEE,* UNDER SENATOR *O'FALLON,* WHO'D SUCCEEDED TO ITS HEAD AFTER THE CAR CRASH WHICH KILLED SEN. *JOSEPH McCARTHY.*

"YES, THAT'S THE *FATHER* OF THE *JSA-HATER* WHO NOW PUBLISHES THE *CAPITAL-GLOBE* HERE IN WASHINGTON.

"IT WAS A *SPECIAL HEARING* INTO OUR POSSIBLE ALLIANCE WITH THE HEAD OF *ELIMINATIONS, INC.*--WHO WAS ACCUSED OF BEING AN *ENEMY AGENT...*

THIS INDIVIDUAL IS A *KNOWN AGENT* OF A *HOSTILE FOREIGN POWER...* A VERY *HIGHLY PLACED* AGENT, I MIGHT ADD.

THIS COMMITTEE DEMANDS TO KNOW YOUR *CONNECTION* WITH THIS MAN.

HE--TRIED TO *KILL US,* SIR. THAT'S ALL.

*SO YOU SAY!* BUT WHAT *PROOF* HAVE WE? YOUR DOSSIERS INCLUDE MANY SUCH UNCLEAR EVENTS.

11

"THAT'S WHEN O'FALLON, SR., ZAPPED US WITH THE CLINCHER...

WE KNOW *NOTHING* ABOUT ANY OF YOU EXCEPT THE *FEW* FACTS YOU HAVE GIVEN REPORTERS. THAT IS *NOT* ENOUGH.

THIS IS A *CLOSED SESSION* OF A CONGRESSIONAL COMMITTEE-- AND BY THAT *AUTHORITY*, I ASK YOU--

IF YOU ARE *GOOD* AMERICANS, YOU WILL *SHOW* THIS COMMITTEE YOUR *FACES*, SO WE MAY BEGIN THE PROCESS OF *CLEARING* YOU.

"THE SHOCK WAS ALMOST PALPABLE.

"IT TOOK ONLY A MOMENT'S CONFERENCE FOR ME TO ANNOUNCE THE RESULT:

WE RESPECTFULLY *DECLINE,* SENATOR. OUR FACES-- OUR *NAMES*--OUR *LIVES*-- ARE OUR OWN BUSINESS.

BUT DON'T WORRY--

--BECAUSE YOU *WON'T* BE HEARING FROM US *AGAIN!*

POOF

"AT LEAST, WITH THE HELP OF GREEN LANTERN'S RING, WE MADE A DRAMATIC IF *SORROWFUL* EXIT.

"THEREAFTER, EXCEPT FOR A FEW VERY-EXCEPTIONAL CASES, THERE WAS NO MORE JUSTICE SOCIETY FOR *TWELVE YEARS.*

"THE WORLD *SPUN* ON: O'FALLON PERISHED IN A FIRE A FEW YEARS LATER... SPACE SATELLITES AND TELE-VISION BECAME EVERYDAY REALITY.

"*SUPERMAN... BATMAN* AND *ROBIN... WONDER WOMAN,* REMAINED ACTIVE... BUT IT WAS NOT A *TIME* FOR OUR KIND OF HERO."

12

VERY INTERESTING. BUT, *UH*--WASN'T *MRS. TREVOR* ONE OF THOSE WHO *RETIRED* IN '51?

YES, SENATOR. BUT LATER, SHE DECIDED HER VOW TO *FIGHT FOR FREEDOM* WHEN SHE'D LEFT *PARADISE ISLAND* TEN YEARS EARLIER HAD AN EVEN *STRONGER* CLAIM ON HER.

I SEE. NOW, MAY I ASK--*WHAT,* PRECISELY, MADE THE REST OF THE JSA BECOME *ACTIVE* AGAIN IN THE EARLY 1960'S?

THAT'S... A BIT *HARD* TO EXPLAIN, SENATOR.

*TRY. PLEASE.*

"VERY WELL. BUT FIRST, YOU'LL JUST HAVE TO *ACCEPT* OUR *WORD* FOR IT THAT THERE'S A *PARALLEL EARTH* EXISTING IN A DIMENSION *NEXT* TO OURS...

"...ONE ON WHICH THERE WAS *NEVER* A JUSTICE SOCIETY OF AMERICA, EXCEPT IN COMIC-BOOKS."

"IN 1961, SEVERAL OF MY OLD FOES CAME OUT OF THEIR *OWN* BRAND OF RETIREMENT:

"THE *FIDDLER*--THE *SHADE*--AND THE *THINKER.*

"A CHAIN OF CIRCUMSTANCES LED A YOUNG *SUPER-HERO* OF THAT OTHER EARTH--ITS OWN *FLASH,* IN FACT--TO COME TO OUR WORLD, AND EVEN BRING ME OUT OF MOTH-BALLS.

"I'M NOT *SURE,* BUT IT MAY HAVE BEEN *LATER* THAN '61 ON THAT EARTH--THINGS GET A BIT *CONFUSED* WHEN YOU START MUCKING ABOUT WITH SPACE AND TIME.

"SOON, ANYWAY, *VANDAL SAVAGE*--AN IMMORTAL ENEMY OF GREEN LANTERN'S--LURED THE *OTHERS* INTO CLIMBING INTO COSTUME AGAIN.

"HE CAPTURED THEM BRIEFLY--BUT WE TWO FLASHES *FREED* THEM--

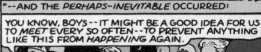

"--AND THE *PERHAPS-INEVITABLE* OCCURRED:

YOU KNOW, BOYS--IT MIGHT BE A GOOD IDEA FOR US TO *MEET* EVERY SO OFTEN--TO PREVENT ANYTHING LIKE THIS FROM *HAPPENING* AGAIN.

I'M IN *FAVOR* OF IT!

LET ME GET THIS *STRAIGHT,* FLASH: YOU EXPECT THIS COMMITTEE TO BELIEVE THERE ARE *TWO EARTHS*--*TWO FLASHES*--?

MR. CHAIRMAN, I THINK *CONGRESSWOMAN VALDEZ* AND I HAVE ALREADY MADE IT CLEAR WE HAVE NO PROBLEM GOING ALONG WITH THE JSA ON THIS ONE.

IF YOU'D *CONTINUE,* MR. GARRICK...?

"CERTAINLY, CONGRESSMAN PHILIPS. BEFORE LONG, THE WORD GOT AROUND--AND OTHER OLDTIME JSAers GOT BACK INTO HARNESS, TOO--INCLUDING, WE MIGHT ADD, SUPERMAN AND EVEN OUR ALLEGED ACCUSER, BATMAN.

"ALONG THE WAY, WE EVEN RESUSCITATED THE SEVEN SOLDIERS OF VICTORY FROM WORLD WAR TWO--AS WITNESS THE STILL-ACTIVE SHINING KNIGHT AND STAR-SPANGLED KID.

"THESE PAST COUPLE OF DECADES, THE JUSTICE SOCIETY AND THAT OTHER EARTH'S 'JUSTICE LEAGUE OF AMERICA' HAVE OFTEN EXCHANGED VISITS--WITH RESULTS BENEFICIAL, I THINK, TO BOTH WORLDS-- STARTING IN SUMMER OF '63.

"A FEW PEOPLE IN THIS CHAMBER MAY RECALL HEROES WITH NAMES LIKE THE RAY--BLACK CONDOR--UNCLE SAM--THE HUMAN BOMB--PHANTOM LADY--DOLL MAN.

"WELL, THOSE AND OTHER WORLD WAR TWO HEROES HAD CROSSED OVER INTO THAT THIRD EARTH WE MENTIONED EARLIER--THE ONE WHERE THE NAZIS WON THE WAR, TROUNCING EVEN THEIR JAPANESE ALLIES.

"BUT I'M PROUD TO SAY THAT THE JSA, THE JLA, AND THOSE HEROES--THE FREEDOM FIGHTERS--SET THINGS RIGHT AGAIN ON THAT WORLD, WHICH WE CALL 'EARTH-X' FOR NO PARTICULAR REASON.

"I WISH YOU COULD MEET THE JUSTICE LEAGUE, SENATOR. ONE OF ITS MEMBERS-- THE BLACK CANARY--WAS EVEN BORN ON THIS PLANET, AND IS THE DAUGHTER OF THE ORIGINAL.

SO THAT IS THE SECRET OF THOSE OTHER COSTUMED SUPER-HEROES WHO'VE SHOWN UP HERE, FROM TIME TO TIME.

MAYBE YOU JSAers HAVE BEEN DOING A BIT MORE GOOD THAN IT LOOKED LIKE FROM MY DISTRICT.

THEN WHY DIDN'T YOU TELL THE WORLD ABOUT THIS "JUSTICE LEAGUE," FLASH?

SURELY YOU'RE KIDDING, MR. CHAIRMAN! WE'VE GOT A HARD ENOUGH TIME GETTING PEOPLE TO BELIEVE IN US!

STILL, MAYBE IT WAS A MISTAKE TO--

KRAKK!

DON'T ADMIT ANYTHING, FLASH--

--NOT TILL POWER GIRL HAS HER SAY!

WELL--SO MUCH FOR OUR NEW SECURITY PRECAUTIONS!

HOLY--!

CRASSHHH

SEE HERE, YOUNG LADY--THIS IS A CONGRESSIONAL HEARING, NOT A CIRCUS!

GOOD THING YOU KEEP REMINDING EVERYBODY OF THAT, SENATOR--

OTHERWISE, SOME OF US COULDN'T TELL THE DIFFERENCE!

KARA--!

DON'T WORRY, COUSIN--I'M NOT GOING TO HURT ANYBODY.

SORRY I WAS OUT OF THE COUNTRY ON A MISSION FOR THE PAST COUPLE OF WEEKS--BUT I PRESUME I'VE ARRIVED IN TIME TO TESTIFY.

LIVE
UBS NEWS

ER--OF COURSE, POWER GIRL. GO AHEAD.

GOOD--BECAUSE IT'S TIME SOMEBODY SPOKE UP FOR THE JSA--FROM THE INSIDE!

YOU TELL 'EM, P.G.!

MAKES ME WISH I COULD BE THERE MYSELF!

15

THE JUSTICE SOCIETY KNOWS YOU HAD IMPORTANT BUSINESS *HERE*, SYLVESTER.

BESIDES, YOU SENT IN A *DEPOSITION*. THEY COULDN'T ASK FOR ANYTHING *MORE*.

MAYBE SO, BUT I *STILL*--

COUSIN SUPERMAN AND I'VE TOLD THE WORLD HOW I CAME TO EARTH ONLY A FEW YEARS AGO--HAVING BEEN RAISED IN SPACE BY MACHINES AFTER OUR NATIVE KRYPTON WAS DESTROYED--

--BUT THE *JSA'S* NEVER REALLY GONE *PUBLIC* WITH DETAILS OF THEIR *CASES* SINCE I JOINED A FEW YEARS BACK.

IN ALL THESE DECADES, THEY'VE NEVER HAD *SENSE* ENOUGH TO HIRE A *PUBLIC-RELATIONS* EXPERT-- SO MAYBE IT'S TIME *I* TRIED MY HAND AT BEING ONE.

"MY DEBUT ON EARTH COINCIDED WITH *ROBIN* BECOMING ACTIVE AS A JSAer AGAIN--AND WITH THE *STAR-SPANGLED KID* JOINING UP.

"RIGHT OFF, WE ALL GOT INVOLVED IN FOILING A PLOT BY THE LATE *BRAIN WAVE* TO CREATE *NEW* BODIES FOR HIMSELF AND HIS OLD BUDDY, *PER DEGATON*--SINCE THEIR OWN WERE PRETTY MUCH OVER THE HILL.

"WITH ME PROVIDING SOME OF THE MUSCLE, WE PUT THE LID ON THEM BOTH AND PACKED THEM OFF TO JAIL--AND I TOOK CARE OF THE *SATELLITE* BRAIN WAVE WAS USING TO BLACKMAIL THE EARTH.

16

"SOON AFTERWARD, A SECOND PSYCHO-PIRATE USED HIS POWERS TO MAKE GREEN LANTERN START ACTING LIKE PUBLIC ENEMY #1."

"THAT'S WHAT SEEMS TO HAVE SET GOTHAM CITY POLICE COMMISSIONER BRUCE WAYNE OFF ON A TANGENT-- MADE HIM DECIDE THE TIME FOR THE JSA'S 'VIGILANTE TACTICS' WAS OVER--"

"--SO THAT HE USED ROBIN'S SIGNAL-DEVICE--"

"--TO BRING SEVERAL LESS ACTIVE MEMBERS INTO THE FRAY, CONVINCING THEM THE 'NEW JSA' HAD BECOME A MENACE TO LAW AND ORDER."

"I OUGHT TO KNOW--SINCE I GOT ZAPPED IN THE MIDDLE OF IT ALL."

"BY THE WAY, JUST IN CASE EVERYBODY'S FORGOTTEN--WE WERE CALLED THE SUPER-SQUAD, EVEN THE ALL-STAR SUPER-SQUAD, FOR A TIME THERE--BUT BY NOW, WE WERE JUST PLAIN JUSTICE SOCIETY AGAIN--"

--AND THAT'S THE NAME, THE HERITAGE, WE'RE PROUDEST OF!

I'M NOT ACCUSED OF ANYTHING--AND IF WE EVEN SUSPECTED THE JSAers OF BEING TRAITORS--WOULD THE HUNTRESS AND I HAVE RESIGNED FROM THE NEW INFINITY, INC. TO COME BACK TO THE FOLD?

UNLESS YOU WERE DECEIVED BY THEM, TOO, KAREN--JUST AS ROBIN WAS, ALL THOSE YEARS!

BUT-- WHAT IF SHE AND HELENA ARE RIGHT?

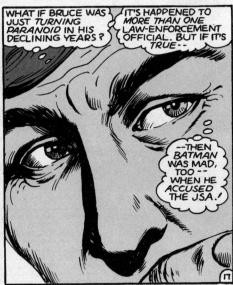

WHAT IF BRUCE WAS JUST TURNING PARANOID IN HIS DECLINING YEARS?

IT'S HAPPENED TO MORE THAN ONE LAW-ENFORCEMENT OFFICIAL. BUT IF IT'S TRUE--

--THEN BATMAN WAS MAD, TOO -- WHEN HE ACCUSED THE JSA!

17

AND, ACROSS THE ROOM FROM RICHARD GRAYSON:

POOR DICK! ALL THIS TALK ABOUT DAD WILL TARNISH NOT ONLY HIS NAME BUT BATMAN'S--IF I HAVE TO REVEAL THEY WERE ONE AND THE SAME.

GOD HELP ME--EVEN IF IT'S THE ONLY WAY TO SAVE THE JSA--I DON'T KNOW IF I CAN DO IT!

IF THE HUNTRESS FEELS AS YOU DO, POWER GIRL--WHY HAS THIS COMMITTEE NOT BEEN ABLE TO LOCATE HER TO TESTIFY?

I ASSURE YOU, SENATOR, NOTHING WOULD KEEP HER AWAY--

--IF SHE DIDN'T HAVE EXTREMELY URGENT BUSINESS-- IN ANOTHER CAPACITY!

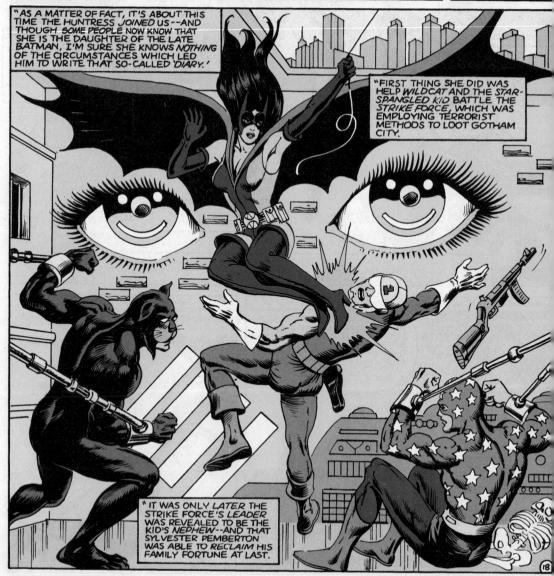

"AS A MATTER OF FACT, IT'S ABOUT THIS TIME THE HUNTRESS JOINED US--AND THOUGH SOME PEOPLE NOW KNOW THAT SHE IS THE DAUGHTER OF THE LATE BATMAN, I'M SURE SHE KNOWS NOTHING OF THE CIRCUMSTANCES WHICH LED HIM TO WRITE THAT SO-CALLED 'DIARY.'"

"FIRST THING SHE DID WAS HELP WILDCAT AND THE STAR-SPANGLED KID BATTLE THE STRIKE FORCE, WHICH WAS EMPLOYING TERRORIST METHODS TO LOOT GOTHAM CITY.

"IT WAS ONLY LATER THE STRIKE FORCE'S LEADER WAS REVEALED TO BE THE KID'S NEPHEW--AND THAT SYLVESTER PEMBERTON WAS ABLE TO RECLAIM HIS FAMILY FORTUNE AT LAST.

18

"THAT'S WHEN *THE THORN* POPPED UP FOR THE FIRST TIME SINCE THE 1940'S--TRYING TO TURN *KEYSTONE CITY* INTO HER PERSONAL TURF--

"--WHILE THE *HUNTRESS* WAS BUSY DEFEATING HER EARLIER NAMESAKE AND HER CRIMINAL HUBBY, THE *SPORTSMASTER.*

A FEW WEEKS LATER, AN ALIEN WEIRDIE CALLED THE *MASTER SUMMONER* CAUSED ALL KINDS OF *CHAOS* TO ERUPT--BRINGING THE WORLD TO THE BRINK OF *DESTRUCTION...*

I REMEMBER THE *CHAOS*, ANYWAY--BUT I SEEM TO RECALL THE JSA JUST SITTING ON THEIR *HANDS* FOR DAYS ON END!

PRECISELY-- BECAUSE THEY'D LEARNED THE SUMMONER WAS USING *THEIR* VERY SUPER-POWERS--TO *FUEL* THE EARTH'S OBLITERATION!

WAY TO GO, *KARA*!

IF I EVER DECIDE TO *TOTALLY* RETIRE-- EVEN ABANDON MY ADOPTED PLANET--

--I'LL KNOW IT'S IN GOOD *KRYPTONIAN HANDS!*

BUT NOW, MR. CHAIRMAN, I COME TO THE *SADDEST* EVENT IN JSA HISTORY...

...THE DAY IN 1979 WHEN TWO OF THE BRAVEST MEN IN GOTHAM CITY--OR THE WORLD--*DIED* IN THE VERY SAME HOUR!

"I'LL NEVER FORGET OUR ANSWERING THE CALL TO GOTHAM'S *TRADE TOWER.*

"WE CAME *FLYING*-- BOTH UNDER OUR OWN STEAM, AND IN THE JSA'S *SKY-SKIMMER...*

"...BUT THE CRAZED MAN *ATOP* IT, HIS HANDS CRACKLING WITH SUPERHUMAN *ENERGY*, WAS MORE THAN A *MATCH* FOR US.

GET *USED* TO IT, WORLD! FROM NOW ON, *BILL JENSEN* GETS WHAT HE WANTS--

--AND WHAT I WANT IS-- *BRUCE WAYNE!*

BRING HIM TO ME-- *NOW*--OR YOUR WHOLE CITY WILL *DIE!*

19

143

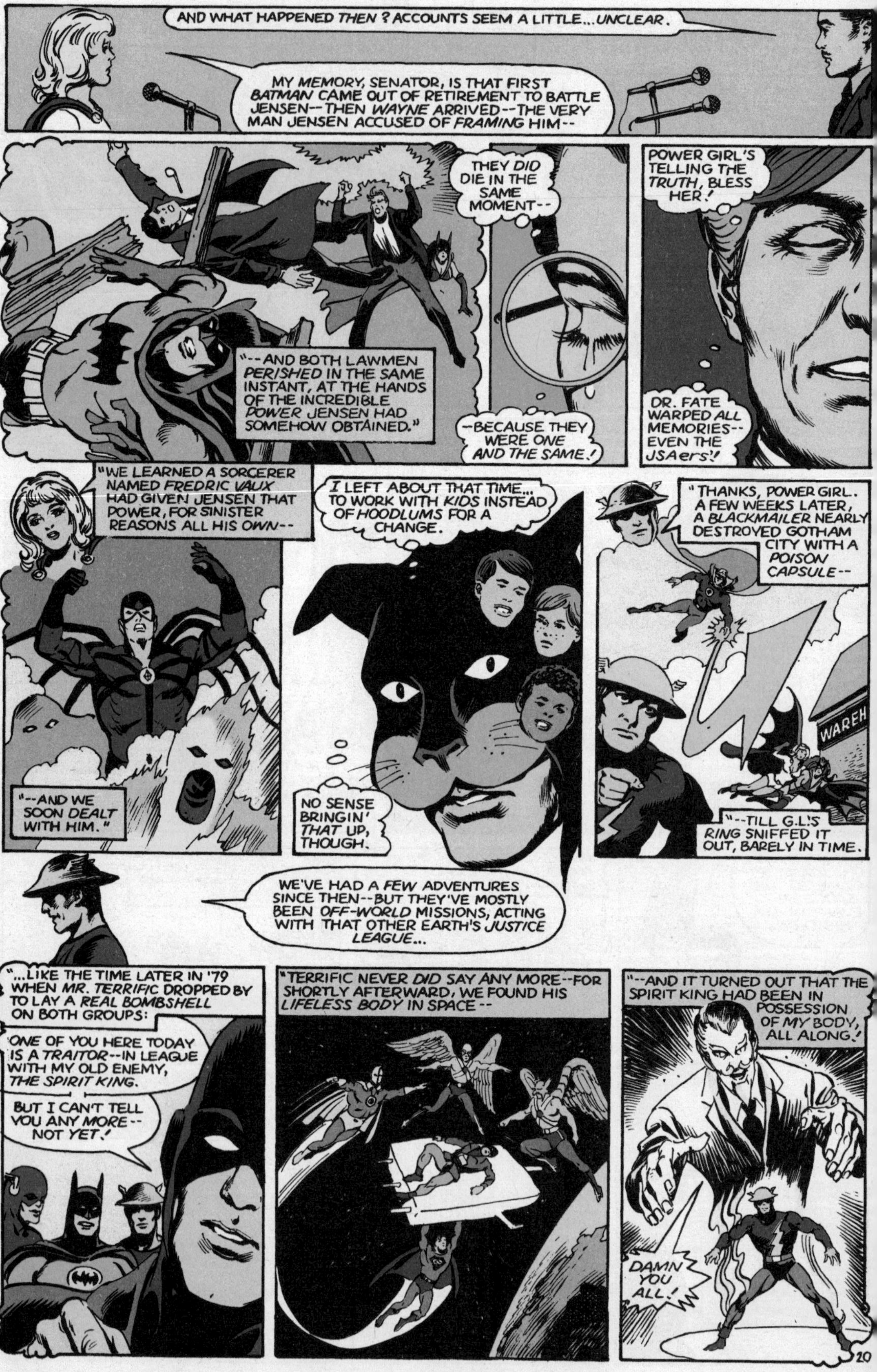
AND WHAT HAPPENED THEN? ACCOUNTS SEEM A LITTLE... UNCLEAR.
MY MEMORY, SENATOR, IS THAT FIRST BATMAN CAME OUT OF RETIREMENT TO BATTLE JENSEN-- THEN WAYNE ARRIVED--THE VERY MAN JENSEN ACCUSED OF FRAMING HIM--
"--AND BOTH LAWMEN PERISHED IN THE SAME INSTANT, AT THE HANDS OF THE INCREDIBLE POWER JENSEN HAD SOMEHOW OBTAINED."
THEY DID DIE IN THE SAME MOMENT--
--BECAUSE THEY WERE ONE AND THE SAME!
POWER GIRL'S TELLING THE TRUTH, BLESS HER!
DR. FATE WARPED ALL MEMORIES-- EVEN THE JSAers'!
"WE LEARNED A SORCERER NAMED FREDRIC VAUX HAD GIVEN JENSEN THAT POWER, FOR SINISTER REASONS ALL HIS OWN--
"--AND WE SOON DEALT WITH HIM."
I LEFT ABOUT THAT TIME... TO WORK WITH KIDS INSTEAD OF HOODLUMS FOR A CHANGE.
NO SENSE BRINGIN' THAT UP, THOUGH.
"THANKS, POWER GIRL. A FEW WEEKS LATER, A BLACKMAILER NEARLY DESTROYED GOTHAM CITY WITH A POISON CAPSULE--
WAREH
"--TILL G.L.'S RING SNIFFED IT OUT, BARELY IN TIME.
WE'VE HAD A FEW ADVENTURES SINCE THEN--BUT THEY'VE MOSTLY BEEN OFF-WORLD MISSIONS, ACTING WITH THAT OTHER EARTH'S JUSTICE LEAGUE...
"...LIKE THE TIME LATER IN '79 WHEN MR. TERRIFIC DROPPED BY TO LAY A REAL BOMBSHELL ON BOTH GROUPS:
ONE OF YOU HERE TODAY IS A TRAITOR--IN LEAGUE WITH MY OLD ENEMY, THE SPIRIT KING.
BUT I CAN'T TELL YOU ANY MORE-- NOT YET!
"TERRIFIC NEVER DID SAY ANY MORE--FOR SHORTLY AFTERWARD, WE FOUND HIS LIFELESS BODY IN SPACE--
"--AND IT TURNED OUT THAT THE SPIRIT KING HAD BEEN IN POSSESSION OF MY BODY, ALL ALONG!
DAMN YOU ALL!
20

WE'RE NOT TRYING TO WHITEWASH THE *MISTAKES* WE'VE MADE OVER THE YEARS--WHETHER IT'S OUR *FAILURE*, TO DATE, TO CAPTURE MR. TERRIFIC'S MURDERER--

--OR OUR REFUSING TO VOTE INTO MEMBERSHIP SOME *YOUNGER* HEROES WHO WANTED TO JOIN, NOT LONG AGO.

FORTUNATELY, ONE OF OUR NUMBER, THE *STAR-SPANGLED KID*, HAD MORE FORESIGHT--

--AND *INFINITY, INC.* NOW OPERATES OUT OF LOS ANGELES.

WELL, MR. CHAIRMAN--*THAT* IS PRETTY MUCH THE FULL *RECORD* OF THE *JUSTICE SOCIETY* OF AMERICA, FOR BETTER OR FOR WORSE.

IF YOU OR THE *AMERICAN PEOPLE* WANT TO BELIEVE THAT WE--ANY OF US *BETRAYED* THIS NATION DURING WORLD WAR TWO, AND COVERED UP THAT BETRAYAL LATER--SO BE IT!

BUT WE HOPE YOU'LL LOOK AT THAT RECORD--NOT JUST AS THE TARNISHED TESTIMONY OF A FELON LIKE *THE WIZARD*, OR EVEN JUST AT *BATMAN'S* ALLEGED DIARY.

I--I ONLY WISH WE HAD SOME SORT OF *EXPLANATION* AS TO *WHY* BATMAN FELT HE HAD TO ACCUSE US OF *TREASON*--AND EVEN AT A PARTICULAR *TIME*--

--BUT--WE JUST DON'T HAVE ONE.

NOW, THE DECISION RESTS WITH THIS *COMMITTEE*... AND WITH THE *AMERICAN PEOPLE*.

JAY GARRICK SITS...AND FOR A LONG MOMENT, THE CHAMBER IS COVERED IN A DEEP, PROFOUND SILENCE.

THEN--IT ERUPTS:

THAT'S TELLING 'EM, FLASH!

THE JSA'S THE BEST THERE EVER WAS!

THAT'S FOR SURE!

SILENCE, PLEASE! THAT MAY CONCLUDE, FOR THE TIME BEING, THE TESTIMONY OF THE JUSTICE SOCIETY--BUT IT DOES *NOT* NECESSARILY CONCLUDE THESE HEARINGS.

THEN MAY I SUGGEST WE RECESS, MR. CHAIRMAN-- WHILE CONGRESSMAN PHILIPS AND I DISCUSS *PRECISELY* THAT WITH YOU.

UH--CERTAINLY, MS. VALDEZ. THIS COMMITTEE WILL MEET AGAIN *TOMORROW* MORNING.

OR ELSE WE'LL HOLD A PRESS CONFERENCE TO SAY IT'S BEEN *DISBANDED!*

21

ER... THIS HEARING IS NOW RECESSED!

BAM BAM

HOPKINS WON'T NEED ME FOR THAT POWWOW...WHICH SHOULD GET PRETTY HEATED.

AND THE U.S.A AND HELENA SURE DON'T HAVE ANY REASON TO LINE UP TO TALK TO ME.

WONDER IF THE MAN I PHONED EARLIER WILL SHOW--

MR. GRAYSON? OVER HERE, PLEASE!

NO PARKING

BUS STOP

THERE HE IS--

--OR AT LEAST, THAT'S HIS CHAUFFEUR HAILING ME.

DR. NICHOLS HOPES YOU WON'T MIND HIS REMAINING SEATED, MR. GRAYSON. HE'S NOT FEELING WELL THESE DAYS.

HE ISN'T!? I FEEL LIKE I'M A HUNDRED YEARS OLD.

I'M FAR CLOSER TO THAT AGE THAN YOU, DEAR RICHARD... BUT I FEAR I'LL NOT BE THE ONE MEMBER OF THE HUNDRED-YEAR CLUB TO REACH IT.

THE WHAT?

ACTUALLY, DR. NICHOLS, I JUST WANTED TO TALK WITH YOU ONE MORE TIME ABOUT THE NIGHT BATMAN GAVE YOU THAT DIARY... BUT WHAT'S THIS CLUB YOU MENTIONED?

A SILLY THING, REALLY, I SUPPOSE--BUT THEN WE SCIENTISTS ARE NO LESS PRONE TO SILLINESS THAN OTHER MEN, I SUPPOSE.

AS YOU MAY RECALL, I WASN'T A MEMBER OF THE SO-CALLED "TIME TRUST" THAT INCLUDED GREAT MEN LIKE DR. EVERSON...PROF. ZEE...THOUGH THEY HAD HEARD OF MY THEORIES OF INDUCING TIME TRAVEL BY HYPNOSIS.

EVEN AFTER THE DISSOLUTION OF THE TRUST IN '42, EACH OF US STILL PURSUED OUR SEPARATE ATTEMPTS TO TRAVEL THROUGH TIME...

"...AND WE AGREED TO TEST OUR METHODS BY EACH TRYING TO REACH HIS OWN HUNDREDTH BIRTHDAY--

--AND COME BACK TO TELL ABOUT IT!

HEAR, HEAR!

"EVERSON AND STANLEY ARE DEAD NOW, POOR SOULS...

"...AND ZEE VANISHED IN '47, LEAVING BEHIND A NOTE SAYING HIS FAILURE HAD CAUSED HIM TO OPT FOR A SECLUDED LIFE IN THE SOUTH PACIFIC.

"FUNNY THING, THOUGH--THE LAST I HEARD OF OUR INFORMAL LITTLE GROUP WAS WHEN POOR COMMIS-SIONER WAYNE TOLD ME HE WAS OFF TO SEE PER DEGATON IN PRISON.

"ON A WHIM, I ASKED TO COME ALONG WITH HIM."

22

THIS WAS IN '79?

OH, YES. I REMEMBER IT DISTINCTLY, BECAUSE THAT'S WHEN MR. WAYNE'S DISTRUST OF THE JUSTICE SOCIETY HAD REACHED ITS HEIGHT.

DEGATON HAD BEEN ONLY AN ASSISTANT TO ZEE AND THE OTHERS, OF COURSE, NOT A MEMBER OF OUR LITTLE CLIQUE...

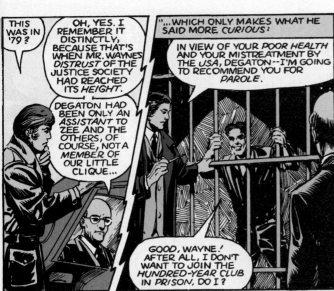

"...WHICH ONLY MAKES WHAT HE SAID MORE CURIOUS:

IN VIEW OF YOUR POOR HEALTH AND YOUR MISTREATMENT BY THE USA, DEGATON -- I'M GOING TO RECOMMEND YOU FOR PAROLE.

GOOD, WAYNE! AFTER ALL, I DON'T WANT TO JOIN THE HUNDRED-YEAR CLUB IN PRISON, DO I?

"DEGATON WAS PAROLED, SHORTLY AFTERWARD -- NOT LONG BEFORE THE NIGHT BATMAN BROUGHT ME THAT STRANGE JOURNAL ..."

-- TO BE GIVEN, IN THE EVENT OF MY DEATH, TO CLARK KENT, EDITOR OF THE METROPOLIS DAILY STAR.

MY GOD! IT -- IT'S TOO FANTASTIC TO BE TRUE, BUT -- I THINK I'M STARTING TO GET IT!

DR. NICHOLS -- IT'S EXTREMELY URGENT THAT YOUR CHAUFFEUR DRIVE ME AT ONCE TO A CERTAIN ADDRESS HERE IN WASHINGTON --!

HE'LL DRIVE US BOTH, DEAR BOY. HOP IN.

TELL ME, SIR -- IS TODAY, BY ANY CHANCE, THE BIRTHDAY OF ONE OF THE "TIME TRUST" MEMBERS?

BIRTHDAY? WELL, LET ME -- WHY, YES, NOW THAT YOU MENTION IT -- PROFESSOR ZEE'S, POOR MAN --

-- IN FACT, IF HE WERE ALIVE, IT WOULD BE HIS HUNDREDTH BIRTHDAY! BUT HOW DID YOU --?

THIS IS THE PLACE! WHATEVER YOU DO, DR. NICHOLS, DON'T GET OUT OF THE CAR!

AND IF ANYTHING STRANGE HAPPENS WHILE I'M IN THIS WRECK OF AN OLD BUILDING --

-- TELL YOUR CHAUFFEUR TO GET YOU OUT OF HERE!

23

YEP, THIS IS THE PLACE!

'COURSE, I'M STILL WHISTLING IN THE DARK. EVEN IF HE'S HERE, I'M ONLY GUESSING AS TO WHAT IT MIGHT HAVE TO DO WITH THE JUS--

UP WITH YOUR HANDS!

YOU!? THEN I WAS RIGHT--

--PER DEGATON!

YOU SAW MY PICTURE DURING THOSE HEARINGS, DIDN'T YOU?

JUST AS I SAW YOU ON TV-- RICHARD GRAYSON!

ALL DRESSED UP IN YOUR STORMTROOPER OUTFIT, EH? HOW COME?

YOU WILL SEE -- IN PRECISELY ONE-HALF HOUR.

ANY ADVANCE CLUES?

WHY NOT? AS YOU WELL KNOW, I MADE THREE ATTEMPTS IN 1947 TO CONQUER THE WORLD BY ALTERING PAST EVENTS.

THREE TIMES I VIRTUALLY SUCCEEDED-- ONLY TO BE UNDONE BY SO-CALLED SUPER-HEROES.

AND EACH TIME, ONLY MY MEMORY RETURNED LATER--GIVING ME ANOTHER CHANCE, YET ALSO TORTURING ME BY MAKING ME FEEL I WAS FOREDOOMED TO FAILURE!

THINGS COULD HAVE GONE ON THAT WAY AD NAUSEUM, OF COURSE -- WITH ME FEELING AS IF I WERE ON A MOEBIUS STRIP, REPEATING THE SAME ACTS OVER AND OVER.

THE FOURTH TIME--THE FINAL TIME-- I WAITED UNTIL PROFESSOR ZEE HIMSELF HAD PUT THE FINISHING TOUCHES ON HIS PRECIOUS TIME MACHINE, HERE IN THIS VERY LAB. THEN--

NOW, DEGATON, I SHALL GO INTO THE FUTURE --TO MY OWN 100th BIRTHDAY --AND RETURN TO THE SAME INSTANT I LEFT!

NO, YOU WON'T, ZEE!

INSTEAD, YOU WILL WRITE WHAT I TELL YOU TO WRITE!

WHY-- YOU TRULY MEAN THAT, DON'T YOU?

--THERE! I'VE WRITTEN I AM LEAVING THE COUNTRY. AND NOW?

AND NOW--

ARRGH

--YOU DIE!

BLAM

"BUT THE FOOL STAGGERED BACKWARD--

"--AND, FALLING INTO HIS TIME MACHINE, SOMEHOW MANAGED TO ACTIVATE IT!

POP!

NO!

24

IT ISN'T *FAIR!* THE *PERFECT CRIME*--NOT EVEN A *BODY* FOR ANYONE TO FIND--YET, EVEN IN DYING, THAT OLD FOOL'S TAKEN HIS MACHINE *WITH HIM!*

--SO ALL I'VE HAD TO DO IS *BIDE MY TIME* SINCE THAT DAY IN '47, UNTIL THE TIME MACHINE MATERIALIZES *RIGHT HERE*--IN THE RUINS OF ZEE'S LAB!

BUT--*WAIT!* I'M NOT BEATEN *YET!* I KNOW THE PRECISE *DAY* AND *HOUR* HE'D ALREADY SET IT TO *REAPPEAR*--

SO *THAT'S IT!*

DON'T *STALL*, GRAYSON! YOU MUST HAVE *SUSPECTED* MOST OF WHAT I TOLD YOU--OR YOU WOULDN'T BE HERE.

UH--*RIGHT.* IN FACT, THAT EXPLAINS WHY THE *FIRST* OF YOUR CRIMES THAT ANY-BODY'S EVER *KNOWN* ABOUT--

--IS WHEN YOU TRIED TO TAKE OVER THE *CAPITAL*, NOT AS A TIME TRAVELER--BUT AS JUST ANOTHER GAUDY MEMBER OF THE *WIZARD'S* FIRST LITTLE COMBO!

## THE INJUSTICE SOCIETY OF THE WORLD!

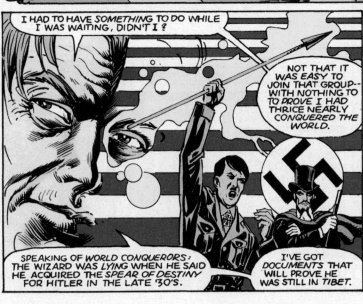

I HAD TO HAVE *SOMETHING* TO DO WHILE I WAS WAITING, DIDN'T I?

NOT THAT IT WAS *EASY* TO JOIN THAT GROUP--WITH NOTHING TO PROVE I HAD *THRICE* NEARLY CONQUERED THE WORLD.

SPEAKING OF WORLD CONQUERORS: THE WIZARD WAS *LYING* WHEN HE SAID HE ACQUIRED THE *SPEAR OF DESTINY* FOR HITLER IN THE LATE '30'S.

I'VE GOT *DOCUMENTS* THAT WILL PROVE HE WAS STILL IN *TIBET.*

OR, AT LEAST, THEY *WOULD*--IF I WEREN'T GOING TO *KILL* YOU, AND DISPOSE OF *YOUR* BODY AS FULLY AS *ZEE'S.*

OKAY--BUT JUST FOR *LAUGHS*, DEG--

--YOU KNOW ANYTHING ABOUT THAT *BOMB DEFENSE FORMULA* BUSINESS BACK IN '41?

OF COURSE! AS ASSISTANT TO THE "TIME TRUST," I WAS THE ONE WHO *SABOTAGED* IT, SO THAT IT *FAILED* ITS SECOND TEST, AND THUS WAS *SCRAPPED.*

I NEVER DREAMED, NATURALLY, THAT ONE DAY, BATMAN--FOR REASONS OF HIS OWN--WOULD CLAIM THE *JUSTICE SOCIETY* DID IT.

"--BUT HAD I KNOWN, IT WOULD HAVE MADE THE *YEARS* PASS MORE QUICKLY-- THE YEARS I SPENT IN *PRISON* AFTER THE CAPTURE OF THE INJUSTICE SOCIETY.

"EVEN SO, I KNEW THAT ALL THAT *REALLY* MATTERED WAS THAT I *SURVIVE* ANOTHER 37 YEARS--TO BE AROUND WHEN THE *TIME MACHINE* REAPPEARED!

"TIME AND CIRCUMSTANCE TOOK THEIR *HEAVY TOLL,* HOWEVER--AND I HAD BECOME A *HUMAN DERELICT* BY THE TIME THE BRAIN WAVE FOUND ME IN '76.

"HE AND I HAD STRUCK UP A *FRIENDSHIP* OF SORTS EARLIER-- THOUGH I'VE NO DOUBT HE MOSTLY JUST *SUSPECTED* I HAD A *FINAL* ACE UP MY SLEEVE.

LONETTI'S ROTTEN PIES

"FOR THAT REASON, HE *REVITALIZED* ME-- EVEN GAVE ME WHAT AMOUNTED TO A *NEW BODY* FOR A TIME--

"--NOT MY OWN, THOUGH! WHAT DID I WANT WITH *BLACK HAIR?* PHAUGGH!

"AT ANY RATE, THE RECON- STITUTED *JSA* PROVED TO BE TOO MUCH FOR THE BOTH OF US--

"AND SO I SPENT A COUPLE MORE YEARS IN PRISON--UNTIL I MANAGED, SOMEHOW, TO CONVINCE *BRUCE WAYNE* TO GO TO BAT FOR ME.

"WAYNE WAS A *DISTURBED* MAN AT THAT TIME, I DON'T MIND TELLING YOU--

"--OR HE'D HAVE SEEN *THROUGH* ME IN AN INSTANT!

26

"BUT HE WAS NEVER MORE DISTURBED THAN WHEN HE SHOWED UP TO GREET ME ON THE DAY OF MY RELEASE, AND--

YOU'RE A FOOL, WAYNE! I'VE SPENT MY REDUCED SENTENCE JUST WAITING--AND I'VE GOT LESS THAN SIX YEARS MORE TO WAIT!

I'M GOING TO BECOME MASTER OF THE WORLD YET, COMMISSIONER--

--AND YOU'LL NEVER STOP ME--NOT IN A HUNDRED YEARS!"

SO THAT'S IT! AFTER DEGATON'S TWO NOT-SO-SUBTLE "HUNDRED-YEAR" HINTS, BRUCE MUST'VE CHECKED WITH DOC NICHOLS--LEARNED ABOUT THE "CLUB"--ZEE'S DISAPPEARANCE--HIS HUNDREDTH BIRTHDAY--AND PUT TWO AND TWO TOGETHER!

I CAN SEE HOW YOU GOT INVOLVED, GRAYSON-- AS WAYNE'S FORMER WARD. BUT THAT BATMAN DIARY JUST ABOUT MESSED UP MY GAME PLAN.

HOW SO?

HOW DO YOU THINK? TO CLEAR THEM- SELVES, THE JSA HAD TO GO OVER THEIR PAST WITH A FINE-TOOTH COMB...

...AND THAT MEANT THAT, SOONER OR LATER, SOMEBODY MIGHT ASK JUST THE RIGHT QUESTIONS ABOUT PER DEGATON.

LIKE, WHETHER PROF. ZEE REALLY TOOK OFF FOR PARTS UNKNOWN-- OR WHETHER I KILLED HIM.

WAYNE COULDN'T BRING HIMSELF TO GO TO THE JSA-- BUT BATMAN'S LITTLE BLACK BOOK ALMOST BROUGHT THEM TO ME.

WELL, WELL... ONLY FIVE MINUTES LEFT TILL SHOWTIME.

SO WHAT IS THIS "ULTIMATE PLAN"?

SAME AS EVER, OF COURSE-- TO CONQUER THE WORLD, BY PLUNGING IT BACK INTO THE DARK AGES.

ONLY THIS TIME, I'VE HAD NEARLY FOUR MORE DECADES TO SALT AWAY THE LATEST WEAPONS--SO THAT EVEN THE JUSTICE SOCIETY WON'T BE ABLE TO STAND AGAINST ME!

I KNOW! NOW, SAY YOUR PRAYERS, GRAYSON, BECAUSE HERE'S WHERE I LAY YOU DOWN TO--HUH?

THE TIME MACHINE-- REAPPEARING!

POP!

YOU WISH!

27

DAMN WATCH MUST BE SLOW AGAIN. OH WELL...

HOLD IT! THE DOOR'S ARE OPENING -- AND --

SOMEONE'S INSIDE!

P-PROFESSOR ZEE--!?

YOU!?

Y-YOU DID THIS-- TO ME --PER DEGATON!

YOU-- SHOT ME-- BUT I'VE MANAGED TO STAY ALIVE --

--THESE FEW --PRECIOUS-- SEC!.--

I'M DISAPPOINTED IN YOU, DEGATON. DIDN'T YOU EVER SEE A BATARANG BEFORE?

'COURSE, I'VE ADAPTED THEM A BIT, SINCE DAD DIED...

THE JUSTICE SOCIETY-- AND EVEN THE COMMITTEE!

28

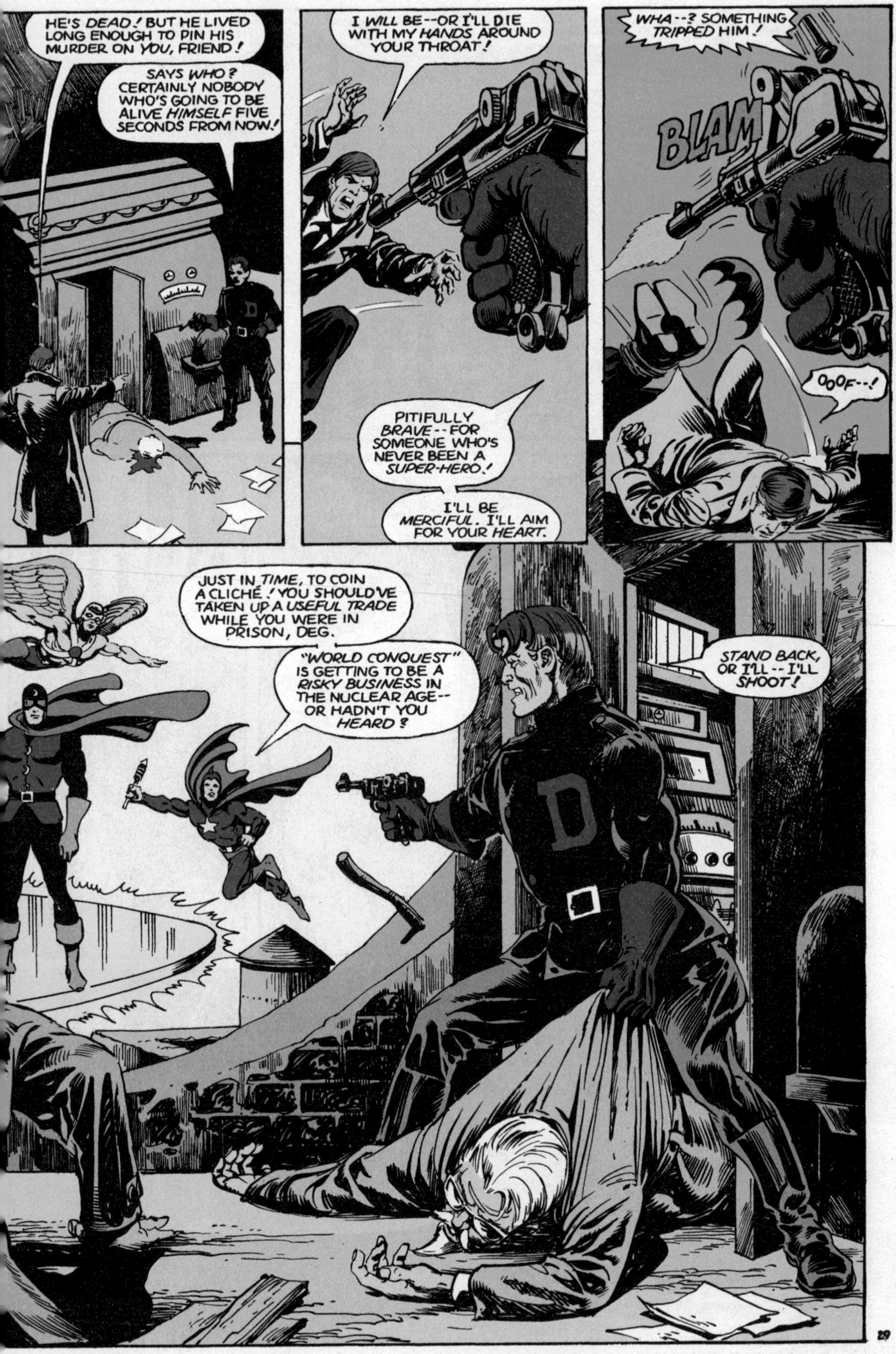
HE'S DEAD! BUT HE LIVED LONG ENOUGH TO PIN HIS MURDER ON YOU, FRIEND!
SAYS WHO? CERTAINLY NOBODY WHO'S GOING TO BE ALIVE HIMSELF FIVE SECONDS FROM NOW!
I WILL BE--OR I'LL DIE WITH MY HANDS AROUND YOUR THROAT!
PITIFULLY BRAVE--FOR SOMEONE WHO'S NEVER BEEN A SUPER-HERO!
I'LL BE MERCIFUL. I'LL AIM FOR YOUR HEART.
WHA--? SOMETHING TRIPPED HIM!
BLAM
OOOF--!
JUST IN TIME, TO COIN A CLICHÉ! YOU SHOULD'VE TAKEN UP A USEFUL TRADE WHILE YOU WERE IN PRISON, DEG.
"WORLD CONQUEST" IS GETTING TO BE A RISKY BUSINESS IN THE NUCLEAR AGE--OR HADN'T YOU HEARD?
STAND BACK, OR I'LL--I'LL SHOOT!
29

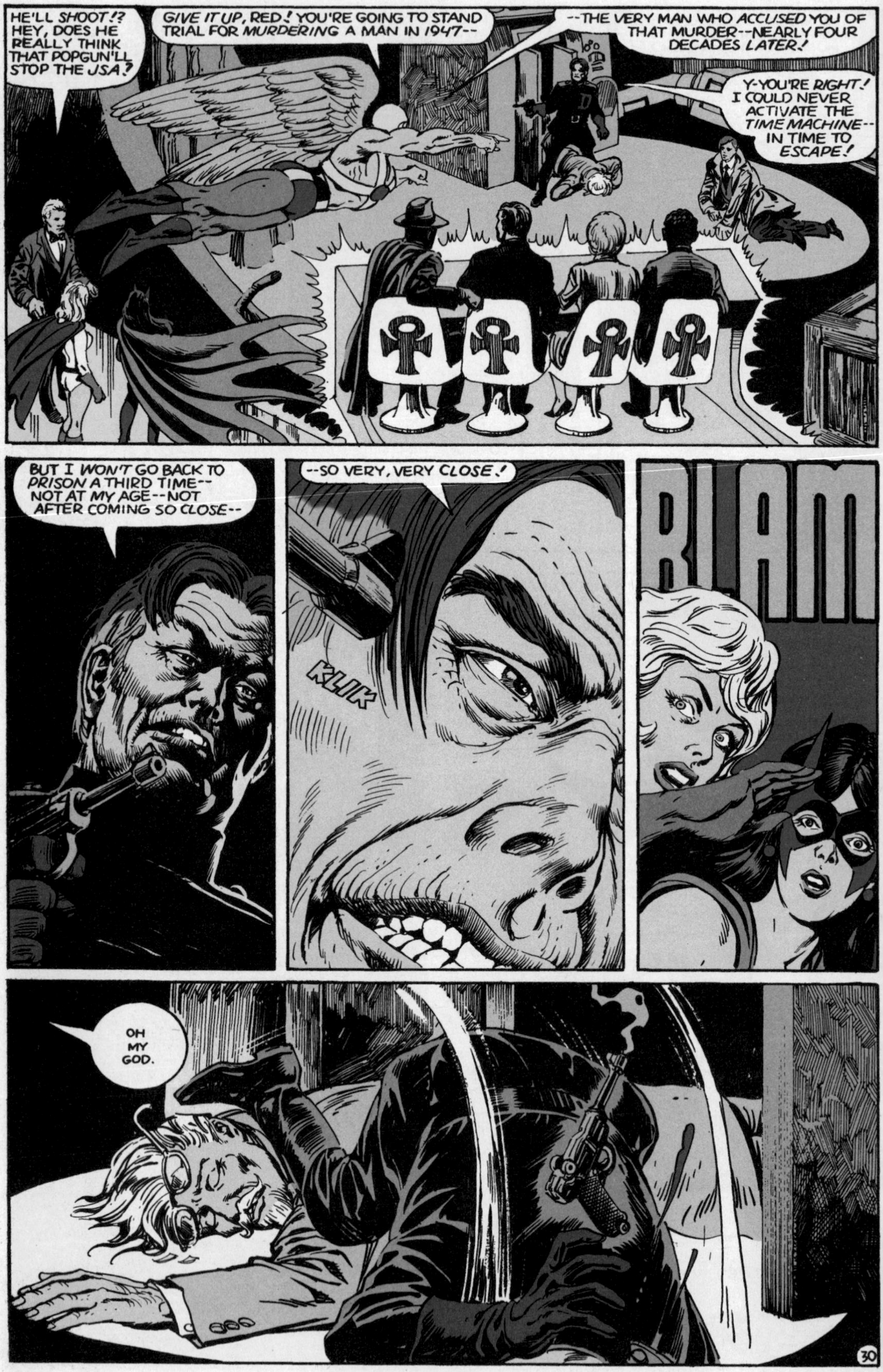
HE'LL SHOOT!? HEY, DOES HE REALLY THINK THAT POPGUN'LL STOP THE JSA?
GIVE IT UP, RED! YOU'RE GOING TO STAND TRIAL FOR MURDERING A MAN IN 1947--
--THE VERY MAN WHO ACCUSED YOU OF THAT MURDER--NEARLY FOUR DECADES LATER!
Y-YOU'RE RIGHT! I COULD NEVER ACTIVATE THE TIME MACHINE--IN TIME TO ESCAPE!
BUT I WON'T GO BACK TO PRISON A THIRD TIME--NOT AT MY AGE--NOT AFTER COMING SO CLOSE--
--SO VERY, VERY CLOSE!
KLIK
BLAM
OH MY GOD.
30

SOON, AS THE AMBULANCE ARRIVES...

IRONIC, ISN'T IT--THAT THIS SHOULD ALL HAPPEN JUST *AFTER* WE OF THE COMMITTEE DECIDED TO *DISCONTINUE* OUR HEARINGS.

AND ISSUE A *STATEMENT*, SENATOR--

--A STATEMENT DECLARING WE FEEL THE JUSTICE SOCIETY ARE *INNOCENT* OF THE CHARGES IN BATMAN'S DIARY--DON'T FORGET ABOUT *THAT!*

UH--I WON'T, CONGRESSMAN.

YOU BETTER NOT ... OR WE'LL START INVESTIGATING *YOU!*

WHILE, OUT OF THE *OTHERS'* HEARING...

...I GUESS THE JSA MEANT MORE TO BRUCE THAN HE COULD *LET* ON HELENA ... EVEN TO *HIMSELF.*

SO WHEN HE COULDN'T BRING HIMSELF TO *TELL* THEM WHAT HE SUSPECTED ABOUT DEGATON--HIS *SUBCONSCIOUS* TOOK OVER--AS *BATMAN*--AND WROTE THAT *"DIARY".*

BUT WHY'D HE GIVE IT TO *DR. NICHOLS* IN '79--LIKE HE *KNEW* HE WAS GONNA DIE?

BECAUSE, DICK ... HE *DID* KNOW.

HE MADE ME PROMISE NOT TO *TELL* ANYONE THIS, NOT EVEN *YOU,* SO I HAVEN'T ... TILL NOW.

DAD WAS *DYING,* DICK... DYING OF *CANCER.*

THEN--HE'D HAVE *DIED*--

WITHIN THE YEAR, EVEN IF BILL JENSEN AND FREDRIC VAUX HAD *NEVER* EXISTED.

THE CANCER'D *CAUSED* HIS HOSTILITY TO THE JSA. HIS *BATMAN* PERSONA KNEW THAT, SOMEHOW--EVEN IF *BRUCE WAYNE* DIDN'T.

I GUESS HE JUST FOUND A CONVOLUTED WAY OF LETTING THE JSA PROVE THEMSELVES--AND *STOP* DEGATON--EVEN AFTER HIS DEATH.

HELENA, I--I'M SO *ASHAMED...*

DON'T BE, DICK. YOU'VE SPENT A *LIFETIME* THINKING BRUCE WAYNE--AND BATMAN--WERE *PERFECT.*

NO MAN IS THAT--NOT EVEN THE *BATMAN!*

31

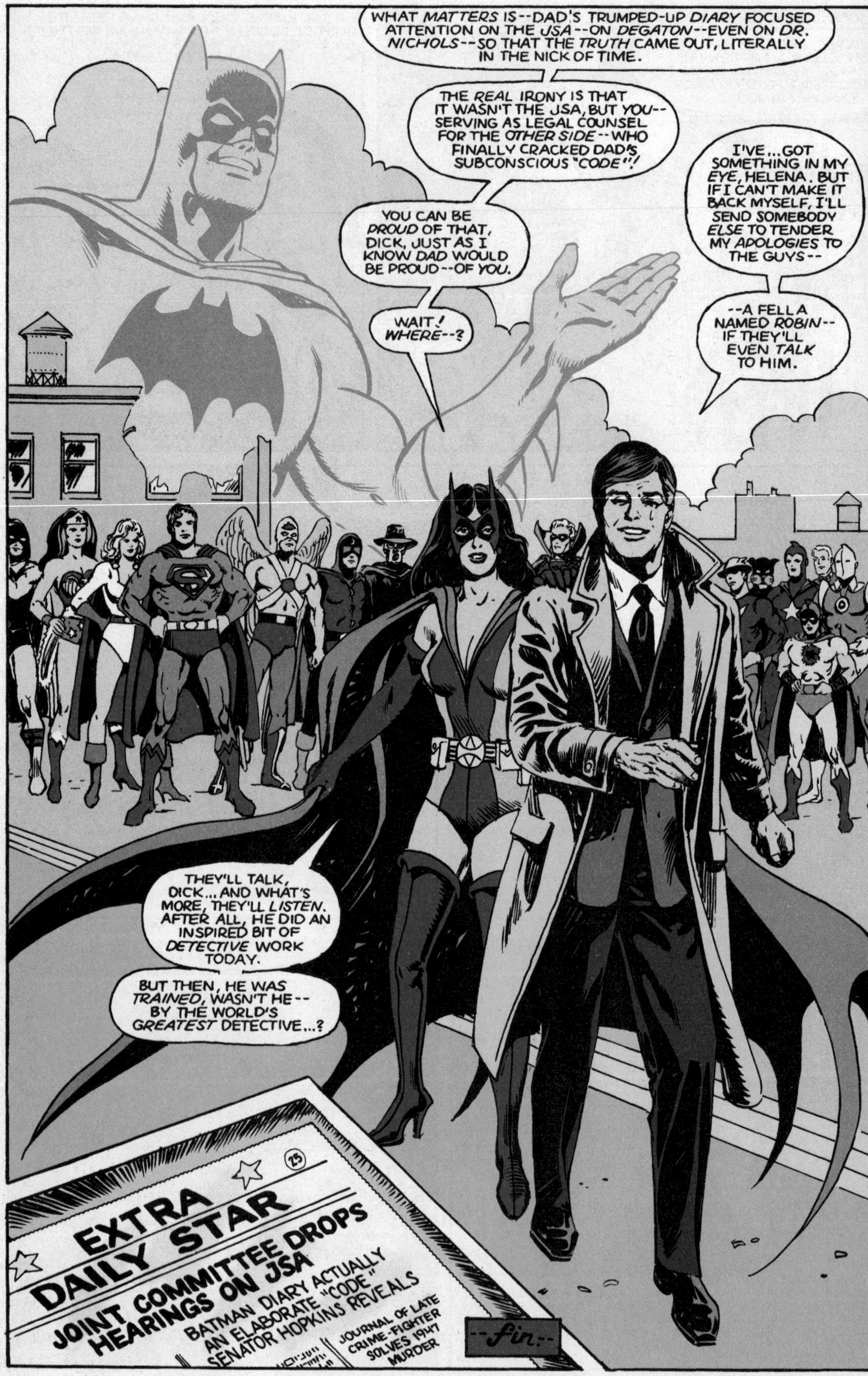
WHAT MATTERS IS--DAD'S TRUMPED-UP DIARY FOCUSED ATTENTION ON THE JSA--ON DEGATON--EVEN ON DR. NICHOLS--SO THAT THE TRUTH CAME OUT, LITERALLY IN THE NICK OF TIME.
THE REAL IRONY IS THAT IT WASN'T THE JSA, BUT YOU--SERVING AS LEGAL COUNSEL FOR THE OTHER SIDE--WHO FINALLY CRACKED DAD'S SUBCONSCIOUS "CODE"!
YOU CAN BE PROUD OF THAT, DICK, JUST AS I KNOW DAD WOULD BE PROUD--OF YOU.
WAIT! WHERE--?
I'VE...GOT SOMETHING IN MY EYE, HELENA. BUT IF I CAN'T MAKE IT BACK MYSELF, I'LL SEND SOMEBODY ELSE TO TENDER MY APOLOGIES TO THE GUYS--
--A FELLA NAMED ROBIN--IF THEY'LL EVEN TALK TO HIM.
THEY'LL TALK, DICK...AND WHAT'S MORE, THEY'LL LISTEN. AFTER ALL, HE DID AN INSPIRED BIT OF DETECTIVE WORK TODAY.
BUT THEN, HE WAS TRAINED, WASN'T HE--BY THE WORLD'S GREATEST DETECTIVE...?
EXTRA
DAILY STAR
JOINT COMMITTEE DROPS HEARINGS ON JSA
BATMAN DIARY ACTUALLY AN ELABORATE "CODE" SENATOR HOPKINS REVEALS
JOURNAL OF LATE CRIME-FIGHTER SOLVES 1947 MURDER
--fin.--

*"This is a flawless book."*
*—PHILADELPHIA DAILY NEWS*

*"Though Geoff Johns has been involved in many of DC's most notable titles over the last half decade, there is arguably no group of heroes he's more associated with, or more adept at writing, than the Justice Society of America."*
*—IGN*

## FROM THE *NEW YORK TIMES* #1 BEST-SELLING WRITER OF *JUSTICE LEAGUE* & *GREEN LANTERN*

# GEOFF JOHNS

## with DALE EAGLESHAM

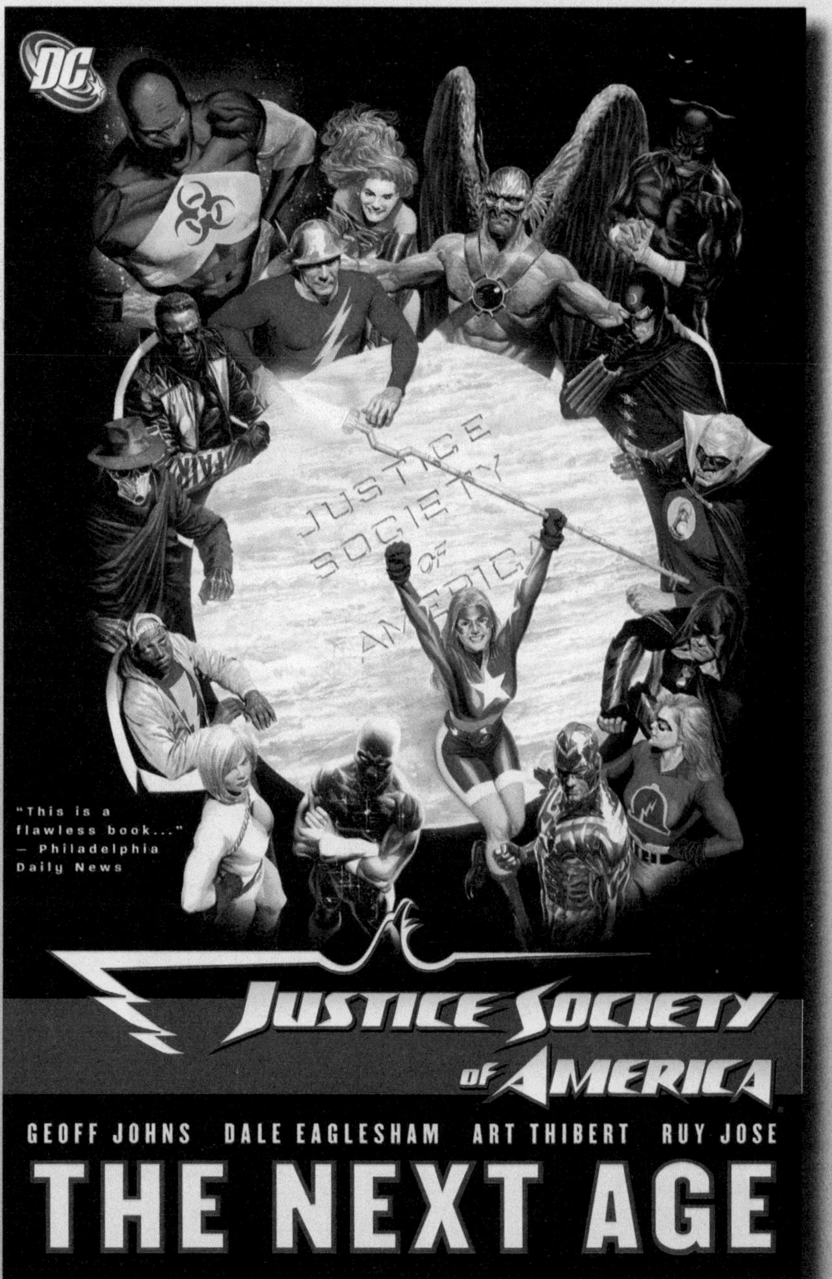
"This is a flawless book..." – Philadelphia Daily News
JUSTICE SOCIETY of AMERICA
GEOFF JOHNS DALE EAGLESHAM ART THIBERT RUY JOSE
THE NEXT AGE

THY KINGDOM COME
PART 1

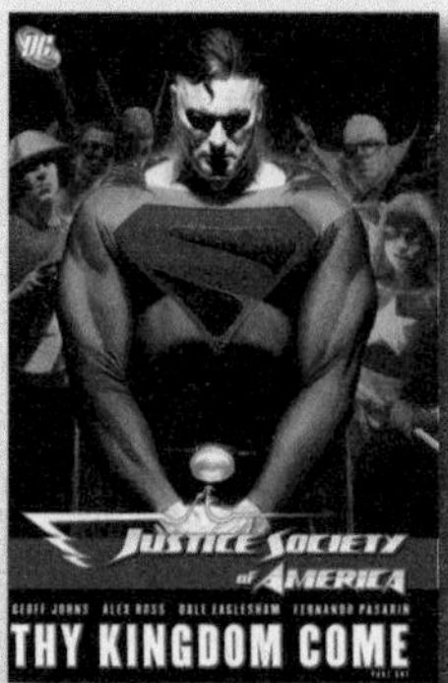
JUSTICE SOCIETY of AMERICA
GEOFF JOHNS ALEX ROSS DALE EAGLESHAM FERNANDO PASARIN
THY KINGDOM COME

with ALEX ROSS and
DALE EAGLESHAM

THY KINGDOM COME
PART 2

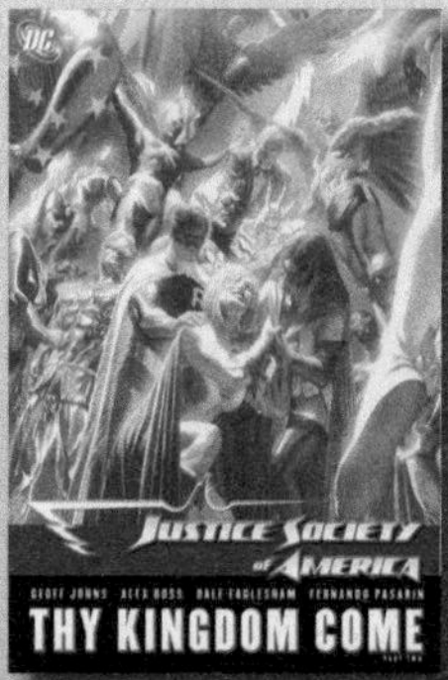
JUSTICE SOCIETY of AMERICA
GEOFF JOHNS ALEX ROSS DALE EAGLESHAM FERNANDO PASARIN
THY KINGDOM COME

with ALEX ROSS and
DALE EAGLESHAM

THY KINGDOM COME
PART 3

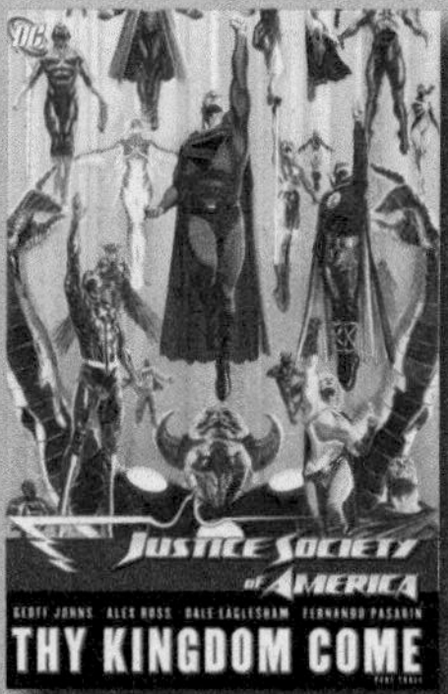
JUSTICE SOCIETY of AMERICA
GEOFF JOHNS ALEX ROSS DALE EAGLESHAM FERNANDO PASARIN
THY KINGDOM COME

with ALEX ROSS and
DALE EAGLESHAM

# THE DARK KNIGHT. THE MAN OF STEEL. TOGETHER.
# SUPERMAN/BATMAN: PUBLIC ENEMIES
## JEPH LOEB & ED McGUINNESS

JEPH LOEB | ED McGUINNESS | DEXTER VINES